THE CIVIL WAR AND
RECONSTRUCTION IN
INDIAN TERRITORY

The Civil War and Reconstruction in Indian Territory

Edited and with an
introduction by
BRADLEY R. CLAMPITT

UNIVERSITY OF NEBRASKA PRESS
Lincoln and London

© 2015 by the Board of Regents of the University of Nebraska

A portion of the introduction originally appeared as "'For Our Own Safety and Welfare': What the Civil War Meant in Indian Territory," by Bradley R. Clampitt, in *Main Street Oklahoma: Stories of Twentieth-Century America* edited by Linda W. Reese and Patricia Loughlin (Norman: University of Oklahoma Press, 2013), © 2013 by the University of Oklahoma Press. Reproduced with permission.

All rights reserved
Manufactured in the United States of America

Library of Congress Cataloging-in-Publication Data
The Civil War and Reconstruction in Indian Territory / Edited and with an introduction by Bradley R. Clampitt.
pages cm
Includes bibliographical references and index.
ISBN 978-0-8032-7727-4 (pbk.: alk. paper)
ISBN 978-0-8032-7887-5 (epub)
ISBN 978-0-8032-7888-2 (mobi)
ISBN 978-0-8032-7889-9 (pdf)
1. Indians of North America—Indian Territory—History—19th century. 2. Indians of North America—History—Civil War, 1861–1865. 3. United States—History—Civil War, 1861–1865—Participation, Indian. 4. Indian Territory—History—19th century. I. Clampitt, Bradley R., 1975–, editor.
E78.I5C53 2015
973.7089'97—dc23
2015002790

Set in Minion by Westchester Publishing Services

CONTENTS

Map of the Civil War in Indian Territory   vii

Introduction: The Civil War and Reconstruction in Indian Territory   1
Bradley R. Clampitt

1. Bitter Legacy: The Battle Front   19
Richard B. McCaslin

2. Hardship at Home: The Civilian Experience   38
Clarissa Confer

3. Our Doom as a Nation Is Sealed: The Five Nations in the Civil War   64
Brad Agnew

4. "The Most Destitute" People in Indian Territory: The Wichita Agency Tribes and the Civil War   88
F. Todd Smith

5. Who Defines a Nation?: Reconstruction in Indian Territory   110
Christopher B. Bean

6. "We Had a Lot of Trouble Getting Things Settled after the War": The Freedpeople's Civil Wars   132
Linda W. Reese

7. Hearth and Home: Cherokee and Creek Women's Memories of the Civil War in Indian Territory   153
Amanda Cobb-Greetham

8. To Reach a Wider Audience: Public Commemoration of the Civil War in Indian Territory   172
Whit Edwards

Contributors   183

Index   185

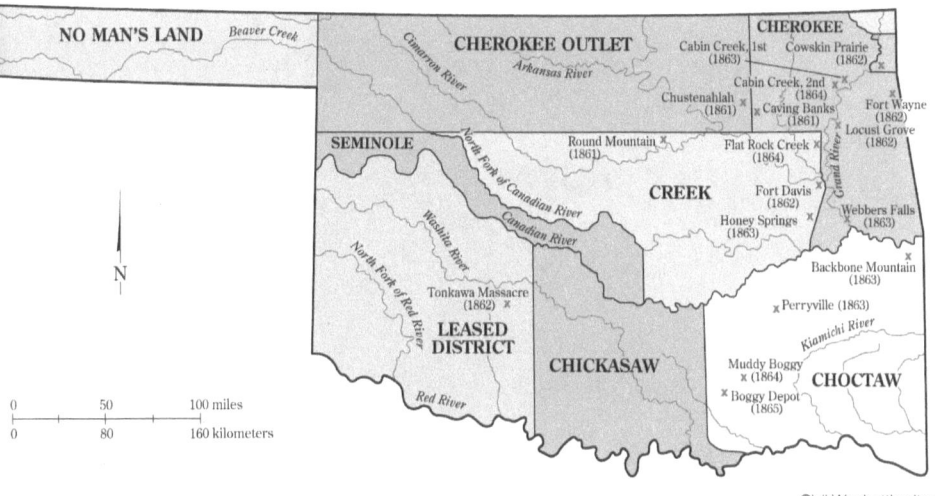

Civil War battle sites

The denizens of Indian Territory found themselves caught between two powerful belligerents during the American Civil War. In the eastern half of the territory, numerous battles raged among Indian, black, and white troops. The conflict ravaged the home front for members of the Five Nations there and for the Plains tribes who resided in the western portion of the territory. From *The Story of Oklahoma: Revised Second Edition*, by W. David Baird and Danney Goble. Reproduced with permission. All rights reserved.

Introduction

The Civil War and Reconstruction in Indian Territory

Bradley R. Clampitt

From 1861 to 1865 the American Civil War raged after decades of sectional animosity between North and South, and the fratricidal bloodbath lives on in the imaginations of countless Americans. The endless public fascination with the Civil War has prompted one prominent historian to describe it as "The War That Never Goes Away."[1] One need not be a native of a former Confederate state to fall spellbound to the tragic "War for Southern Independence," and one need not hail from a Northern state to appreciate the Union's heroic effort to preserve the nation and eventually dismantle the abomination of chattel slavery. But where does that leave individuals who seek to understand the violent conflict in Indian Territory, a region populated predominantly by people who were neither Northern nor Southern and indeed were not U.S. citizens?

In recent years scholars have brought a degree of geographical balance to the study of the war by looking beyond the famed battles and leaders of the eastern theater and dedicating increased attention to the endless war in the western and Trans-Mississippi regions.[2] This volume continues that admirable trend and contributes to the relatively sparse scholarly literature of the Civil War and Reconstruction in Indian Territory.[3] The contributors approach the subject from multiple perspectives in eight essays that incorporate modern scholarship and interpretations into a readable narrative designed for students and scholars alike.

The Civil War began forty-six years before Oklahoma statehood, but the ravages of war transcended political distinctions such as statehood. The residents of what was then known as Indian Territory experienced the horrors of civil war as vividly as almost any other population. So, when historians and students consider the region's role in the Civil War, do they think first of individuals who remained loyal to the United States or those who struggled for Southern independence? Perhaps the answer should be "Neither." Instead, the conflict in Indian Territory presents a unique interpretive framework, what one might call a series of "wars within a war." The American Indian population waged its own wars for independence, and indeed survival, within what began as someone else's fight. That quest for sovereignty most accurately frames the story of the Civil War in Indian Territory. The war witnessed brutal conflicts within and between Indian nations and tribes, numerous battles that involved Union and Confederate military forces, and debilitating struggles for civilians on the home front. It left a legacy in the region as bitter as that experienced almost anywhere in the country. The story of the Indians' Civil War also serves as a reminder that history is rarely about heroes and villains and that people in history frequently defy simple categorization.

Relative to the war's primary theaters of operations and the economic and political centers of the Union and the Confederacy, wartime Indian Territory must be considered remote and sparsely populated. Approximately seventy thousand individuals resided primarily in the territory's eastern half on lands claimed by Native American groups now known as the Five Nations—Chickasaws, Choctaws, Creeks (Muscogees), Seminoles, and Cherokees—who had been forcibly relocated from the southeastern United States decades earlier. The Chickasaw Nation occupied the south-central portion of the territory immediately west of the Choctaw Nation, which covered the southeastern corner of the region. Creeks and Seminoles claimed tracts of land near the center of the territory, while the Cherokee Nation possessed the northeastern portion. Smaller reserve groups and members of Plains tribes occupied the western portions of the territory, and a few other tribes lived on small tracts adjacent to the Cherokee Nation.[4]

Each of the Five Nations' governments had evolved during the decades between removal and the Civil War. Although some variation existed between the nations, by the time of the war, the Cherokees, Chickasaws, Choctaws, and Creeks had instituted republican governments similar to that of the United States with elected executives and assemblies. The Cherokees, Choctaws, and Creeks designated their executives principal chiefs, while the Chickasaws referred to their leader as governor. The Seminole Nation operated a more localized government, in part because of a lack of funding from their federal treaties that might have financed more significant government restructuring. Among the Seminoles a chief led each town, and a general council governed the nation overall. Each nation in the eastern half of the territory and the tribes who resided near the Wichita Agency in the western portion received annual payments from the federal government. Indian agents employed by the United States supervised payments, enforced treaty provisions, and served as liaisons between the federal government and Indian nations and tribes.[5]

The territory attracted the attention of Union and Confederate officials who hoped that the region might provide resources that they could ship to more important locations east of the Mississippi River, but claims that the two belligerents desperately sought to control an Indian Territory rich in resources exaggerate reality. In that regard what Indian Territory offered paled in comparison with the resources found in other contested border grounds such as Kentucky. Two other factors—geography and the question of the Indian population's allegiance—contributed far more to the territory's significance. Its location made Indian Territory potentially important and placed its residents in a precarious situation. Union-controlled Kansas bordered the territory to the north, while the Confederate states of Texas and Arkansas loomed to the south and east, respectively. To the northeast, Missouri included residents with divided loyalties. A Confederate-controlled Indian Territory might serve as a military buffer zone to protect the more important Texas and could potentially provide a base of operations for Confederate invasions of Kansas or even the rich gold fields of Colorado. Conversely, Union officials viewed the territory as a buffer to protect those regions and as a potential highway of invasion to Texas. Therefore, simple geography increased the likelihood of competition for control of Indian Territory and virtually guaranteed the involvement of the region's Native American population in the conflict.[6]

Neither belligerent could realistically assume that the Indian nations and tribes sympathized with its cause. Union officials could hardly be surprised if Indian leaders exhibited no great affection for the U.S. Army. Confederate officials certainly recognized that the southeastern states bore great responsibility for the removal of the Five Nations to Indian Territory decades earlier and that several tribes in the western portions of Indian Territory understandably harbored resentment toward the residents of Texas, who had forcibly removed them to the territory in more recent years. Still, because Union and Confederate officials displayed interest in Indian Territory, Indian leaders needed to be concerned about the looming war.

Neutrality therefore appeared virtually impossible and was perhaps ill advised anyway because the war threatened to envelop the Indians' homelands. Perhaps the Indians' best course of action was to enter the war on their own terms. The vast majority of the residents of Indian Territory chose a side, but they did so for myriad reasons unique to their own experience, not necessarily out of affection for the Union or the Confederacy. Old grievances made a united front unlikely, and each group acted individually, with most leaders motivated by what they considered the best course of action for their people.

Of course the Native American occupants of the region as a whole proved neither ardent Confederates nor staunch Unionists. Most supported the Confederacy, some chose the Union, a relative few changed allegiance during the war, and others at least attempted to remain neutral. Beyond the fundamental desire to take the course of action deemed best for their respective people, numerous concerns factored into the groups' decisions. Existing treaties with the United States and dependence upon the federal government for a degree of financial support and reliance upon its military for physical security motivated some to remain loyal to the Union, while resentment of the United States, a genuine belief in the propriety of slavery, and a stronger cultural connection with the American South motivated others to support the Confederacy.[7]

Members of the Chickasaw, Choctaw, Cherokee, and Creek Nations collectively owned approximately seventy-seven hundred slaves. The plantation culture among those four nations strongly resembled that of white Southerners to the south and east of the territory. Similar to legislation in slaveholding states in the American South, laws in the Indian nations restricted the education of slaves and severely punished those who attempted to escape. However, one distinct characteristic emerged in the Indian Territory version of the Southern plantation complex. Native planters followed the traditional custom of communal use of land beyond individual plantations. Indian planters valued and protected their private property as much as any white landowner, but as one historian described it, "An Indian citizen could clear, improve, fence, and cultivate as much land as he wished, provided he did not interfere with his neighbor's holdings."[8] (In chapter 3 of this collection, Brad Agnew discusses the role of slavery in the conflict among members of the Five Nations and explains what prompted certain groups and individuals to support the Union.)

In addition to questions of security, money, legal obligations, and slavery, potential threats to continued possession of Indian lands concerned leaders of the Five Nations. An 1860 speech by Republican William H. Seward, who would become Abraham Lincoln's secretary of state, alarmed many Indian leaders. Seward pointed to American expansion into western lands as the key to suppressing the intense sectional conflict and called for yet another relocation of Native Americans to clear the way for white settlement. Therefore, while a Republican victory in the presidential election of 1860 likely promised an end to the expansion of slavery into the western territories, it guaranteed absolutely nothing to the inhabitants of Indian Territory. For all of these reasons, the Civil War would explode into more than simply a "white man's war."[9]

Indeed, events far and near in the spring of 1861 presented thousands with the reality of civil war. The famous events at Fort Sumter, South Carolina, in April and Lincoln's subsequent call for volunteers to suppress the rebellion forced the hand of the eight slave states that had not seceded in the aftermath of the presidential election of 1860. Four states—Missouri, Kentucky, Maryland, and Delaware—remained officially loyal to the Union, while the other four—Virginia, North Carolina, Tennessee, and Arkansas—seceded and joined the Confederacy. Meanwhile, activities in and near Indian Territory in April 1861 more immediately affected the course of the war there. As war loomed that spring, Federal soldiers occupied three forts in the territory and Fort Smith, just across the Arkansas border. Fort Smith served as a supply depot to the three other posts, which helped to protect the Five Nations from raiding Plains tribes, who considered the Five Nations invaders. Fort Washita stood in the southeastern portion of the Chickasaw Nation, about sixty miles southeast of Fort Arbuckle. Farther west, Fort Cobb was located in present-day Caddo County, approximately forty miles north of present-day Lawton. Fort Cobb supplied the nearby Wichita Agency, which served a number of small bands that had been removed from Texas, including Wichitas, Caddos, Anadarkos, Penateka Comanches, and others and protected them against bands of Comanches, Kiowas, and Kickapoos.[10]

After a sequence of orders that initially called for the concentration of Federal forces at Fort Washita, Union officers ultimately ordered the evacuation of the military posts in the territory, thus leaving the Five Nations without the military protection guaranteed them by treaties with the United States. From the American perspective, this action did not represent a calculated decision to abandon Indians. Union officials ordered the evacuation of military posts elsewhere in areas threatened by Confederates and considered the soldiers' presence in the East more important.[11]

Not surprisingly, however, some Native Americans considered the evacuation tantamount to abandonment by the United States. The withdrawal of Union soldiers certainly cleared the way for Confederate diplomats who sought to form official alliances with the Five Nations and other groups within the territory. Considering conditions in Indian Territory in 1861, the cultural connections between many members of the Five Nations and the Southern states, and the perception that the federal government had abandoned them, it is hardly surprising that most members of the Five Nations cast their lot with the Confederacy.[12] An even simpler point should not be overlooked—in the minds of many Native Americans, the Confederacy offered at least the opportunity to fight for the lands supposedly reserved for Indians.

What followed that historic spring brought years of tragedy and bloodshed to Indian Territory. In chapter 1 of this volume, Richard B. McCaslin chronicles the military narrative of the Civil War in Indian Territory and in the process establishes invaluable context for the other essays in the collection. McCaslin explicates the nuanced conflicts that blurred the lines of battle and created and destroyed fleeting alliances. He narrates the battles and campaigns of Indian Territory, explains their significance within the region, places the results within the larger context of the war, and situates the territory within the Trans-Mississippi theater specifically. The military events exacerbated existing conflicts within and between nations and tribes, struggles that often proved as severe as those between the Union and Confederacy. McCaslin illustrates how these conflicts played out on the field of battle and demonstrates that both Union and Confederate war efforts suffered from crippling command failures and personal rivalries among leaders.

Though the Union and the Confederacy competed for control of the territory and the allegiance of its residents, both ultimately abandoned serious interest in the region after the midpoint of the war. None of the military activity in the territory significantly affected the outcome of the war, and neither the military campaigns nor the civilian suffering proved especially urgent to officials in Richmond or Washington. In fact, with certain exceptions, both the Union and Confederate governments largely ignored the region and its inhabitants after the Union secured control of the Mississippi River in 1863. Still, as McCaslin and others in this volume demonstrate, the war raged on in the territory and transformed the lives of thousands there regardless of waning interest among officials to the east. Indians and whites on both sides and black Union soldiers fought battles and skirmishes, while Stand Watie gained a degree of recognition for his exploits in guerilla warfare on behalf of those Cherokees who supported the Confederacy. Civilians suffered intensely at the hands of forces on both sides and because neither government adequately provided for Indians.[13]

Indeed, the battles and campaigns described in McCaslin's essay brought terror and suffering to the territory's home front. Clarissa Confer examines the experience of civilians—Indian, white, and black—in Indian Territory and illustrates the uncertainty of life in a border region caught between two belligerent powers. Civilians found themselves in the direct path of military actions from the outset of the war, and many fled the territory in search of security, while others lacked the basic resources necessary to relocate. Left to fend for themselves against armies from both sides, as well as irregular forces and outlaws, men, women, and children suffered from a range of material deprivations, including shortages of food, clothing, and shelter. As with the military conflict, the struggles of the home front widened existing chasms among noncombatants within the Five Nations. As Confer explains, the chronic lack of stability and security plagued the residents of Indian Territory long after the war.

The brutality of civil war divided Native Americans just as it fissured North and South. That crisis of division began with the important decision of which side to support and continued through years of tragedy and devastation wrought by warfare. Brad Agnew closely examines the

Five Nations' decision making, experiences, and perspectives during the Civil War era, beginning with his assessment that the decades between removal and the war do not represent a "golden age" in Five Nations history. Serious rifts remained within the nations after removal, and the divisions were only exacerbated by the rise of Christianity among the communities and the escalation of tensions related to slavery. The 1840s and 1850s brought immediate threat to the lands supposedly reserved to the nations in the form of cattle drives and railroads. Agnew delineates the complex disputes between the nations and within individual communities and adroitly explains the motivations for each group in their formation of alliances during the Civil War. Agnew's essay is particularly enlightening for its analysis of the multifaceted motives and actions of Cherokee leader John Ross. Ultimately, Agnew concludes that the war, Reconstruction, and the influx of outsiders into the territory further undermined Indian sovereignty and resulted in the greatest tragedy to befall the Five Nations since initial European contact.

Meanwhile, inhabitants of Indian Territory outside the Five Nations survived their own trials of the Civil War. F. Todd Smith focuses his essay on the experiences of the Plains tribes who resided at the Wichita Agency in the western portion of the territory. Smith chronicles the often-overlooked story of the western tribes' arrival in Indian Territory shortly before the Civil War and demonstrates that these individuals suffered as much as their counterparts in the eastern half of the territory and, like the Five Nations, responded to the crisis of civil war in myriad ways. Smith explains that before the war, agency tribes found themselves "between two fires," with hostile Texans on one side and Comanches and Kiowas on the other. The Civil War introduced a "third fire" in the form of the contest between the Union and the Confederacy and those belligerents' competition for the agency tribes' allegiance. Thus the residents of the Wichita Agency and those Comanches who signed the treaties clearly did so out of concern for their own well-being rather than as a display of affection for the new Confederacy. During the remainder of the conflict, some agency tribes fled to Union-controlled

Kansas, others attempted to persevere in western Indian Territory, and still others searched for independence away from either belligerent. Smith scrutinizes the relationship between the agency tribes and the Confederacy, an association that proved short lived because the Confederacy could not adequately provide for the tribes and because the Indian leaders did not trust their new allies to protect them from Texans. The agency tribes' struggles continued after the war when the federal government forced them to share their lands with other tribes, including their traditional enemies.

Thus when the war ended in 1865, it proved a mixed blessing to the residents of Indian Territory. Peace and stability eventually returned, but the war's end also meant surrender negotiations and yet another round of treaties with the federal government. As the war's closing scenes played out, Confederate-allied Indians, Plains Indians, and Confederate officials held an important conference May 25–27 at Camp Napoleon, near the Washita River and present-day Verden, Oklahoma. Confederate officials sought peaceful relations with all Native groups and vowed to honor Indian demands for the right to surrender their own forces. Confederate Indians also turned their attention to their postwar fate. Before the meeting, Choctaw principal chief Peter P. Pitchlynn revealed those concerns and expressed the Confederate Indians' position when he insisted upon separate surrenders for Indian forces, "that we may be enabled to take steps for our own safety and welfare."[14]

Thus events at Camp Napoleon, perhaps more than any other event, illustrate the Indians' ongoing search for sovereignty and their attempt to protect their interests during what began as someone else's war. The delegates pledged peace between the Plains tribes and the Confederate-allied Indians. Indeed, the authors of the remarkable document known as the Camp Napoleon Compact chose for their motto "An Indian shall not spill an Indian's blood" and promised, "The tomahawk shall be forever buried. The scalping knife shall be forever broken." The compact features dramatic and emblematic language that lamented the decline of the Indian populations and placed some of the blame squarely on Indian shoulders. Delegates called for a united front among all Indians in an attempt to protect themselves against their common enemies.[15]

During the next several weeks, all Confederate Indian forces surrendered. If Indian leaders still pondered their postwar fate, U.S. emissaries cleared up those uncertainties at a meeting with representatives of the Five Nations and other groups at Fort Smith, Arkansas, in September. Because the Indians had made war against the United States, proclaimed the American envoys, they forfeited all rights and expectations from previous treaties. Nations and tribes would be expected to make peace with each other and with the United States, abolish slavery, surrender portions of their lands for the relocation of other Natives into Indian Territory, and submit to a policy that united all Indian groups in the territory under one government. Federal officials made no distinction between Natives who had supported the rebellion and those who had not. Indian delegates understandably rejected the terms and refused to conclude an official settlement at Fort Smith, though all eventually negotiated Reconstruction treaties with the federal government. Though some tribes fared better than others in negotiations, those Reconstruction treaties essentially made official most of the American demands announced at Fort Smith and enumerated exactly how much land each Indian nation or tribe would cede.[16]

Those bitter postwar years are the focus of Christopher B. Bean's essay on Reconstruction in Indian Territory. Bean chronicles the negotiations between Native American representatives and federal officials and assesses the motives, actions, and successes and failures of each. Federal officials sought to open the region to white settlement, while consolidating Indian governments under congressional rule and taking a significant early step toward the policy of assimilation. Interestingly, Bean demonstrates in detail that resultant treaties varied based on Indian negotiation strategies. Rather than provide a well-ordered postscript to the war, the Reconstruction years witnessed the continuation of antebellum and wartime conflicts with railroad companies and other territorial outsiders and ever-widening rifts between Indian progressives and traditionalists.

The most controversial battle to emerge during the Reconstruction years in Indian Territory remains contentious today—what would be the fate of the Indian nations' former slaves? Linda W. Reese expertly examines the intense and sometimes violent struggle between Indian nation members and freedpeople and demonstrates that, like most issues with the war era in Indian Territory, no simple conclusion applies to every community. Federal officials expected the Indian nations to grant full rights of citizenship to their former slaves, a proposal many leaders and members vehemently opposed. While Native officials verbally sparred with federal representatives in Washington, Indians and freedpeople waged a brutal conflict in Indian Territory. Both Union- and Confederate-affiliated Indian nations endeavored to limit the rights of freedpeople, in some cases even calling for, ironically, the removal of former slaves to segregated areas within the territory. Freedpeople encountered the greatest difficulty and daily uncertainty in the Choctaw and Chickasaw Nations.

The modern continuation of that controversy highlights the importance of public memory of the Civil War, a subject that has garnered much attention from scholars during recent years. Amanda Cobb-Greetham examines memories of Creek and Cherokee women of the war period as recorded in the Indian-Pioneer Papers and places that project in the context of the growing scholarly literature on historical memory. The accounts focus on the difficulties of daily life, material conditions, struggles for food and shelter, and the survivors' return to destroyed homes and devastated landscapes more so than on the war's political causes and consequences or its transformative effects on the country. The women's memories also lend individual voices and perspectives to the larger issues addressed in other essays within this collection.

In an insightful essay that approaches Civil War memory from a modern angle, Whit Edwards lends his expertise in the area of public or applied history and examines commemoration of the war in Indian Territory. Edwards explains where and how the general populace often learns about the conflict in light of its relative obscurity in textbooks and public school curricula. Public historians grapple with the challenge of making the war relevant and accessible to a general audience and to that end employ numerous methodologies. Edwards explains that historical reenactments have emerged as an effective forum through which to inform individuals about the war and to encourage them to pursue further research. Reenactments communicate human dimensions of the conflict in ways that statues and memorials cannot convey.

The diverse population and myriad dimensions of the war in Indian Territory present public historians with unique challenges in their quest to commemorate the war in the territory and to communicate with a large audience the important questions examined throughout this collection.

In the end, Native Americans' determined but problematic pursuit of sovereignty best illustrates the distinctive character of the Civil War and Reconstruction in Indian Territory. Although the territory was geographically similar to border regions such as Missouri and Kentucky, the residents of those states were U.S. citizens who shared their national and cultural identities with other citizens in the North or the South or both. While some Native Americans exhibited genuine loyalties to either the Union or the Confederacy, they were not U.S. citizens, and the protection of their own people understandably motivated them more than any other factor. They found themselves fighting to protect a precarious position as semi-independent nations with the unusual dual status of communities distinct from the American citizenry yet legally considered wards of the federal government.

Unfortunately for Native Americans in Indian Territory, the Civil War presented a threat to their sovereignty more than an opportunity to secure it. A Union victory delivered only a step backward from true independence, while a Confederate victory portended the unknown, though at the very least it would have further divided Indian peoples and prolonged slavery within the Indian nations. Ultimately that paradox demonstrates yet another in the long list of tragedies associated with the Civil War. The Indian nations almost certainly stood to gain nothing from their participation, yet neutrality proved unrealistic for groups of quasi-independent peoples caught between two powerful belligerents. Still, the Indian participants for the most part were not innocent bystanders. They played an active role in their theater of the war, and for that the Union victors punished them severely during Reconstruction. The disastrous dimension of Reconstruction in Indian Territory was not that the Confederate-allied Indians were punished. They had fought an armed rebellion against the United States, and for that they expected and received punishment. The great transgression was that the federal government treated all Natives in the same manner and punished even those who chose not to support the Confederacy. Moreover, as Bean's essay demonstrates, in the long term the U.S. government penalized the Confederate-allied Indians more severely than it punished the residents of the eleven former Confederate states.

The same U.S. government that waged a heroic war effort to preserve the nation and destroy slavery perpetrated the moral crimes of the Indian Reconstruction treaties. Some of the same Indian groups who fought courageously to protect the interests of their peoples switched sides when it proved convenient, Indians on both sides owned slaves, and certain Indian participants willfully endeavored to preserve chattel slavery. The story of the Civil War in Indian Territory is one of shades of gray rather than black and white or heroes and villains.

The eight essays that follow examine this nuanced story of layered conflicts within the larger war from multiple angles. These include the military front and the home front, the experiences of the Five Nations and those of the agency tribes in the western portion of the territory, the severe conflicts between Native Americans and the federal government and between Indian nations and their former slaves during and beyond the Reconstruction years, and the concept of memory through the lenses of Native American oral traditions and the modern craft of public history. The essays are carefully crafted to provide accessible summaries and analyses of the subject matter for students, general readers, and scholars. In an attempt to preserve the readability of the essays yet provide materials useful to scholars and those who wish to pursue further research, the authors have provided detailed sources and have restricted historiographical dialogue to the endnotes. It is our hope that this collection provides a crossroads of sorts for scholars and especially students interested in the Civil War, Native American history, and Oklahoma history.

NOTES

1. James M. McPherson, "The War that Never Goes Away," in McPherson, *Drawn with the Sword: Reflections on the American Civil War* (New York: Oxford University Press, 1996), 55–65.
2. Earl J. Hess, *The Civil War in the West: Victory and Defeat from the Appalachians to the Mississippi* (Chapel Hill: University of North Carolina Press, 2012); Bradley R. Clampitt, *The Confederate Heartland: Military and Civilian Morale in the Western Confederacy* (Baton Rouge: Louisiana State University Press, 2011); Charles D. Grear, ed., *The Fate of Texas: The Civil War and the Lone Star State* (Fayetteville: University of Arkansas Press, 2008); Kenneth W. Howell, *The Seventh Star of the Confederacy: Texas during the Civil War* (Denton: University of North Texas Press, 2009); Richard Lowe, *Walker's Texas Division, C. S. A.: Greyhounds of the Trans-Mississippi* (Baton Rouge: Louisiana State University Press, 2004); Gary D. Joiner, *Through the Howling Wilderness: The 1864 Red River Campaign and Union Failure in the West* (Knoxville: University of Tennessee Press, 2006); Stephen A. Townsend, *The Yankee Invasion of Texas* (College Station: Texas A&M University Press, 2005); Jeffrey S. Prushankin, *A Crisis in Confederate Command: Edmund Kirby Smith, Richard Taylor, and the Army of the Trans-Mississippi* (Baton Rouge: Louisiana State University Press, 2005); Stephen A. Dupree, *Planting the Union Flag in Texas: The Campaigns of Major General Nathaniel P. Banks in the West* (College Station: Texas A&M University Press, 2008).
3. Mary Jane Warde, *When the Wolf Came: The Civil War and the Indian Territory* (Fayetteville: University of Arkansas Press, 2013); Lary C. Rampp and Donald L. Rampp, *The Civil War in the Indian Territory* (Austin TX: Presidial, 1975); LeRoy H. Fischer, ed., *The Civil War Era in Indian Territory* (Los Angeles: Lorrin L. Morrison, 1974); Laurence M. Hauptman, *Between Two Fires: American Indians in the Civil War* (New York: Free Press, 1995); John C. Waugh, *Sam Bell Maxey and the Confederate Indians* (Abilene TX: McWhiney Foundation,

1998); Clarissa W. Confer, *The Cherokee Nation in the Civil War* (Norman: University of Oklahoma Press, 2007); Annie Heloise Abel, *The American Indian in the Civil War* (3 vols.) (Cleveland OH: Arthur H. Clark, 1915–1925). Abel's three volumes have been reprinted by the University of Nebraska Press as *The American Indian as Slaveholder and Secessionist* (Lincoln, 1992); *The American Indian in the Civil War, 1862–1865* (Lincoln, 1992); and *The American Indian and the End of the Confederacy, 1863–1865* (Lincoln, 1993).

4. Douglas Hale, "Rehearsal for Civil War: The Texas Cavalry in the Indian Territory, 1861," *Chronicles of Oklahoma* 68 (Fall 1990): 233–34; Robert L. Kerby, *Kirby Smith's Confederacy: The Trans-Mississippi South, 1863–1865* (New York: Columbia University Press, 1972), 4; Rampp and Rampp, *Civil War in the Indian Territory*, 1; Confer, *Cherokee Nation in the Civil War*, 4–7; Fischer, *Civil War Era in Indian Territory*, 1. In this collection the term "Five Nations" is used instead of "Five Tribes" or "Five Civilized Tribes." For some historians, "Five Tribes" has generally replaced the traditional "Five Civilized Tribes" in scholarly usage in large part because of the elusive definition of "civilization" and because of judgments of other cultures implicit in the term. The traditional "Five Civilized Tribes" reference, used by whites and the tribes themselves, referred to the parallels between Five Nations' cultures and mainstream American cultures. The nations also used the terms in part to distinguish between themselves and Plains tribes, whom they considered more "wild" or "savage." The Five Nations individually and collectively fit the definition of nation in that they pursued and preserved political sovereignty and controlled specific regions through a commitment to written, codified governments. For the evolution of the use of "tribe," see David La Vere, *Contrary Neighbors: Southern Plains and Removed Indians in Indian Territory* (Norman: University of Oklahoma Press, 2000), 21–22.

5. Fischer, *Civil War Era in Indian Territory*, 11–14; F. Todd Smith, *The Caddos, the Wichitas, and the United States, 1846–1901* (College Station: Texas A&M University Press, 1996), chaps. 3 and 4.

6. Hale, "Rehearsal for Civil War," 233–34; Kerby, *Kirby Smith's Confederacy*, 4; Rampp and Rampp, *Civil War in the Indian Territory*, 1; Confer, *Cherokee Nation in the Civil War*, 4–7.

7. Hauptman, *Between Two Fires*, ix–xii, 1–13; Rampp and Rampp, *Civil War in the Indian Territory*, 3.

8. Fischer, *Civil War Era in Indian Territory*, 15, 16 (quotation); Hauptman, *Between Two Fires*, ix–xii, 1–13; Rampp and Rampp, *Civil War in the Indian Territory*, 3; Waugh, *Sam Bell Maxey and the Confederate Indians*, 29–30.

9. George E. Baker, ed., *The Works of William H. Seward* (Boston: Houghton, Mifflin, 1853–1884), 4:346–67.

10. E. D. Townsend to Secretary of War, March 27, 1861, in United States War Department, *The War of the Rebellion: A Compilation of the Official Records*

of the Union and Confederate Armies, 128 vols. (Washington DC: Government Printing Office, 1880–1901) (hereafter cited as *Official Records*) ser. 1, vol. 1, 659–60; Smith, *Caddos, Wichitas, and the United States*, 78–84; La Vere, *Contrary Neighbors*, 62–90; A. M. Gibson, "Confederates on the Plains: The Pike Mission to Wichita Agency," *Great Plains Journal* 4 (Fall 1964): 8. Fort Gibson, in the Cherokee Nation, had been abandoned in 1857 but would witness extensive wartime activity. Fort Towson, in the Choctaw Nation, had been turned over to the Choctaw Indian Agency in 1854 and ceased operation as an active military post. It was occupied temporarily by Confederates during the war.

11. See various orders, reports, and correspondence in *Official Records*, ser. 1, vol. 1, 648–53, 656–57, 659–67; see also Dean Trickett, "The Civil War in Indian Territory, 1861," *The Chronicles of Oklahoma* 17 (September 1939): 318–22 and n30.

12. Hauptman, *Between Two Fires*, 25–26; Confer, *Cherokee Nation in the Civil War*, 45–46.

13. Steven E. Woodworth and Kenneth J. Winkle, eds., *Atlas of the Civil War* (New York: Oxford University Press, 2004), 310; Arrell Morgan Gibson, "Native Americans and the Civil War," *American Indian Quarterly* 9 (Fall 1985): 390–93; Rampp and Rampp, *Civil War in Indian Territory*, 11–146.

14. Brad R. Clampitt, "'An Indian Shall Not Spill an Indian's Blood': The Confederate-Indian Conference at Camp Napoleon, 1865," *Chronicles of Oklahoma* 83 (Spring 2005): 34–53; J. J. Reynolds to James Harlan, June 28, 1865, *Official Records*, ser. 1, vol. 48, pt. 2, 1018; Camp Napoleon Compact, May 26, 1865, *Official Records*, ser. 1, vol. 48, pt. 2, 1102–3; Edmund Kirby Smith to Albert Pike, April 8, 1865, *Official Records*, ser. 1, vol. 48, pt. 2, 1266–69; C. S. West to W. D. Reagan, *Official Records*, ser. 1, vol. 48, pt. 2, 1279–80; Kirby Smith to D. H. Cooper, *Official Records*, ser. 1, vol. 48, pt. 2, 1270; Cooper to James W. Throckmorton, May 16, 1865, *Official Records*, ser. 1, vol. 48, pt. 2, 1307; Cooper to W. P. Adair, May 16, 1865, *Official Records*, ser. 1, vol. 48, pt. 2, 1307–8; Cooper to Throckmorton, May 22, 1865, *Official Records*, ser. 1, vol. 48, pt. 2, 1317; James C. Veatch to J. Schuyler Crosby, July 20, 1865, *Official Records*, ser. 1, vol. 48, pt. 2, 1095–97; Interview with Charles Stewart Lewis, March 11, 1938, in Indian-Pioneer History, ed. Grant Foreman, 112 vols., unpublished manuscript, 109:157, Research Division, Oklahoma Historical Society, Oklahoma City; Testimony of James Webb Throckmorton, *Congressional Record*, 49th Cong., 1st sess., March 9, 1886, ser. 2236, pt. 3, 17; Maurice Boyd, *Kiowa Voices: Myths, Legends, and Folktales* (Fort Worth: Texas Christian University Press, 1981), 163; Council Minutes, May 13, 16, 20, 1865, Peter P. Pitchlynn Papers, Gilcrease Institute, Tulsa OK; William P. Adair to Stand Watie, May 13, 1865, in *Cherokee Cavaliers: Forty Years of Cherokee History as Told in the Correspondence of the Ridge-Watie-Boudinot Family*, ed. Edward E. Dale and

Gaston Litton (Norman: University of Oklahoma Press, 1939), 224–25; Pitchlynn to Smith, May 17, 1865, Peter P. Pitchlynn Papers, Western History Collections, University of Oklahoma, Norman.

15. Clampitt, "Camp Napoleon," 43–47; Camp Napoleon Compact and Camp Napoleon Minutes, May 25–27, 1865, Pitchlynn Papers, Gilcrease Institute; Reynolds to Harlan, June 28, 1865, *Official Records*, ser. 1, vol. 48, pt. 2, 1018; Cooper to S. S. Anderson, May 15, 1865, *Official Records*, ser. 1, vol. 48, pt. 2, 1306; Camp Napoleon Compact, May 26, 1865, *Official Records*, ser. 1, vol. 48, pt. 2, 1102–3; U.S. Commissioner of Indian Affairs, *Annual Reports*, 39th Cong., 1st sess., 1865, H. Ex. Doc., vol. 2, pt. 1, serial 1248, 202.

16. Gibson, "Native Americans and the Civil War," 405; M. Thomas Bailey, *Reconstruction in Indian Territory: A Story of Avarice, Discrimination, and Opportunism* (Port Washington NY: Kennikat, 1972). Several Plains tribes, including Comanches, Kiowas, Cheyennes, Arapahos, and Kiowa-Apaches, played a relatively minor role in the war. At a meeting in Kansas in October 1865, American officials assigned those tribes to various reservations in Indian Territory, Kansas, and the Texas Panhandle.

1   Bitter Legacy

The Battle Front

Richard B. McCaslin

Abraham Lincoln never read Clausewitz, but if he had, he would have found much that sounded quite familiar. The embattled president pursued a Clausewitzian strategy during the Civil War that blended political with military objectives. His four steps to a Union victory became to secure the border states, isolate the Confederacy diplomatically, defeat the Confederate armies, and eliminate the South's will to resist. In order to win, he had to do this throughout the Confederacy, which included Indian Territory. As long as Confederate forces operated there, threatening the adjacent border states, undermining Lincoln's diplomatic claims of military primacy, and encouraging violent resistance to Federal authority, the Civil War would continue. Confederates seized the initiative from the Federals several times in Indian Territory, but they lacked effective leaders and military resources. By the war's end, Federals occupied much of the territory, and Indians, Unionist and Confederate alike, had yet another bitter legacy to contemplate.[1]

For Indians who remained loyal to the Union, life became complicated when the U.S. Army in 1861 abandoned its three active forts in Indian Territory—Arbuckle, Washita, and Cobb—and withdrew north into Kansas. These outposts were occupied by Texans under the command of Col. William C. Young, who advanced slowly in May. His entry into the territory was facilitated by the efforts of commissioners sent by the Texas secession convention to meet with the Five Nations. The governor of the Chickasaws, Cyrus Harris, readily cooperated, and the envoys were welcomed by Choctaw leaders as well. Cherokee leader John Ross did not welcome the agents, but at a council in April with Cherokees, Creeks, Seminoles, and others, the commissioners were told that all those present would support the Confederacy.[2]

The Texas commissioners were soon joined by an official agent of the Confederacy. Albert Pike was a former captain in the U.S. Army who had settled in Arkansas as a lawyer and an Indian agent. He was known to be eccentric, but Confederate authorities chose him as their commissioner to secure alliances with the Five Nations. Pike expected to work with Ben McCulloch, a Texas Ranger who was appointed as a brigadier general and told to organize Confederate forces in the territory. McCulloch had been promised a regiment from each of three adjacent states—Texas, Arkansas, and Louisiana—and was also expected to raise several regiments of Indians with Pike's help.[3]

Both sides wanted the support of the powerful Cherokees. McCulloch and Pike together went to Ross's home near Tahlequah, but Ross refused to muster even a home guard. He was in a difficult position. His supporters were deeply divided, with reasons to support either faction in the national conflict. At the same time he was opposed by Cherokees led by Stand Watie, who quickly recruited a mounted regiment and was appointed as a Confederate colonel by McCulloch. Ross subsequently convened his executive council in August 1861 and signed an alliance with the Confederacy. He then authorized the muster of a second regiment of Cherokee cavalry led by John T. Drew, who had friends among the followers of both Watie and Ross. In October 1861, with two regiments of Cherokee troopers already in the field, Pike signed alliances with Ross, Watie, Drew, and other Cherokee leaders.[4]

While Pike and McCulloch mustered the Cherokees, Pike also organized other Confederate forces within the Five Nations. He found the Creeks split into hostile factions like the Cherokees. Opothleyahola and his allies remained loyal to the Union, while his opponents did not. Prominent among the latter were Daniel N. and Chilly McIntosh, half-brothers whose father, William, had been killed by Opothleyahola's followers. Pike during July 1861 signed a treaty with the McIntosh brothers, promising them that they would serve only in Indian Territory. Pike's meeting with the Choctaws and Chickasaws went more smoothly thanks to Col. Douglas H. Cooper, who convinced both groups to support the Confederacy before Pike arrived. Cooper also enlisted a mounted regiment, which Pike again pledged would stay in the territory. The Seminoles divided as well over supporting the Confederacy, but John Jumper convinced some to fight for the South, and Pike agreed that they would serve with the McIntosh brothers.[5]

Pike's diplomatic efforts sparked bloody clashes. When the Creeks quarreled, Pike ordered Cooper to use his Choctaws and Chickasaws to crush the Unionists. Many who opposed the pro-Confederate Creeks fled to Kansas, along with pro-Union Cherokee refugees, but many others joined Opothleyahola. When the latter led his group, about two-thirds of which were noncombatants, north toward Kansas, Cooper attacked. He struck first at Round Mountain on November 16, 1861, but his command, which included the McIntosh brothers and Jumper as well as Texas cavalry, was repulsed. Opothleyahola retreated that night, so Cooper claimed a victory. Drew joined Cooper with his Cherokees, but in a clash at Bird Creek on December 9 the new arrivals refused to fight, and the Creeks again bested their pursuers. Cooper begged for reinforcements to replace Drew's unreliable men and received almost 1,400 troops from Arkansas and Texas, including Young's command. Cooper hit the Creek camp at Chustenahlah, near the site of the Bird Creek battle, on December 26. Texas troopers dismounted and drove the Creeks, along with some Seminoles, from a steep, rocky ridge. The retreating warriors were joined by panic-stricken women and children, and Confederate riders killed many.[6]

Chustanahlah marked a gloomy end to the first year of the war for pro-Union Indians. Watie arrived late in the fighting and led the pursuit the next day, when many more Unionists were killed and others were captured. When Watie tired of the chase, Cooper continued to hunt stragglers, who had no food, or shelter from snow and sleet. Several thousand sad survivors, including Opothleyahola, stumbled into Kansas, where they and other Indian refugees starved in makeshift shelters through a bitter winter. Lucky ones settled near military outposts, where some officers provided supplies on their own initiative.

The Indians' plight complicated Federal efforts to press the Confederates in the territory as well as elsewhere in the far west. Lincoln, to improve his prospects, assigned Maj. Gen. Henry W. Halleck to command the new Department of Missouri and sent Maj. Gen. David H. Hunter to direct the new Department of Kansas, where Hunter worked hard to support the refugees. On the Confederate side, Pike became a brigadier general in the late fall of 1861 and took command of all Indian troops. Concerned like his Federal counterparts about the failure of his superiors to support Indian allies, by February 1862 Pike established a headquarters at Fort Davis, on the southern side of the Arkansas River near Fort Gibson, abandoned since 1857. There he continued to bicker with Confederate authorities.

Seeking like Lincoln to improve his prospects in the far west, Jefferson Davis sent Maj. Gen. Earl Van Dorn to command the Trans-Mississippi District. Van Dorn was eager to regain Missouri, so he merged the forces of Pike, McCulloch, and Brig. Gen. Sterling Price, the former governor of Missouri, for a campaign. Union troops had driven Price out of Missouri in February 1862, and McCulloch settled with him in northern Arkansas, along with Van Dorn. Pike was told to join them with most of his Indian units, including troops from all of the Five Nations. He struggled to supply his men and convince them to fight outside Indian Territory despite his earlier promises. In the end he marched with only the two Cherokee regiments led by Watie and Drew; the McIntosh brothers lagged behind to locate Cooper, and all three arrived too late for the fighting at Pea Ridge. At that place Van Dorn fought a battle on March 7 and 8, 1862, but he did not win the victory he sought.[7]

The engagement at Pea Ridge began with a clash between Pike's Cherokees and Union cavalry. The Federal troopers were shocked by the fierce appearance of their enemy, and a Missouri regiment balked when ordered to charge. The Indians, joined by Texans, swarmed over a three-gun battery and threw the Federals into a panicked retreat. Rallying Union troops drove back Pike's men but failed to recover the guns. The fight degenerated into a melee, with Cherokees sniping from the woods while Texas cavalry and infantry from Arkansas and Louisiana engaged other Federals. Union reinforcements flanked the Confederates, McCulloch was killed, and the Southern attack collapsed. Pike led some of his Cherokees to the Confederate far left, where he arrived after nightfall. Others straggled in later, but Drew's men actually left for home. Both sides reorganized during the night, and Van Dorn put Pike's Indians (Watie's regiment and some newly arrived Creeks) in his lines. After an artillery duel, during which most of the Confederate guns ran out of ammunition or were disabled, the Federals advanced on the morning of March 8. The Southern lines broke, and Van Dorn ordered a withdrawal that became a rout, with Confederates being chased deep into the Arkansas hills while a freezing rain fell.

After Pea Ridge, reports of Indian atrocities surfaced. Brig. Gen. Samuel R. Curtis, the commander of the Union army at Pea Ridge, accused Pike's Indians of scalping Federal dead and wounded. Others said the mutilated bodies numbered as high as forty, and the culprits were said to be Drew's Cherokees. Pike denounced the behavior of his Cherokees, and he forbade them to kill any wounded soldiers or take scalps. What was not commonly reported was that Indian prisoners were killed by Federals while allegedly trying to escape and that the Indian dead, unlike the bodies of white Confederates, were left unburied on the field. Pvt. William H. Marsh of the Thirteenth Illinois Infantry observed that "a pile of dead Indians" lay "in a hollow near the ridge," where he assumed they had been "overlooked when the dead were buried." In other words, Indians became unwelcome in Confederate armies, while their own experiences on battlefields dominated by white men discouraged many from seeking further service outside their own lands.[8]

Pike left Pea Ridge alone and found his men on the border of Indian Territory. Both Cherokee regiments were there, as well as Cooper's Choctaws and Chickasaws and a detachment of Daniel N. McIntosh's Creeks, who had arrived too late to fight. Watie's Cherokees served as the rearguard as Pike retreated to within a day's ride of the Red River. There Pike established a headquarters, Fort Ben McCulloch, on the Texas Road, the main path from Kansas through Indian Territory into Texas. Pike resented broken promises of supplies and reinforcements, as well as having to bring Indians out of their homelands in violation of formal agreements. He was further infuriated when Van Dorn went east of the Mississippi River, where his men were needed after the Confederate defeat at Shiloh. This left the Indians virtually alone against Federals, again in contradiction to promises of protection. Furthermore, Van Dorn took with him materials intended for the Indians, and he did not defend Pike against charges that Pike's Cherokees had committed atrocities. In a foul mood, Pike ignored instructions to defend Arkansas and instead furloughed many of his men.

Pvt. Edward H. Ingraham of the Thirty-Third Illinois Infantry wrote from Arkansas in May 1862, "No further bloodshed is expected here except occasional skirmishes with the wandering half civilized hordes in the south west." Confederate operations during that summer in Indian Territory were primarily left to Watie and Drew, who led a few hundred men in guerilla raids within the Cherokee Nation. Senator James M. Lane of Kansas, an abolitionist veteran of the violence that wracked his state before the war, pressed for decisive action to quash Indian support for the Confederacy. He provided an example of what he wanted by raiding Missouri, killing many people and bringing back freed slaves and wagons filled with loot. He also pushed hard to change the military commanders in Kansas, and Lincoln replaced Hunter with Brig. Gen. James G. Blunt during May 1862. Blunt was another Kansas abolitionist and had commanded some of Lane's irregulars, but his objectives differed from those Lane advocated. Blunt intended to eliminate Confederate raiders in the territory, pressure the Confederates in Arkansas, and return Unionist Indians to their lands, where they would be protected in part by Indian regiments.[9]

When Federals marched down the Texas Road into Indian Territory in June 1862, Blunt stayed behind, giving command of the advance to Col. William Weer, another of Lane's Jayhawkers. Weer had a pair of Indian regiments, Cherokees and Creeks; two regiments of white infantry; three regiments of white cavalry; and two artillery batteries. Confederate Cherokees called for help, but Pike sent just a few companies under Cooper, while a single Missouri battalion came from Arkansas. Federals scattered Watie's men and surprised the Missourians, most of whom became prisoners. Drew's Cherokees defected; so many joined Weer that he organized an Indian regiment led by Maj. William A. Phillips, an abolitionist newspaper reporter who declined a lucrative job offer from Horace Greeley to remain in the west as an officer. A Federal detachment visited Ross, presenting him with a dilemma. He wanted to ally with the Union, but Confederates expected him to honor his treaty with them. The Federals solved the riddle by arresting Ross, making it impossible for him to obey Confederate orders. He was sent to Fort Leavenworth, whence he traveled to Washington to meet Lincoln.

Cooper struggled to organize an effective resistance, but the Federals beat themselves. Weer camped for days, apparently trying to decide what to do while abusing his subordinates and drinking. Morale dwindled until Col. Frederick C. Salomon, a former Prussian officer, arrested Weer and took charge. Salomon told Blunt that Weer "was either insane, premeditated treachery to his troops, or perhaps that his grossly intemperate habits long continued had produced idiocy or monomania."[10] Weer in fact was a notorious alcoholic, and Blunt had ignored that. Salomon then led most of his troops north, leaving behind the three Indian regiments under the command of Col. Robert W. Furnas. Some of Furnas's troopers, led by Phillips, routed a Confederate force near Fort Gibson in July 1862. But Salomon's withdrawal into Kansas forced Furnas to move his headquarters to Baxter Springs. Furnas was followed by thousands of miserable refugees from among the Unionist Cherokees.

Weer's collapse did not save Pike's military career. Maj. Gen. Thomas C. Hindman returned to Arkansas, for which he had previously served as a U.S. congressman, in the summer of 1862 as the Confederate commander of the Trans-Mississippi. He labored to restore order, but his harsh measures generated many protests. Pike accused Hindman of stealing supplies meant for Indians, while Hindman fumed because Pike would not join in campaigns from Arkansas into Missouri. To mollify protesters, Davis in July 1862 appointed Maj. Gen. Theophilus H. Holmes to supersede Hindman, but Holmes let Hindman remain in command of Arkansas, Missouri, and Indian Territory. Pike submitted such a hostile letter of resignation that Cooper called for his arrest. Pike then picked a fight with Holmes and disappeared into Texas. When Pike resurfaced Holmes had him arrested and then let him resign. As Holmes explained to Davis, "Genl. Pike has ruined us in the Indian Country, and I fear it will be long before we can reestablish the confidence he has destroyed." Holmes added, "Please accept Pike's resignation as he has head enough to do us great injury with the Indians but has not judgment enough to do us good anywhere."[11]

Similar command tangles hindered Union efforts to expand upon Weer's meager success. A furious Blunt met Salomon at Fort Scott, declined to hold a court martial, and then appointed Salomon and Weer as brigadier generals. But Union plans to return to Indian Territory had to be postponed when Blunt's command became a district in the new Department of Missouri. Most important, Blunt was made subordinate to Maj. Gen. John M. Schofield, whose principal concern was Missouri. In the fall of 1862 Schofield ordered Blunt to support his operations there.

Ironically, Blunt's troops encountered some old foes in Missouri. After Pike left, Cooper brought about two thousand Texans and Indians—including his own Choctaws and Chickasaws and Watie's Cherokees—to northern Arkansas. Hindman added Missouri cavalry led by Col. Joseph O. Shelby to Cooper's command and then ordered him north to forage around Newtonia. Blunt sent Weer and Salomon to scout, but when they met the Confederates, the outnumbered Union troops had to withdraw. Schofield reinforced and struck again on October 4, routing the Southerners. Cooper led his Indians back to Indian Territory, chased by Blunt, while Schofield rode east in pursuit of the primary Confederate force. Blunt attacked Cooper once more on October 22 in the Cherokee Nation, driving the Confederates and taking their artillery. Cooper retreated to Fort Davis, thus conceding control of the territory north of the Arkansas River.[12]

Federal authorities were determined to eliminate Hindman's army, so Blunt marched into Arkansas in the late fall of 1862. Capt. Jacob D. Brewster described Blunt's Indian troops as "a queer set, mounted on ponies and most of them have their squaws & children with them & on the march the family all ride on the one pony." Blunt struck a Confederate cavalry force at Cane Hill on November 28 and then waited for Hindman to attack. When Hindman tried to flank the Federals, a tangled fight erupted on December 7 at Prairie Grove, and the Confederates had to withdraw. Blunt surprised Hindman three weeks later at Van Buren, scattering the Confederates. Hindman retreated toward Little Rock, where he requested and received a transfer. Schofield chastised Blunt for letting Hindman escape, but others applauded the victory at Prairie Grove, and Blunt got a promotion to major general.[13]

While Blunt chased Hindman, Phillips, now a colonel in charge of the Indian regiments formerly commanded by Furnas, led them and some Kansas cavalrymen into Indian Territory in an attempt to finish Cooper and Watie. He destroyed Fort Davis and heavily damaged the property of pro-Confederate Indians who fled as he advanced, but he could not force a showdown. He shuttled between Arkansas and the territory for months and then settled by April 1863 at Fort Gibson (which he called Fort Blunt). Under Phillips's supervision, the Cherokee executive council met and repudiated the Cherokees' 1861 treaty with the Confederacy. In response, Cherokee Confederates assembled at Webber's Falls and elected Watie to be their leader. This attracted the notice of Phillips, who routed Watie and destroyed his camp in a dawn attack. During the next few months Watie raided the Federals several times in retaliation but accomplished little.

The loss of Arkansas Post in January 1863 convinced Davis that another change was needed in the Trans-Mississippi. Lt. Gen. Edmund Kirby Smith took charge of the department, while Holmes, also promoted to lieutenant general, replaced Hindman in command of Arkansas. Brig. Gen. William Steele, a West Point graduate from New York who lived in Texas, took charge of Indian Territory. He established his headquarters at Fort Smith, while Cooper stayed in the southern part of the territory. When Schofield sent thousands of Federals from the Trans-Mississippi theater to the Vicksburg campaign, Holmes decided to attack. The effort failed; Holmes was repulsed at Helena, while Watie tried to take a wagon train at Cabin Creek and was beaten. Phillips, alarmed at the approach of Cooper with a superior force, had asked Blunt for support. In response Blunt sent two regiments of infantry and a section of artillery along with three hundred wagons loaded with supplies. These Federals, joined by six hundred of Phillips's Indians, found Watie dug in across the Texas Road in June 1863. Rattled by cannon fire and discouraged when reinforcements did not arrive, the Confederates quit the field after several days of fighting and allowed the Union column to reach Fort Gibson.

The Confederacy suffered heavy blows in early July 1863 at Gettysburg and Vicksburg, and Kirby Smith tried to boost morale by winning a quick victory. He sent Arkansas troops to reinforce Watie and ordered Cooper to join them as well. Their target was Fort Gibson, but Blunt hurried there with his soldiers after the fight at Cabin Creek. The reinforced Federals attacked at Honey Creek on July 17, before the Arkansans arrived. Watie's and Cooper's Confederates outnumbered their attackers and had entrenched across the Texas Road, but a rainstorm wet their powder. At the same time Union artillery pounded them. The First Kansas Infantry (Colored) led the main Federal assault, flanked by dismounted Colorado and Cherokee troopers. When the Union advance halted to let the Cherokees adjust their position, the Twenty-Ninth Texas

Cavalry mistook this for a retreat and charged into the black infantry's volleys. Devastated, the surviving Texans and others began to flee. Blunt pressed his attacks, forcing the Confederates to burn their supply depot at Honey Springs and abandon the field to him in the largest engagement of the Civil War in Indian Territory. Arkansas troops did arrive late in the day, but they could do nothing in the chaos.

Blunt pressed his advantage after Honey Springs. He returned to Fort Gibson, where he was reinforced by the Second Kansas Cavalry under Col. William F. Cloud. With about 4,500 men, Blunt crossed the Arkansas River on July 22, 1863, and moved south to find Cooper, Watie, and Brig. Gen. William L. Cabell, the West Point graduate from Virginia who had led the Arkansas troops to Indian Territory. Allegedly the three Confederates together had more than nine thousand soldiers, but they scattered as Blunt approached. Cabell marched for Fort Smith with three thousand, while the McIntosh brothers led the Confederate Creeks west. Cooper and Watie stayed with Steele, retreating south toward the Red River. Blunt chased Steele, skirmishing with him and destroying his supply depot at Perryville. Steele planned to attack at least a part of Blunt's forces, but a lack of reinforcements, destruction of his supplies, and persistent desertion forced him to cancel his scheme. Instead, his command dispersed. Blunt sent a detachment to harass Watie, dispatched another to maul the Creeks, and joined Cloud to chase Cabell. After clashing briefly with the Federals, Cabell retired into southwestern Arkansas, allowing Blunt to occupy Fort Smith.[14]

Blunt succumbed to illness and briefly transferred command to Cloud at Fort Smith, but his quick return to service allowed the Confederates to get a measure of revenge. After he recovered at Fort Scott, Blunt left that post for Fort Smith in the first week of October 1863, having heard that Confederate forces in southern Arkansas posed a threat. His slow-moving wagon train was escorted by fewer than one hundred troopers. On October 6 his group unexpectedly joined a fight between the Union garrison at Baxter Springs and a much larger guerilla force led by William C. Quantrill. The raiders, who had sacked Lawrence,

Kansas, in August 1863, had failed to take the outpost, and they eagerly descended upon Blunt's more vulnerable Federals arriving on the Texas Road. The Union force was overwhelmed, and few escaped alive. Blunt eluded his pursuers, gathered survivors, and did his best to harass his attackers. He also followed them to make certain he knew where they went and sent couriers to gather units for a counterstrike. But Quantrill escaped south to Texas for the winter. Soon after this humiliation Blunt was removed from district command.[15]

The Confederates had little time to savor their triumph over Blunt. Cooper, trying to maintain a presence north of the Arkansas River, sent Watie on a raid. Watie had an agenda as well: to disrupt a meeting of Cherokee Unionists. He scattered the assembly at Tahlequah and burned Ross's home. In December 1863 Colonel Phillips at Fort Gibson sent some of his Indian troopers in pursuit of Watie, and they found him on Barren Fork Creek. Watie outnumbered his pursuers, but the latter were well led and had a howitzer, which they used to good effect. Three dozen of Watie's troops were killed or wounded before the rest finally ran. That same month a frustrated Steele asked to be relieved. He was replaced with Brig. Gen. Samuel Bell Maxey, a West Point graduate who had moved from Kentucky to Texas before the war.

Maxey's efforts to organize a campaign were hindered by Cooper, who resented being superseded again, and by Phillips, who in February 1864 rode down the Texas Road from Fort Gibson with almost two thousand cavalry, laying waste to Choctaw and Chickasaw communities. Confederate casualties mounted as scattered units scrambled to confront the Union threat—Cooper established his headquarters at Fort Washita, directly in the Federals' path, but Quantrill refused to join him, claiming his men were not ready. Phillips wanted to raid Texas and did occupy Boggy Depot, but he canceled his attack on Fort Washita and retired north, leaving several hundred dead in his wake. Phillips also offered a treaty to the Choctaws, Chickasaws, and Seminoles, and their delegates met to discuss it. Both Maxey and Cooper attended the meeting, apologizing for the lack of Confederate support and promising to do better. Davis sent this same message, and the Indians renewed their allegiance.[16]

Maxey's plans for Indian Territory were next disrupted by orders from Kirby Smith to help block Maj. Gen. Frederick Steele's march south from Little Rock in support of Maj. Gen. Nathaniel P. Banks's drive up the Red River in Louisiana. Maxey led Brigadier General Richard M. Gano's Texans and Col. Tandy Walker's Choctaws to southern Arkansas, where they joined Brig. Gen. John S. Marmaduke in attacking a wagon train on April 18, 1864, at Poison Spring. In this engagement, Walker placed his Choctaws on the road between Steele's wagons and the Union base at Camden. When the train approached, the Indians participated in routing the escort, capturing 170 wagons and a four-gun battery. Many of the Federals were black, and some of them were killed after the battle by the Confederates. But the Choctaws could also recall that Phillips just months earlier had told his men to take no prisoners as they marched through Indian Territory. The war in the far west had become a blood feud. Steele, after losing more wagons and troops at Marks's Mill and learning of Banks's defeat, withdrew to Little Rock, suffering heavy casualties again in a last engagement at Jenkins Ferry.[17]

Maxey did not want to lose the initiative he believed he had gained with the victory over Steele. Returning to Indian Territory, he ordered Cherokee Col. William Penn Adair to lead several hundred mounted Indians (Cherokees, Creeks, Choctaws, and Seminoles) north across the Arkansas River. Quantrill was to join Adair but took another route. Both of them caused some damage while outdistancing their pursuers, and both returned south of the Arkansas by the first week of May 1864.

Maxey next turned to Watie. The Cherokee leader responded by capturing a steamboat bound for Fort Gibson in June 1864. For several months Federal authorities had pressed for using the Arkansas River to ship vital supplies to the post, but Phillips opposed the idea. A rise in the river seemed to negate many of his arguments, and $120,000 in cargo was loaded aboard the *J. R. Williams*, a stern-wheeler. Only one officer and twenty-five soldiers served as an escort. When Watie ambushed the vessel with three pieces of artillery, the Union troops abandoned the grounded boat and retreated toward Fort Smith, leaving the goods to Watie. Sadly for him, many Creeks and Seminoles departed with their loot, which left Watie without enough men to haul the rest of the cargo or defend it from Federal reinforcements, who soon approached. A flood provided a solution by washing away most of Watie's prize. He was encouraged by the arrival of Chickasaws, but when a detachment of them was overwhelmed by Union infantry, he burned his remaining booty and rode south. Watie was promoted to brigadier general for this feat, while Federal authorities at Fort Gibson worried about feeding thousands of Indian refugees left hungry by Watie's attack.

Maxey was heartened by these successes, as were some pro-Confederate Indians. In late June 1864 Watie's Cherokees and Walker's Choctaws reenlisted for the duration of the war. More summer raids followed by Gano, who captured more than a hundred Federals in an attack near Fort Smith, and Watie, who scattered a Union foraging party north of the Arkansas River. Maxie even probed the defenses of Fort Smith itself in early August. Gano provided a diversion while Watie and Cooper struck the pickets. Watie drove them into the main Union lines, and the Confederates continued to fight when a mounted detachment counterattacked. Nightfall allowed the raiders to retire in good order, carrying captured food and other supplies. Cooper, who managed most of the fighting, was pleased, but Watie was disappointed that the attack had not been pressed. The arrival of more Federals at Fort Smith during late August ended any discussion of another assault among the Confederates.

Watie and Cooper had been pushing for a large-scale raid north across the Arkansas River since midsummer 1864, and in September Maxey agreed. Told about the proposal, Kirby Smith also approved as part of a larger operation that included Maj. Gen. Sterling Price pushing north into Missouri. Kirby Smith considered the effort in Indian Territory to be a diversion for the primary campaign by Price, but he was intrigued by the claims of Watie and Cooper that they might reach Kansas. To add strength to the raid, Gano joined Watie and Cooper, and so by seniority Gano commanded the expedition in the field when Cooper elected to stay behind as the overall commander. Gano brought three Texas cavalry regiments and a partisan battalion. Watie had his brigade, which included two regiments of Cherokees and two of Choctaws, as well as Jumper's Seminole battalion. The Confederates thus totaled about two thousand men, along with six guns. Just before their departure, Cooper amended the plan to exclude Kansas; that would be the goal of a later operation. For the immediate future the targets were Union units and a supply train said to be traveling from Fort Scott to Fort Gibson.

Watie and Gano crossed the Arkansas River above Fort Gibson and found 125 Union soldiers cutting hay. The Federal commander, a captain, chose to fight; many of his troops were black, and it was commonly reported that the Confederates did not take black prisoners. The Federals repulsed the first assaults by Gano but were soon overwhelmed. Forty Federals were killed, while sixty-six were missing, wounded, or captured. Of the forty dead, thirty-three were black; only four survived the engagement. Gano and four hundred Texans found the train two days later, on September 18, 1864, at Cabin Creek on the Texas Road. The three hundred wagons were guarded by about six hundred Federals, Indian and white. Expecting an attack, they had taken cover inside a stockade.

Gano brought up his entire command, arranged with Watie's brigade on the left and his on the right, and then attacked before daylight on September 19. The Federals fought hard until after sunrise, but their lines broke after several attacks and a heavy rain of shot and shell from the Confederate artillery. They fled in disorder without their wagons; the desertion of the civilian teamsters, many of whom took their mules, prevented the recovery of any wagons not already taken by Watie's Confederates. About half of the wagons were driven away by the victors; others were destroyed after being looted. A Union brigade approached Gano's column as it rode south, but the Federals were exhausted after a hurried march and did not attack. After three days of hard work by their men, Gano and Watie delivered their wagons to Cooper. It was the most valuable prize ever taken by the Confederates in Indian Territory, and the raiders were commended by not only their military superiors but also the Confederate Congress.[18]

Maxey might well have expected a Union campaign against him during the summer and fall of 1864, especially after the raid by Gano and Watie, but quarrels among Federal commanders precluded any such operation. Blunt and Lane focused more on politics than soldiering, and Phillips became a target of their ire and was temporarily removed from command by late July. The success of Gano and Watie increased the bickering among Federal commanders, who believed that both Fort Gibson and Fort Smith might be the targets of an even greater Confederate attack. In fact, Cooper's plans for a raid into Kansas after Gano and Watie returned had to be canceled because of a lack of men and material. That was just as well for the Union leaders who had to cope with Price's raid into Missouri. The climax came on October 23 at Westport, in the largest battle of the Civil War west of the Mississippi River. Price, outnumbered two to one, was beaten and retired in a cold rain. Among his pursuers was Blunt, who also played a prominent role at Westport. The Federals caught Price at Mine Creek and scattered his forces, but the Confederates continued their flight south, losing men to Union attacks and desertion. Price entered Indian Territory west of Fort Scott and, left alone by Federals, made his way to Texas by way of Boggy Depot.

Cooper finally became the overall commander of Confederate forces in Indian Territory in February 1865, when Maxey was transferred to Texas at his own request. Watie succeeded Cooper in charge of all Indian troops. But it was too late for either man to accomplish much, and Watie concentrated the units under his control at Boggy Depot, conducting occasional patrols until the war's end. Confederates in the territory began surrendering in May 1865, while negotiations were underway for the Trans-Mississippi as a whole, and the process continued until July.

Cooper could surrender only the white troops; each of the Five Nations governments insisted upon surrendering separately. The Choctaws were first, on June 19 at Doaksville. Four days later, at the same place, Watie became the last Confederate general to surrender his men, who included Cherokees, Creeks, Seminoles, and Osages. The last to quit were the Chickasaws, who along with the Caddos agreed to terms on July 14. Lincoln did not live to see it, but when these last Confederate Indians laid down their arms, his Clausewitzian plan for victory was complete. Never again would Confederates from Indian Territory challenge the national government, while residents and refugees alike thought more about recovery than resistance.

NOTES

1. The standard study of military operations in Indian Territory during the Civil War has been Lary C. Rampp and Donald L. Rampp, *The Civil War in the Indian Territory* (Austin TX: Presidial, 1975). A more culturally nuanced perspective into the Five Nations at war is offered by Mary Jane Warde in her award-winning *When the Wolf Came: The Civil War and the Indian Territory* (Fayetteville: University of Arkansas Press, 2013). Another intriguing Indian perspective is provided by Laurence M. Hauptman in *Between Two Fires: American Indians in the Civil War* (New York: Free Press, 1996). Much about the Civil War in the territory within a regional context can be found in Jay Monaghan, *Civil War on the Western Border, 1854–1865* (Boston: Little, Brown, 1955); and Alvin M. Josephy, Jr., *The Civil War in the American West* (New York: Alfred A. Knopf, 1992). The classic work on the residents of Indian Territory in the Civil War remains the two volumes produced by Annie H. Abel: *The American Indian as Slaveholder and Secessionist* (Cleveland OH: Arthur H. Clark, 1915) and *The American Indian as a Participant in the Civil War* (Cleveland OH: Arthur H. Clark, 1919).
2. For more on William C. Young and his troopers, see Allen G. Hatley, *Reluctant Rebels: The Eleventh Texas Cavalry Regiment* (Hillsboro TX: Hill College, 2006).
3. More detailed information can be found in Walter Lee Brown, *The Life of Albert Pike* (Fayetteville: University of Arkansas Press, 1997). Thomas W. Cutrer's *Ben McCulloch and the Frontier Military Tradition* (Chapel Hill: University of North Carolina Press, 1993) provides great perspectives on both the man and the events in which he participated.
4. Clarissa W. Confer, in *The Cherokee Nation in the Civil War* (Norman: University of Oklahoma Press, 2012), recounts the hard decisions made by the Cherokees. This work is based upon her Penn State dissertation, which provided

information on all of the Five Nations in Indian Territory during the Civil War. The best works on John Ross are by Gary E. Moulton: *John Ross, Cherokee Chief* (Athens: University of Georgia Press, 1978) and *The Papers of Chief John Ross*, 2 vols. (Norman: University of Oklahoma Press, 1985). Stand Watie has drawn much attention as the only Indian to be a Confederate general. Among the best books on him, in chronological order, are Frank Cunningham, *General Stand Watie's Confederate Indians* (San Antonio TX: Naylor, 1959); Kenny A. Franks, *Stand Watie and the Agony of the Cherokee Nation* (Memphis TN: Memphis State University Press, 1979); and Wilfred Knight, *Red Fox: Stand Watie's Civil War Years in Indian Territory* (Glendale CA: Arthur H. Clark, 1988). Letters to, from, and about him appear in Edward Everett Dale and Gaston Litton, eds., *Cherokee Cavaliers: Forty Years of Cherokee History as Told in the Correspondence of the Ridge-Boudinot-Watie Family* (Norman: University of Oklahoma Press, 1939). W. Craig Gaines's book, *The Confederate Cherokees: John Drew's Regiment of Mounted Rifles* (Baton Rouge: Louisiana State University Press, 1989), enhances the perspectives offered by those who focus primarily on Ross and Watie.

5. For differing perspectives, see Christine S. White and Benton R. White, *Now the Wolf Has Come: The Creek Nation in the Civil War* (College Station: Texas A&M University Press, 1996); and Billy J. McIntosh, *From Georgia Tragedy to Oklahoma Frontier: A Biography of Scots Creek Indian Chief Chilly McIntosh* (Franklin TN: American History Press, 1988). The latter is a very personal perspective, but it presents some interesting arguments.

6. Lela J. McBride offers much detail on the Chustenahlah campaign in *Opothleyaholo and the Loyal Muscogee: Their Flight to Kansas in the Civil War* (Jefferson NC: McFarland, 1999).

7. William L. Shea has coauthored two good books on Pea Ridge: *Pea Ridge: Civil War Campaign in the West* (Chapel Hill: University of North Carolina Press, 1992), with Earl J. Hess, and *War in the West: Pea Ridge and Prairie Grove* (Abilene TX: McWhiney Foundation, 1996), with Grady McWhiney. Sterling Price spent some time in Indian Territory in 1864, after his forces were routed in the Westport campaign. For more about him, see Albert Castel, *General Sterling Price and the Civil War in the West* (Baton Rouge: Louisiana State University Press, 1968).

8. William H. Marsh to "Father," March 21, 1862, William H. Marsh Papers, Illinois State Historical Library, Springfield.

9. Edward H. Ingraham to "Alice," May 20, 1862, E. H. Ingraham Papers, Illinois State Historical Library, Springfield. Robert L. Collins, in *General James G. Blunt, Tarnished Glory* (Gretna LA: Pelican, 2005), tries to provide a balanced analysis of this effective but corrupt leader.

10. *The War of the Rebellion: A Compilation of the Official Records of the Union and Confederate Armies*, 128 vols. (Washington DC: U.S. Government Printing Office, 1880–1901), ser. 1, 13:485.

11. Theophilus H. Holmes to Jefferson Davis, August 28, 1862, Theophilus H. Holmes Papers, Special Collections, Perkins Library, Duke University, Durham NC.
12. Indians fought on both sides at Newtonia. See Larry Wood, *The Two Civil War Battles of Newtonia* (Charleston SC: History Press, 2010).
13. Jacob D. Brewster to "Sister," October 19, 1862, Jacob D. Brewster Papers, Dolph Briscoe Center for American History, University of Texas at Austin. For more about the battle, see William L. Shea, *Fields of Blood: The Prairie Grove Campaign* (Chapel Hill: University of North Carolina Press, 2009), as well as the previously referenced book *War in the West* that Shea coauthored with Grady McWhiney.
14. There is a good description of these operations in Mark K. Christ, *Civil War Arkansas, 1863: The Battle for a State* (Norman: University of Oklahoma Press, 2010). See also Dale Cox, *The Battle of Massard Prairie: The 1864 Confederate Attacks on Fort Smith, Arkansas* (privately printed, 2008).
15. There are many books on William C. Quantrill, but one of the best remains Edward E. Leslie, *The Devil Knows How to Ride: The True Story of William Clark Quantrill and His Raiders* (New York: Random House, 1996).
16. Only a single chapter of Louise Horton, *Samuel Bell Maxey: A Biography* (Austin: University of Texas Press, 2009), concerns the Civil War, but more can be found in John C. Waugh, *Sam Bell Maxey and the Confederate Indians* (Abilene TX: McWhiney Foundation, 1998).
17. The classic study of Nathaniel P. Banks's 1864 operation, Ludwell H. Johnson's *The Red River Campaign: Politics and Cotton in the Civil War* (Baltimore MD: Johns Hopkins University Press, 1958), devotes one chapter to events in Arkansas. Gregory J. W. Urwin provided good essays on Poison Spring to two anthologies: Anne J. Bailey and Daniel E. Sutherland, *Civil War Arkansas: Beyond Battles and Leaders* (Fayetteville: University of Arkansas Press, 2000), and Mark K. Christ, *"All Cut to Pieces and Gone to Hell": The Civil War, Race Relations, and the Battle of Poison Spring* (Little Rock: Butler Center for Arkansas Studies, 2003). Urwin included more information in his own work, entitled *Black Flag over Dixie: Race Atrocities and Reprisals in the Civil War* (Carbondale: University of Southern Illinois Press, 2004).
18. For more about this engagement, see Steven L. Warren, *The Second Battle of Cabin Creek: Brilliant Victory* (Charleston SC: History Press, 2012).

2 Hardship at Home

The Civilian Experience

Clarissa Confer

Indian Territory proved to be an extremely difficult place to live during the American Civil War. The residents faced many trials, their experiences mirroring neither Union nor Confederate territory entirely but rather existing in a state of constant change, turmoil, and insecurity. The territory remained a true border area for most of the conflict, which led to the sense of uncertainty that permeated daily life.[1]

From the very beginning of the war, civilians felt the full effects of military action. The first military engagement of the Civil War in Indian Territory, Confederate pursuit of Opothleyahola's group in 1861, was an act of warfare primarily aimed against civilians. This established a trend that continued throughout the war. The Union army, the Confederate army, Jayhawkers, bushwhackers, William Clarke Quantrill's guerilla band, and numerous other outlaws frequented the region.[2] This produced a volatile and dangerous situation for combatants and residents alike. Those who joined the armies of the contending nations naturally faced hardships and the possibility of death, but those who remained at home dealt with an equally uncertain future. Murder, theft, shortage of food, inadequate medical aid, and lack of transportation and communication combined to challenge civilians in Indian Territory. Naturally, not all residents shared the same experiences. The category of civilians included the Indian members of the Five Nations as well as the minority of whites and African Americans who resided in the territory at the start of the war, so there is no overall civilian experience. However, all who stayed in Indian Territory faced similar disruptive forces brought by war.[3]

The arrival of the conflict in 1861 immediately brought changes to daily life.[4] As the nation chose sides in the impending conflict, so too did Indian Territory divide along sectional lines. However, these sectional lines ran along even more convoluted paths than those in the larger nation. The simple division of geography did not work well in the Indian nations. All five of the sovereign nations signed treaties with the Confederate States of America in 1861, pledging their loyalty to the Southern cause and thus their alliance with one another. However, even diplomatic efforts could not smooth over the divisions plaguing Native societies. The tensions over removal simmered just beneath the surface, and old grudges, suspicions, and the desire for revenge gained new life as national pressures intruded. The Confederate alliance did not hold up for long in the face of intratribal divisions. Cherokees, Creeks, and Seminoles all split along former fracture lines and provided troops to both the Union and Confederacy. This left their families back home in a truly divided region.[5]

As tensions grew, communities split. Former friends and even relatives now regarded each other in a new light. As in other border states, men from the same family might join two different armies, leaving their wives and children behind to deal with the ramifications of such choices. The ties that formerly bound people—kinship, religion, economic status—frayed under the pressures of war.

The challenges to life on the home front came almost immediately on the heels of the national crisis. At the onset of the war, people tended to react very strongly. The issues and debates were current, the fervor for the cause strong. In this atmosphere, respect for freedom of speech disappeared, at least in matters of politics. In the early years of the Southern alliance, any indication that an individual did not support the Southern cause invited violence from Confederate supporters.

Speaking out against the Confederacy would brand a man as a troublemaker and a person to be avoided. In the Cherokee Nation an employee heard his boss criticize the Confederacy, so he quit, citing the danger of living with a Northern man and threatening to report him as such to authorities, "which is the same as a man's death warrant." A drunken man accused Isaac Hitchcock of being a spy simply because he received a letter with a Washington DC postmark. Confederate supporters nervously protected their nations' commitment to the Southern cause. Daniel Dwight Hitchcock suffered capture by the Confederates for admitting his preference for the Union. Confederate colonel Douglas Cooper implied that he held Hitchcock for his own safety because of "the state of feeling in the country." Perhaps Cooper genuinely cared about Hitchcock's fate; more likely, he was considered a harmful influence as an educated, well-respected figure who might voice opposition to Confederate alliance.[6]

These types of confrontations reveal the numerous divisions on the home front. One of the first choices to be made in 1861 centered on military service—to fight or not to fight, with the Union or Confederacy? As individuals made their choices about the war, they had to deal with the consequences. It is always difficult to try to remain neutral or disengaged during a conflict, particularly a civil conflict. Both warring factions expect, and at times demand, allegiance. Those remaining undecided or unwilling faced a constant balancing act in order to live peacefully in the war-torn region. Travel became dangerous for men who, like Isaac Hitchcock, had chosen not to join the army. Conscription into the military might result from a trip to get supplies. Hitchcock consciously avoided areas and roads where military men traveled. More than once he was unwillingly pressed into temporary service as a soldier.[7] Rejecting military duty was not a popular choice in Indian Territory. Nancy Jane Rider's father "did not believe in fighting" and so did not enlist. He paid a high price for his defiance. Along with other nonenlistees, he remained in seclusion for the duration of the war, hiding in the dense woods, sleeping in caves, and subsisting on wild game and the meager food supplies smuggled to them by their families. Men who had already run into trouble with the enemy found it difficult to return home because of the possibility of being surprised by troops. Daniel Dwight Hitchcock's mother rejoiced at his release and return home, only to fear for his life a few days later when Southern forces passed by her farm.[8]

Those who chose not to fight often found it easier to leave the area rather than deal with the ramifications of their choices. Men sought work in other states until the war was over, or entire families moved out to escape the conflict.[9] However, this option worked for only a minority. Relocation frequently did not represent a viable choice. Most families or individuals did not have the economic ability to move, and family ties and responsibilities bound them as well. Women, especially those with husbands dead or away, just did not have the means to leave. So the majority of residents of Indian Territory remained at home and prepared for the unknown times that lay ahead.

The future was unlikely to be positive. For much of the war, Indian Territory was an occupied region. Before the war, the Five Nations had existed as nearly autonomous entities, providing their own legislative, judicial, and law enforcement systems. Federal governmental presence was limited to small garrisons in a few forts intended to protect "civilized" Indians from "uncivilized" tribes. The largest installation, Fort Gibson, recently had been decommissioned and Federal troops withdrawn, and smaller garrisons pulled out in 1861; thus the arrival of various military units in the area represented a drastic change. From 1862 to 1864 the opposing forces contended for control of northeastern Indian Territory—Confederates could never completely hold the area north of the Arkansas River; neither could the Federals secure it. The contested region included much of the Creek and Cherokee Nations, including the Cherokee national capital at Tahlequah and the residential area of some of the nation's wealthiest citizens at Park Hill.[10] The Choctaw and Chickasaw Nations to the south experienced fewer incursions by the enemy until later in the war.

All five Native nations enlisted men in the Confederate States Army (C.S.A.), and the Creeks, Cherokees, and Seminoles officially provided men to the U.S. Army. Their initial C.S.A. alliance had pledged Natives to fight only within their nations, but demands changed quickly during the war. Units often ranged widely throughout Indian Territory and occasionally into neighboring states. This extensive travel meant soldiers, the able-bodied men in families, did not reside in the nations. With neither the pro-Union nor pro-Confederate leaders in the area, many civilians of Indian Territory had been left to their own devices. Women and children made up the majority of the remaining residents. They faced numerous challenges as a result of wartime conditions in addition to the normal burdens of nineteenth-century life in a rural area. The uncertainty of supplies, threats of hostile raids, and isolation caused by poor communications were magnified by the conflict.

Residents of Indian Territory endured having two separate armies and numerous outlaws frequent their nation, with the resulting violence and hardships. Guerilla raiders such as Quantrill rode through the region with impunity, and regiments or fragments of commands could show up with little or no warning. Indian civilians suffered many of the same problems that white Confederates endured in occupied areas of the South. We know that mobility in occupied areas was critically curtailed by the uncertainties of travel. Civilians journeying for supplies or visits might find themselves on the road with several hundred soldiers or accompanied by a rough-looking band of thieves. This could be especially alarming for women, who generally moved about without male companionship during the war.[11]

The uncertainty of mobility greatly restricted the lives of civilians and forced an even greater self-reliance on solitary farming communities. Formerly simple tasks such as taking wheat to a mill or visiting friends became anxious trips undertaken only through necessity. With two armies on the move accompanied by the usual shirkers, no one seemed safe. Everyone had heard stories of travelers who never came home.

A dearth of horses and wagons also limited travel. Nearly every serviceable horse in the area, and some less sound, found its way into military service. A horse named Teasle saw action with both the Union and Confederate armies. Apparently not pleased with military treatment, Teasle made periodic trips home, only to be picked up again on the next sweep. Rights of ownership made little difference to those conscripting horses and mules. After Isaac Hitchcock's horse was stolen, he borrowed a neighbor's to finish plowing, only to have *it* taken off to haul cannon. Failing to hide a horse during a raid doomed residents to walk for the rest of the war. Imagine the frustration of a woman when she found her horse had been shot right in her pasture.[12]

Home became the only refuge for civilians who could not travel safely. In many cases the situation there was dire. Living off the land, armies stripped the countryside as they went, bivouacking in fields, burning fences, and trampling crops. After a few encounters, civilians knew what to expect from their temporary neighbors. In 1862 Hannah Hicks noted Confederates camped one-half mile from her farm, and thus she expected to lose her livestock. The situation in Indian Territory differed from much of the South because many soldiers from both sides lived in the region. Confederate Cherokee troops occasionally patrolled the Park Hill vicinity. This gave rise to situations where Confederate Cherokee soldiers "requisitioned" supplies from people they had known all their lives. Thus Hannah knew the Confederates who arrived in her house demanding dinner in December 1862 and received civil treatment from most of them.[13] The dispensing of hospitality, even in strained circumstances, was ingrained in Native culture, and most Indian Territory residents did their best to cope with the situation. Locals forced to travel would stop and stay at the homes of acquaintances regardless of whether anyone was home. Sharing of resources with relatives and other tribal members remained a tradition although strained by wartime changes.

However, it could be difficult to act equitably during war. Old grudges and animosities often surfaced, and resentment or jealousy of material success produced vindictive destruction or theft.[14] The Cherokee capital of Tahlequah and the nearby residential areas are excellent examples. With the Cherokee leadership bitterly divided between John Ross and Stand Watie, the political divisions spilled over into military and social discord. Ross supporters serving in a Union regiment burned homes in Webber Falls where Watie supporters lived, and in turn Watie's men flying the Confederate flag raided the community of Park Hill, burning the Cherokee Council house and John Ross's fine mansion Rose Cottage. In this case of mutual destruction, only one Park Hill mansion survived the civil conflict.[15]

Theft may have been the most widespread and most difficult feature of army occupation. Those who were armed knew that they could easily take what they desired from others. It requires strong leadership based on allegiance, discipline, and superior power to restrain soldiers from looting and pillaging easy targets. Indian societies did not produce that kind of leadership and followers, and few white leaders achieved it either. Thus a type of anarchy reigned in much of the region.

Women remaining at home could expect to see armed parties of men at any time. Word usually spread around a neighborhood about impending raids, but little could be done to prevent or prepare for them. Residents might try to hide valuables if given enough advance warning. The types of possessions that could be buried in the yard or hidden in the hollow of a tree were those that had value in peacetime, such as china and silverware, but had little worth in the daily life of war-torn Indian Territory. Few women sought to impress callers with their best luxury items anymore. The valued goods in 1862 were those that kept the household functioning—oxen, pigs, home furnishings, and stored food—and did not lend themselves to easy concealment. In November 1862 soldiers robbed Hannah Hicks of nearly everything she owned. Apparently having plenty of time for the task, the men thoroughly ransacked every closet, drawer, trunk, and box they could find. Perhaps most infuriating for Hannah, the Cherokee leaders of the group often had eaten at her house. Her belief that an associate directed the looters to Hannah's house reflected the bitter division of friends and acquaintances.[16] In all Hannah endured five robberies during the war, losing a little more each time.

Hannah's experience certainly was not unique. She recorded her shock and sorrow at the destruction of friends' homes throughout the nation as she passed ransacked houses that once offered hospitality. Numerous survivors recalled the frequent robberies of the period. Dozens of residents reported "losing everything," or mentioned that raiders "took anything they wanted." Some recorded that the thieves ransacked their house as they watched. Little could be done by women and children to stop the violence of an armed gang of men.[17] In many cases the destruction was total: all furnishings, clothing, and structures were stolen or went up in smoke.[18]

Although the loss of personal possessions struck deep chords with women, the theft of food and livestock proved a far more serious threat to their existence. Soldiers and bushwhackers methodically stripped Indian Territory of its richest resource—livestock.[19] The soldiers ran off all of Hannah's cattle, although many of the beasts escaped and returned home. Texas troops slaughtered one ox out of each of her three trained pairs. A similar story was repeated across the nations. Women spent laborious hours breaking wild cattle to work, only to have them stolen for food. Few people could replace the pilfered animals. The loss of animals meant a corresponding lack of protein in civilian diets, and the removal of draft animals effectively halted large-scale agriculture. Stripped of much of their meat supply, residents of Indian Territory tried to keep one or two overlooked cows and the hogs that generally ran wild until needed. The shortage of breadstuffs also reached crisis proportions. Soldiers helped themselves to grains and corn in barns and cribs. Replacing that stored food became increasingly difficult. Several of the local mills came under military control or were destroyed. Residents found themselves traveling farther under dangerous conditions to have their few crops processed.[20]

More alarmingly, agricultural production dropped precipitously as the war continued. With men and draft animals gone and fields and fences destroyed by passing troops, women struggled to grow food. Confederates took all the stored wheat from the Ballard family in the Cherokee Nation, leaving them nothing but seed wheat. Such a loss generally forced families to eat the seed and thus leave no means to plant a crop in the following year. The situation became more desperate as each month passed. Union colonel William A. Phillips attempted to alleviate the worst suffering by sending trainloads of flour to civilian areas such as Park Hill. Kindhearted people like Hannah found it hard to refuse requests for help, but any food spared was literally taken from the mouths of her own children. By the spring of 1863 Hannah Hicks could not sustain her own family. In prewar days her family had often helped those in need; now she relied on what flour she was given to feed her children. Hannah noted the impending starvation of the people.[21]

Residents had trouble covering as well as sustaining their bodies. Clothing became scarce when ill-supplied troops ransacked homes for garments, and raw materials for weaving were no longer available. Much of the region experienced bitter winter winds and snow accumulation that foretold hardships for those without shoes and blankets. This lack of adequate clothing may have led to increased sickness and death from exposure.[22]

Illness presented another challenge for Indian people in the territory. In the many single-parent households, an ailing adult could mean disaster for several children. When mothers fell ill they really could not adequately care for their children, but there was no one else to do so. Everyone experienced the loss of family and friends during the war. Diseases such as smallpox remained a problem for Native people in this period, especially at military camps and forts where men gathered in large numbers. Soldiers who survived the close confinement and unsanitary conditions of army camps might return home to find that their family had succumbed to the harshness of civilian life. John Hicks lost two children and his mother in the first year of the war while he and his brothers served with the Federal army.[23] Political choices could bring unintended suffering to people on the edge. When Confederate forces arrested Daniel Dwight Hitchcock they may have caused unexpected suffering among civilians.[24] Hitchcock was his area's only physician. In Indian Territory with its vast spaces and poor communication networks, the removal of one person from the community could trigger ripples felt by many. In many aspects it appeared that the community was falling apart.

The unreliable state of communication added to the grief caused by frequent deaths. Reports of deaths often arrived woefully late or were incorrect, increasing the emotional burden. Isolated from the rest of the country by distance and poor communication, residents of Indian Territory often wished for news of the larger conflict. The lack of accurate information about the movements of the armies frustrated civilians. Their hopes were alternately buoyed or dashed by conflicting reports of battles and skirmishes. Though frequently incorrect, reports that the enemy would arrive in the neighborhood shortly kept everyone upset and on edge. Such alarms disrupted the pattern of everyday life and made it difficult to plan for the future.[25]

Hundreds of families in Indian Territory were caught in a crisis that changed their lives. These noncombatants lived in a constant state of anxiety for the safety and survival of their families. Everything became scarce—food, transportation, medical treatment, community life. Virtually helpless to alter the situation, women and children and a few old and ill men carried on as best they could. The majority of these women failed. Throughout the nations, livestock was stolen; crops were ruined; homes and possessions were destroyed. As men returned from service in either the Union or Confederate army, they found they possessed little more than the meager clothes on their backs. Coming home often meant starting over.

Staying home as most Indian Territory civilians did during the Civil War clearly offered many challenges. However, leaving could provide even more. Most people valued even a meager sense of comfort and security that familiarity with surroundings offered. In general, no one leaves home in a crisis unless forced to. Unfortunately, thousands of Indian Territory civilians did have to leave. They became refugees seeking safety, shelter, and support outside of their homelands. Indian Territory resembled the Southern home front more than the North as a result of this massive displacement. However, Indian Territory refugees suffered far greater hardships because of racial and political divides. They had no welcoming community outside of their nations to provide much-needed support.[26]

Tens of thousands of Indians who fled their homes faced serious problems as refugees. This displacement and suffering followed a general pattern from north to south, corresponding with the tide of military control. Those living in the northern nations initially bore the brunt of wartime upheavals as a result of the pattern of fighting: Creek, Cherokee, and Seminole people constituted the majority of the dislocated residents in 1862. Confederate supporters relocated southward when the Union reestablished control over Indian Territory and the "loyal" element of tribes returned. Many families endured the wartime conditions and then later opted for relocation.

The Creeks who followed leader Opothleyahola became the first large group of refugees from Indian Territory. In 1861 Opothleyahola had rejected Confederate alliance and opposed the McIntosh family leadership of Southern-allied Creeks as he had opposed that family's support of removal in the 1830s. Those who also feared or opposed the Confederate States of America, McIntosh power, or impending conflict flocked to his leadership. They gained the designation "loyal Creeks" for their continued support of the United States.

Politically "loyal," these Creek families faced a long and uncertain journey to find the protection promised by the United States' treaties. Few likely could conceive of a trek that would deposit them in Kansas, helpless and starving for the remainder of the war; however, they prepared for a journey. Seminoles, Delawares, and others fleeing unrest in their nations migrated to the protection of the large gathering.[27]

The violent encounters with the Confederate forces in the winter of 1861 devastated the fleeing civilians. Each engagement and hasty flight cost warriors and personal possessions. Creek civilians suffered a major defeat at the third encounter, Chustenahlah, on December 6, 1861. Opothleyahola's followers ran for their lives as Col. Stand Watie's Cherokee and Cooper's Choctaw soldiers chased men, women, and children over the frozen plains. Civilians panicked and abandoned possessions in a desperate effort to reach safety. Thousands of Creeks and Seminoles who left much of their personal wealth behind at the beginning of the journey subsequently lost the few items they had been able to transport. In the words of one Creek man, this flight was "almost another trail of tears."[28]

Headlong flight took thousands of loyal Creeks and Seminoles across the northern border of Indian Territory into Kansas.[29] Recently torn by internal civil strife, Kansas seemed an unlikely prospect for a safe haven.[30] But for refugees with few alternatives, it represented the comparative security of Union lines. The new arrivals came under the sometimes indifferent care of the various Indian agents assigned to the tribes of Indian Territory. Horrified by what they found when they finally reached the refugee camps, the government agents struggled to convey the enormity of the disaster to others. Phrases such as "It would be impossible to give an adequate description of the suffering endured" and "I doubt much if history records an instance of sufferings equal to these" characterize reports from agents in the field. The agents of the Office of Indian Affairs faced the monumental task of ensuring the survival of some eight thousand people who possessed no food, no tools, no clothes, and no shelter and suffered from malnourishment, exposure, and contagious disease. Scattered over a two-hundred-mile strip along the Verdigris River, the refugee camps endured at least a 10 percent death rate for humans and a catastrophic loss of ponies in that long winter of 1862.[31]

As the government struggled to meet its treaty obligations to the refugees' tribes, Indian leaders held their suffering community together.

They continued an active political system, much of which focused on pressuring U.S. officials for help. Tribal chiefs attempted to continue their traditional role of serving the welfare of their people, despite the realities of refugee life that made it difficult to maintain a sense of leadership. They adapted the federal system of relief to mirror Native culture. Under the tribal system, band leaders, who knew where needs were greatest, received the supplies and passed them out to community members. This ability to provide for their people, even if superficial, maintained their status.[32] They strongly resisted attempts to move their people farther from their rightful nations and sought only one remedy to their situation—returning home.[33] This fervent desire to go back to their respective nations constitutes the one constant noted by all involved in the interminable refugee situation. The Union failure to regain control of northern Indian Territory delayed this outcome. In 1863 the Union army finally entered the Indian nations with a force that included the Indian Home Guard regiments. Thousands of displaced Creeks and Cherokees followed the army and attempted to reestablish their homes. The Federals did not control Indian Territory, however, and the newly arrived refugees found themselves in a desolate area fraught with danger. Bushwhackers roamed the area, preying on Indian women and children whose male protectors served in the army. Confederate raids destroyed crops, and refugees had to be fed through long and insecure supply lines. The tenuous position of civilians in Indian Territory continued nearly to the end of the war as the Union struggled to maintain dominance in the region.[34]

The chaos of war came even to those nations south of most of the fighting. The Choctaw and Chickasaw Nations became a haven for fleeing refugees in the last half of the war. Union forces reestablished a measure of control in Indian Territory in 1863 with bases at Fort Gibson, Cherokee Nation, and Fort Smith, Arkansas. Thousands of loyal Creeks, Cherokees, and Seminoles returned to the Indian nations with the Federal army. The return of refugees possibly posed a greater threat to citizens than the army, however, as loyal Creeks and Cherokees arrived after two years in exile from their homes. These former refugees were now in a position to inflict retribution upon Confederate sympathizers. The fellow citizens they encountered had caused the loyal families' flight to Kansas and prolonged refugee status. As thousands of Creeks, Cherokees, and Seminoles rejoiced at the opportunity to return home in 1863, thousands of their brethren fled in terror. The panicked flight sparked by the arrival of Phillips's Federal troops saw rich and poor alike leave homes behind for an unknown life in exile.

The flight of southern refugees differed from that of Opothleyahola's followers. The Confederate Indians traveled south in small family or neighbor groups rather than on an organized trek under a few leaders. No government agencies awaited their arrival; no provisions existed to feed, clothe, and shelter them.[35] Most of the southern refugees sought assistance from family and friends or survived on their own. Lack of transportation posed a huge problem. Wagons, carts, and draft animals remained in short supply throughout the war. Those with money, such as the William Penn Boudinot family, hired ferries to travel downriver and then used ox teams to move overland. But most families lacked those resources. Ingenuity could save the day as people made sleds of poles to transport their few belongings. Foot travel was the last choice for the long journey. Betsy Christie's mother and aunts walked over one hundred miles to reach safety at Doaksville, Choctaw Nation, where they congregated with other women for protection.[36]

Some families chose to relocate after careful deliberation, while others were forced in sudden flight. Northern soldiers looting Creek homes sometimes caught families in the midst of fleeing the turmoil. The soldiers took what they wanted; they cleaned out smokehouses and broke up wagons with impunity as no men remained to oppose them. In one case a sixteen-year-old boy who probably represented the head of the household was shot and killed. Martha Gibson Walker remembered living in Old Town in the Creek Nation during the war. Northern soldiers burned the town and arrested her father. They released him with a warning to move his family north. The decision had been made for the unprepared family; it could not stay at home any longer. Martha's father exercised what little autonomy he retained by hastily loading the family in wagons headed south. At the Red River they noticed that the Choctaws lived in relative peace, and the family chose to remain there. The Gibson family survived by building a log cabin for shelter, farming for subsistence, and spinning yarn for cloth. Perhaps motivated by their harsh treatment at the hands of the Federals, Martha's brothers joined the Confederate army. Despite comparable hardships, most families reached the Choctaw Nation safely.[37]

Even more so than the early Kansas refugee camps, the gender composition of southern refugees was quite skewed. Most pro-Confederate Indian men already rode with Stand Watie in 1863, and their mothers, wives, sisters, and daughters often had to make the long trek south alone. Some men took furloughs to escort their families to safety and then returned to military duty. William Cordray moved his Cherokee family to Big Blue Creek in the Choctaw Nation and then rejoined Stand Watie in the Cherokee Nation. Seeking safety in numbers, people tried to travel in groups of at least extended family or friends. Many traveling groups stayed together while in exile, offering the comfort of familiar faces. However, the relocation of civilians meant long separations for husbands and wives. Normal relations were suspended during the war years. Numerous children born as refugees knew neither a sense of home nor male authority. Dan Smith, a Creek child born at Fort Washita in 1862, did not see his father until he reached the age of four. Although some men remained near the refugee area and helped females obtain food, husbands and fathers could not be with their families for long periods. Alvin Hodge, a Creek Confederate soldier, provided food for a Cherokee girl named Mary Burgess, whom he later married. Circumstances forced women to take on jobs normally assigned to males. Planting and harvesting crops, purchasing supplies, and even defense of property fell to women already discharging their usual responsibilities. The procuring of food constituted the most important task of Indian refugees. Everywhere in Indian Territory, breadstuffs remained scarce throughout the war. Meat could be obtained in the form of wild game, still relatively abundant in the territory. Many families managed to grow a small crop despite their relocation.[38]

The basic challenges of refugee life did not differ significantly between north and south. The demand for sustenance, safety, and shelter dominated survival efforts. In the Choctaw and Chickasaw Nations, as in Kansas, housing was at a premium. Returning soldiers tried to build at least a crude log cabin to shelter women and children in their absence. Few families had tents; some lived in houses made of mud and straw or cottonwood bark. Temporary shelters and often inadequate nutrition and water supplies raised the civilian death count. Large groups of refugees already suffering from want also had to deal with disease. Smallpox swept through refugee camps, as it did through military camps, with deadly results. The loss of valued family members in a time of stress could be particularly hard on refugee families. Any reduction in the number of people able to acquire food might mean hardship for several family members.[39]

Living as a refugee often meant doing without accustomed services. Indians who removed from larger towns found themselves in much more isolated areas during the war. Families had to be more self-sufficient without nearby towns or trading posts. This situation fostered a sense of community among refugees, including those of different tribes and those who had previously been strangers. Communal activities such as hunting and dividing the kills enabled more people to withstand the demands of refugee life. The familiarity of culture that Creeks and Cherokees found in the Choctaw and Chickasaw Nations may have provided some comfort to these displaced people. The relationship among members of the allied nations appears to have remained essentially positive. Certain refugees spoke highly of their Choctaw and Chickasaw neighbors during the war. In some cases Choctaw families clearly aided in the survival of the temporary refugees. A Creek woman credits the Choctaws with being willing to share whatever they had. If they had not shared, her family would not have survived. The invasion by thousands of homeless individuals taxed both the resources and the patience of the hosts. By 1864 Southern Indian Territory felt the pressure of the relocated population. Choctaw chief Peter Pitchlynn described conditions as an unprecedented state of destitution and suffering, but the Choctaw and Chickasaw citizens still did their best to support their displaced brethren from northern Indian Territory.[40]

The most fortunate refugee families had friends or relatives among the Choctaws and Chickasaws on whom they could rely for assistance. Mary Mackey Wilson came from a prominent Cherokee family. The Mackeys owned an important saltworks on the Illinois River and had extensive landholdings in the nation; her father served as a captain in the Confederate commissary department. The women and children of the extended family, living at Fort Gibson and Webber's Falls, loaded into covered wagons and carriages, taking many of their possessions. Wealthy yet now homeless, the Mackey women traveled to the Blue River with countless other displaced families. There they resided in their own cabin on the property of Jonathan Nail, a Choctaw who had a mill, store, and fine home. Despite the more comfortable surroundings, Mrs. Mackey died of pneumonia, leaving her children to the care of others.[41]

Wealth and status may have softened the hardships of refugee life, but they did not exempt the nation's elite from experiencing displacement. In fact it may have been harder to abandon expensive homes filled with fine furnishings than the simple log cabins of the majority of residents. Consider the influential Adair family. George Washington Adair signed the removal treaty and served as Stand Watie's quartermaster until his death, while his son Col. William Penn Adair was one of Watie's trusted officers. The Adairs, staunch Southern Cherokees, would not be comfortable in the nation once Ross's adherents dominated. Fear of attack by political rivals certainly was not new to the family. The Adairs lived in a large home with thick walls and small windows that was easy to defend, and they slept with doors barred and guards posted. The women and children left this home to join the flood of refugees leaving the Cherokee Nation during the war. They rolled their precious oil paintings on broomstick handles and left them with friends in Arkansas in an attempt to protect their valuables. Despite their careful preparations, the Adairs lost nearly everything on the journey to Texas.[42]

As difficult as refugee or occupied status could be for Indian families, the war presented even more uncertainty for the African Americans in Indian Territory. As a legacy of over two hundred years of contact with Europeans, southeastern Native groups included an often overlooked diversity—thousands of African Americans lived in the nations and shared the fate of their Native neighbors.[43] This minority group within minority nations defies easy categorization. Some lived free, although not equal, while others were held in bondage by Indian owners. In almost every case these individuals had even less power than their Native American neighbors when the war came to them.

To an even greater degree than Indian residents, black families in Indian Territory found themselves suddenly caught in the turmoil of warfare. Largely unable to participate in national decision making, black slaves and freedpeople still retained a measure of control over their future. Slaves throughout the American South were denied the privilege of literacy, political standing, or public voice, yet they knew about the division between North and South. Some understood the changes war could bring, and many were poised to take advantage of new situations to obtain freedom.[44]

Slaves' experience varied widely, partly because not all slaveholders sided with the Confederacy. Those who did tended to relocate. Many who moved south to Texas or the Choctaw Nation tried to take along their slaves. The circumstances of hasty flight allowed for the possibility of escape or separation from masters. Additionally, the lifestyle of refugees generally was not conducive to retaining control over slaves. Unexpected journeys and uncertain living arrangements characterized refugee life. John Harrison and his mother traveled with their master from the Creek Nation to Fort Washita, then to Texas, and then returned to Indian Territory. Such mobility undermined traditional measures of behavioral control.[45]

Some Indian slaves seized the wartime opportunity to improve their situation. As in the rest of Confederate territory, Union lines (in this instance in Kansas) proved a strong lure for those daring enough to try escape. Young, healthy, single men had the best chance of surviving the sometimes harrowing trek to a Federal camp. It seemed to masters that all who could survive the journey tried it: "The few [slaves] who have not gone over to the Federals," remarked a slaveholder, "are either old, infirm, or sick."[46] Unhindered by the burden of small children, male slaves benefited from greater mobility than females. In many cases they already enjoyed travel privileges in order to visit their families on other farms. Operating as individuals rather than families, they were better able to take advantage of opportunities for escape.[47]

Although individuals naturally profited from successful escapes, flight from bondage could have repercussions on those left behind. Security might be tightened or punishments meted out. Often the loss of one person's labor meant the rest of the slaves had to pick up the slack. Mary Stinnett found herself in this position while living in Texas with her master. Her husband George took off for the North and the freedom promised by Union territory, leaving Mary to perform his fieldwork in addition to all of her own tasks in the house. To cooking, cleaning, serving, and mending, Mary added breaking ground with an ox team. Slave women could also pay a high price for the loss of male protectors. When the men in her world—master and father—left for the war, Victoria Thompson was stolen by a white man who forced her to live with him and who branded her.[48]

Male slaves also experienced mobility by going to war as personal servants. They accompanied their Indian masters into the army just as many Virginia or South Carolina slaves did. Evidence suggests that a chance to escape a boring routine or the opportunity to see the world may have motivated those who went to war.[49] A Cherokee family, the Taylors, traded some land for a slave named Doc Hayes. The eight members of his extended family were the only slaves on the Taylors' small farm. When the war broke out, Mr. Taylor left his home to fight with

Stand Watie, and Doc Hayes accompanied him. The men left behind Indian and black women to survive as best they could.[50]

The majority of slaves remained at home. Some masters expected slaves to care for the family while they went off to fight, while others commanded servants to guard their property when the family sought safety. The effectiveness of the latter seems dubious, although former slave Ed Butler insisted that they would never abandon this responsibility until the master returned.[51] Being left on one's own in an area bereft of the normal strictures of society might seem like a boon to slaves; however, the reality was often harsh. As Indian Territory suffered from a lack of food and transportation and from a surplus of violence, slaves generally had difficulty acquiring the limited resources necessary for survival. What few supplies households retained could be taken in one raid. Elsie Gardner remembered being entrusted with the responsibility of guarding her master's clothes. Each time she heard soldiers coming, she carried the clothes out into the swamp to hide. One time while she engaged in this exercise, two hundred soldiers raided the smokehouse, fed their horses in the corn crib, killed the turkeys, and stole cooking utensils.[52]

Life changed for many of those who remained in bondage. Slaveholders realized that the value of their chattel hung in the balance of the war. Sarah Watie expected she would have to sell her "boys" if the tide changed in Texas. Some owners were reluctant to continue supporting an investment that they might soon lose. Thus, Jim Threat's master decided to kill off old slaves during the war when resources were scarce. Even when abuse was not that blatant, slaves suffered when food and clothes were in short supply. Additionally, slaveholders could be expected to attempt to tighten control over their property during tumultuous times.[53] Fear induced masters to initiate new restrictions including less travel, more work, heightened discipline, and possibly more violence. Privileges such as visiting family members might be curtailed in an effort to prevent slaves from running away. Furthermore, owners might try to obtain maximum work from a resource they could soon lose. As one eyewitness remembered, "Everybody was harder on their slaves then."[54]

The Union military forces, rather than the owners of Indian slaves, became the most disruptive force in the lives of the slaves.[55] Historians have characterized the Federal army as an army of emancipation west of the Mississippi River. Wherever Federal forces marched they encouraged slaves to seize their freedom. The arrival of the Union army in Park Hill, Cherokee Nation, prompted a general uprising among slaves who asserted their freedom by helping themselves to horses and weapons and joining a "swelling throng on its way to join the Federal army." Liberation also could involve force resulting in soldiers' chasing slaves from the only home they had to an uncertain future. Lonian Moses belonged to Lewis Ross, one of the largest slaveholders in the Cherokee Nation, owning 150 persons. When Union troops came through the nation in 1862 they declared the slaves free. Still, many slaves did not want to leave because they feared retribution by their master and others. The slaves recognized the Union presence as a fleeting one and feared a lack of protection in their new status as freedpeople.[56]

Indian-owned slaves faced the same cruel dilemma as slaves throughout the South. When the news of freedom finally came, the emancipated blacks found themselves without food, shelter, or clothing and with few means with which to acquire them. Children remembered their family's predicament. "Father was stumped for he didn't know what on earth he was going to do with that big family," recalled one witness. "We had no home, no food and mighty few clothes." Some enterprising women turned the skill they had been taught, cooking for their masters, into a means for survival. Others wrested a bare living from the land as they drifted about trying to establish homes for their families. Emancipation was as difficult in some ways as slavery, and it took many years for freedpeople to achieve a level of security.[57]

The Civil War brought immense suffering to Indian Territory. White, black, or Indian, few families remained untouched by the upheavals and horrors of war. The Indian nations had joined the dominant white governments in their war only to experience a brutal baptism by fire. The conditions for civilians varied from place to place and time to time, yet the constantly shifting military front spread the trauma throughout the region. Many who had been secure early in the war fled their homes in the later years. Plagued by shortages of food, clothing, and shelter, terrorized by random violence, and forced into new social and economic roles, civilian residents may have had a worse war experience than Indian soldiers. The Five Nations endured incredible disruption and destruction. Violence, shortages, and endless uncertainty and tension combined to take a heavy toll. The social, political, and economic losses endured by Indian society persisted long after the war.[58]

NOTES

1. The entire larger region surrounding Indian Territory existed as a border area. For in-depth discussions of the peculiarities of the area, see Jay Monaghan, *Civil War on the Western Border, 1854–1865* (Lincoln: University of Nebraska Press, 1955).
2. The literature of the guerillas in the west has focused primarily on a few well-known figures like Quantrill and Anderson, although hundreds of nameless men took advantage of the chaos to engage in extralegal activity. Bryce Benedict, *Jayhawkers: The Civil War Brigade of James Henry Lane* (Norman: University of Oklahoma Press, 2012); Duane Schultz, *Quantrill's War: The Life and Times of William Clarke Quantrill, 1837–1865* (New York: Macmillan, 1997); Paul R. Petersen, *Quantrill of Missouri: The Making of a Guerrilla Warrior; The Man, the Myth, the Soldier* (Nashville: Cumberland House, 2003).
3. Indian Territory has not attracted the kind of scholarly attention that almost every other region involved in the American Civil War has enjoyed. Annie Heloise Abel was really the first to examine the lives of Native peoples here in her three seminal works: *The American Indian as Slaveholder and Secessionist* (1915; repr., Lincoln: University of Nebraska Press, 1992); *The American Indian in the Civil War, 1862–1865* (1919; repr., Lincoln: University of Nebraska Press, 1992); and *The American Indian and the End of the Confederacy, 1863–1866* (1925; repr., Lincoln: University of Nebraska Press, 1993).The historiography in the past century has been limited and focused such as my own *The Cherokee Nation in the Civil War* (Norman: University of Oklahoma Press, 2009) and really not comparative. In *When the Wolf Came: The Civil War and the Indian*

Territory (Fayetteville: University of Arkansas Press, 2013), Mary Jane Warde includes a useful bibliographic essay, 313–22.
4. Clarissa Confer, *Daily Life during the Indian Wars* (Santa Barbara: Greenwood, 2011), 161–66.
5. Other areas had familial and local divisions, especially the border states, but Native allegiances added another layer of identity to the difficult choices people had to make. Amy Murrell Taylor, *Divided Family in Civil War America* (Chapel Hill: University of North Carolina Press, 2009); Christopher Phillips, *The Civil War in the Border South* (Santa Barbara: ABC-CLIO, 2013); John W. Shaffer, *Clash of Loyalties: A Border County in the Civil War* (Morgantown: West Virginia University Press, 2003).
6. Isaac Hitchcock Journal, April 20, 1861, February 1862, Thomas Gilcrease Institute of American History and Art, Tulsa OK.
7. Isaac Hitchcock Journal, April 20, 1861, February 1862, Thomas Gilcrease Institute of American History and Art.
8. Nancy Jane Rider, 76:161, *Indian-Pioneer Papers* (all material from this collection is personal narrative), Western History Collection, University of Oklahoma, Norman; Hannah Hicks Diary, November 16, 1862, Thomas Gilcrease Institute of American History and Art.
9. Unless one had family in another state, Kansas provided the closest refuge for those fleeing the Northern part of Indian Territory, but that state had its own problems. Kristen Tegtmeier Oertel, *Bleeding Borders: Race, Gender, and Violence in Pre-Civil War Kansas* (Baton Rouge: Louisiana State University Press, 2009); Albert E. Castel, *Civil War Kansas: Reaping the Whirlwind* (Lawrence: University Press of Kansas, 1958).
10. Carolyn Foreman, *Park Hill* (Muscogee OK: Star Printery, 1948), 136; U.S. War Department, *The War of the Rebellion: A Compilation of the Official Records of the Union and Confederate Armies*, 128 vols., index, and atlas (Washington DC: Government Printing Office, 1880–1901), ser. 1, 13:161, 138 (hereafter cited as *Official Records*; all references to ser. 1 unless otherwise noted).
11. Stephen V. Ash, *When the Yankees Came: Conflict and Chaos in the Occupied South* (Chapel Hill: University of North Carolina Press, 1995), 104.
12. Isaac Hitchcock Journal, December 3, 1861, Thomas Gilcrease Institute of American History and Art; Hannah Hicks to sister, September 16, 1865, Grant Foreman Collection (GFC), Thomas Gilcrease Institute of American History and Art, box 3, folder 3.
13. Hannah Hicks Diary, September 16, 1862, December 23, 1862, Thomas Gilcrease Institute of American History and Art.
14. Hannah Hicks observed, "The Pins have been robbing some of their enemies." Hannah Hicks Diary, November 7, 1862, Thomas Gilcrease Institute of American History and Art.

15. Chief Ross's niece and her husband, George Murrell, owned one of the few fine homes in the area to escape destruction during the war.
16. Hannah Hicks Diary, November 17, 1862, Thomas Gilcrease Institute of American History and Art.
17. One of the earliest and still the best analysis of the features of guerilla warfare that creates such psychological uncertainty is Michael Fellman's groundbreaking study of nearby Missouri, *Inside War: The Guerrilla Conflict in Missouri during the American Civil War* (New York: Oxford University Press, 1989); see also Richard S. Brownlee, *Gray Ghosts of the Confederacy: Guerrilla Warfare in the West, 1861–1865* (Baton Rouge: Louisiana State University Press, 1984).
18. Hannah Hicks Diary, September 20, 1862, Thomas Gilcrease Institute of American History and Art, n9, n7; Samantha Lane Hillen, George Mayes, 42:410, 61:302, *Indian-Pioneer Papers*, Western History Collection.
19. In 1861 Indian Territory was reported to "have an immense supply of beeves, sufficient to supply the meat for the whole Confederate service." *Official Records*, 3:589.
20. Rider, 76:161, *Indian-Pioneer Papers*, Western History Collection.
21. Hannah Hicks Diary, September 20, 1862, Thomas Gilcrease Institute of American History and Art; Hannah Worcester Hitchcock to A. E. W. Robertson, May 12, 1863, file 133, box 9, Robertson Papers, University of Tulsa, Tulsa OK.
22. Lizzie Clark to A. E. W. Robertson, January 20, 1863, Robertson Papers, University of Tulsa; Hannah Hicks Diary, January 1, 1863, Thomas Gilcrease Institute of American History and Art.
23. Hannah Hicks Diary, September 28, 1862, Thomas Gilcrease Institute of American History and Art.
24. Isaac Hitchcock Journal, April 20, 1861, February 1862, Thomas Gilcrease Institute of American History and Art.
25. Ash, *When the Yankees Came*, 93. For examples of Native interest in the broader war, see Hannah Hicks Diary, September 14, October 5, and November 18, 1862, Thomas Gilcrease Institute of American History and Art.
26. Indian agents located refugee camps far from white settlements so their charges would not be shot by Kansas farmers. John Turner, Commissioner of Indian Affairs, *Annual Report of the Commissioner of Indian Affairs, 1862* (Washington DC: Government Printing Office, 1863), 177–78.
27. Monaghan, *Civil War on the Western Border*, 220–21; James Scott, 9:172, *Indian-Pioneer Papers*, Oklahoma Historical Society, Oklahoma City; Angie Debo, *Road to Disappearance: A History of the Creek Indians* (Norman: University of Oklahoma Press, 1941), 151.
28. Joseph Bruner, 89:266, *Indian-Pioneer Papers*, Oklahoma Historical Society.
29. The refugee count varies by source and date. Most sources point to more than three thousand people traveling with Opothleyahola, but the number of

refugees in Kansas increased monthly in 1862, reaching over seven thousand. *Annual Report of the Commissioner of Indian Affairs, 1862*, 1, 27, 157.
30. Debra Goodrich Bisel, *The Civil War in Kansas: Ten Years of Turmoil* (Charleston, SC: History Press, 2012).
31. Coffin, *Annual Report of the Commissioner of Indian Affairs, 1862*, 136.
32. Captain John Turner, *Annual Report of the Commissioner of Indian Affairs, 1862*, 154.
33. Dole, *Annual Report of the Commissioner of Indian Affairs, 1862*, 155; G. A. Snow, *Annual Report of the Commissioner of Indian Affairs, 1862*, 142.
34. No signature (probably Cherokee Agent Harlan) to Coffin, May 26, 1863, frame 217, reel 835, M234 RG 75. Correspondence of the Office of Indian Affairs, *Letters Received, 1824–1881*, RG 75—Records of the Bureau of Indian Affairs, National Archives, Washington DC.
35. The Confederacy and the individual tribes did allot funds for the purchase of refugee rations, but the people were not contained in a few camps with regular distribution as they were in the North.
36. Elinor Boudinot Meigs, 7:179A, *Indian-Pioneer Papers*, Oklahoma Historical Society; Jim Spaniard, 86:14, Betsy Christie, 18:84, *Indian-Pioneer Papers*, Western History Collection.
37. Martha Walker Gibson, *Indian-Pioneer Papers*, Western History Collection, 4:376.
38. Andy Cordray, 20:81, Elsie Edwards, 27:190, Minnie Wimberley Hodge, 43:107, Betsy Christie, 18:82, *Indian-Pioneer Papers*, Western History Collection.
39. Polly Barnett, 5:401, Jim Spaniard, 86:14, Eliza Breeding, 11:12, *Indian-Pioneer Papers*, Western History Collection.
40. Richard Fields Boudinot, 1:225, *Indian-Pioneer Papers*, Oklahoma Historical Society; Christopher Columbus Choat, 18:5, Martha Walker Gibson, 94:376, *Indian-Pioneer Papers*, Western History Collection; *Official Records*, 53:1035.
41. Mary Mackey Wilson 99:53, *Indian-Pioneer Papers*, Western History Collection.
42. Eliza Adair, T-663, Doris Duke Oral History Collection, Western History Collection; E. F. Dodson, 3:80, *Indian-Pioneer Papers*, Oklahoma Historical Society.
43. Daniel Littlefield, Jr., *Chickasaw Freedmen: A People without a Country* (Westport CT: Greenwood, 1980), 18; Daniel Littlefield, Jr., *The Cherokee Freedmen: From Emancipation to American Citizenship* (Westport CT: Greenwood, 1978), 9.
44. Ira Berlin et al., *Slaves No More: Three Essays on Emancipation and the Civil War* (New York: Cambridge University Press, 1992), 4.
45. Jim Tomm, John Harrison, 91:323, 39:329, *Indian-Pioneer Papers*, Western History Collection.
46. Wm. Ross to Col. Cooper, August 18, 1862, Cherokee Collection–Misc. Letters, John Vaughn Library, Northeastern State University, Tahlequah OK.

47. Berlin, *Slaves No More*, 16.
48. Narrative of J. W. Stinnett, in *The American Slave: A Composite Autobiography*, ed. George P. Rawick, supp., ser. 1, 12 vols. (Westport CT: Greenwood, 1977), 12:296.
49. Berlin, *Slaves No More*, 2.
50. Narrative of Victoria Taylor Thompson, narrative of Patsy Perryman, in Rawick, *American Slave*, 12:320, 252.
51. Narrative of Ed Butler, in Rawick, *American Slave*, 12:88.
52. Elsie Gardner, 3:129, *Indian-Pioneer Papers*, Western History Collection.
53. Ash, *When the Yankees Came*, 163.
54. Sarah Watie to Stand Watie, May 20, 1863, file 5, box 147, CNP; Narrative of Jim Threat, in Rawick, *American Slave*, 12:329, 331; Berlin, *Slaves No More*, 13.
55. Aaron Astor looks at the upheavals in slave-owning regions in Aaron Astor, *Rebels on the Border: Civil War, Emancipation, and the Reconstruction of Kentucky and Missouri* (Baton Rouge: Louisiana State University Press, 2012).
56. Berlin, *Slaves No More*, 34; Isaac Hitchcock Journal, July 7, 1862, Thomas Gilcrease Institute of American History and Art; Narrative of Lonian Moses, in Rawick, *American Slave*, 12:210–11.
57. Narrative of Jim Threat, Narrative of Patsy Perryman, in Rawick, *American Slave*, 12:338, 252.
58. Annie Heloise Abel, *The American Indian and the End of Confederacy, 1863–1866* (1925; repr. Lincoln: University of Nebraska Press, 1993), 363.

3 Our Doom as a Nation Is Sealed

The Five Nations in the Civil War

Brad Agnew

For the Five Nations (Cherokee, Choctaw, Creek, Chickasaw, and Seminole), the twenty years before 1861 represented an interlude between two cataclysmic upheavals—forced removal over the Trail of Tears and the devastation of the Civil War. In describing this period, Oklahoma historian Angie Debo wrote, "Except for the buffeted Seminoles the Civilized Tribes soon conquered their wild frontier and prospered." Wilma Mankiller, first female chief of the Cherokees, referred to the pre–Civil War years in Indian Territory as a golden era.[1] The uprooted Indians made major strides in rebuilding their lives and governments in Indian Territory, but focusing exclusively on their progress excludes currents that drew them into the Civil War and provoked strife within several of the nations.

The Cherokee Nation experienced a bloodbath in the years following removal, hostile Creek factions avoided conflict by settling in different areas of their nation, and removal created a rift within the Seminole Nation. Secession of the Southern states completed the rupture of all three groups. Internal division was not a significant factor in the remaining nations, although some, perhaps a majority, of Choctaws and Chickasaws favored neutrality in the controversy that split the United States.[2]

After removal most of the "Civilized Tribes" established common schools throughout their nations and soon financed boarding schools.

These institutions should have promoted unity. Unfortunately, the effort spent on education may have intensified differences within some of the nations. The lack of Cherokee-speaking teachers meant many of that community's classrooms were staffed by whites who spoke no Cherokee. Most full-blood children could not understand their teachers and were ridiculed by their mixed-blood, English-speaking classmates. Since competency in English was a criterion for admission when the male and female seminaries opened in 1851, few full-bloods attended. Samuel Worcester, longtime missionary to the Cherokees, reported that students who did not speak English "suffer reproach and contempt as 'Indians'" and concluded, "There is a danger that this growing contempt on one side and jealousy on the other, will provide a great obstacle to progress, if not the ruin of the people."[3]

Christianity embraced by some members of the Five Nations should have been a force for reconciliation. In reality the effort of missionaries sometimes had a divisive effect. Relatively few Cherokees joined organized Christian churches, but some who did selected denominations that shared their outlook on the issue of slavery. In the 1850s many mixed-blood Cherokees were affiliated with the Southern Methodists, while most full-bloods who joined a church were Northern Baptists. Religion, like education, had a disruptive influence on the Cherokees and Seminoles, who also split along denominational lines, with Presbyterians favoring the abolition of slavery and Baptists supporting the peculiar institution.[4]

The concept of a pre–Civil War golden age also suggests a period free from rapacious, white land hunger. Relocated Indians were promised that their new nations would not "without their consent, be included within the territorial limits or jurisdiction of any State or Territory." By the 1840s white cattlemen moved their herds slowly through Indian Territory, allowing them to fatten on Indian grass. They ignored tribal demands for compensation and treated Indian land as free range. In October 1853, when the Cherokee Council prohibited the use of tribal land for cattle drives, the commissioner of Indian affairs refused to enforce the measure. The Creeks complained about the same problem with similar results.[5]

The pressure railroad promoters exerted to obtain rights-of-way through Indian land was potentially more threatening, although their schemes were frustrated by financial and sectional problems. Those frustrations provided little comfort for the residents of Indian Territory who realized land-hungry whites would never be satisfied with mere railroad rights-of-way through their land. In 1844 Stephen Douglas, a Democratic representative from Illinois, had proposed turning the northern portion of land set aside for Indians into a Territory of Nebraska. After the Mexican War, the House Committee on Indian Affairs approved a bill to consolidate all Indian tribes and nations between the Platte and Red Rivers into a single administrative unit headed by a federally appointed official.[6]

Neither Douglas's nor the committee's proposals bore immediate fruit. In 1854, however, the region north of Indian Territory was opened by the provisions of Senator Douglas's Kansas-Nebraska Act. At the same time, Senator Robert Johnson of Arkansas proposed a bill that would have ended the governments of the Five Nations and created a State of Neosho. Chief John Ross warned his people that Johnson's measure would "affect their condition and interest through future time" and urged them to take "utmost care and vigilance" to prevent their rights "from being compromised or impaired."[7]

The controversy over slavery blocked Johnson's plan, but the majority of Americans on both sides of the Mason-Dixon Line wanted the remainder of Indian Territory opened. In his first annual message, Democratic president James Buchanan asserted, "At no very distant day they [Cherokees, Choctaws, Chickasaws, and Creeks] will be incorporated into the Union as one of the sovereign States." In 1857 the proslavery territorial governor of Kansas predicted Indian Territory should soon become a state. During his campaign for the Republican nomination for the presidency in 1860, New York senator William Seward demanded that Indian Territory be vacated by the Indians.[8]

In Indian Territory slavery did not become an issue until the passage of the Kansas-Nebraska Act. As Southern whites and mixed-bloods became more outspoken in their defense of slavery, some full-bloods became more antagonistic. Baptist missionaries Evan Jones and his son John played a role in the revitalization of the Cherokee Keetoowah Society. Albert Pike, an Arkansas resident long associated with the Cherokees, claimed Evan Jones had organized the Keetoowahs "for the purpose of abolitionizing the Cherokees and putting out of the way all who sympathized with the southern State." Pike claimed the purpose of the Keetoowah Society was to deprive mixed-bloods of political power. His assessment was probably accurate, but the full-bloods were not merely pawns of white, abolitionist missionaries; they sought to wrest control of the nation from the mixed-bloods, whose influence had been growing for several generations.[9]

Mixed-bloods and intermarried whites considered the Keetoowahs a threat and responded by establishing chapters of the Knights of the Golden Circle, a secret society intent on expanding the institution of slavery. In Indian Territory its members worked to block the full-blood agenda. These rival organizations deepened the division within the nation and were exploited by whites on both sides when the nation went to war.[10]

The Civil War did not mark the end of a golden age in the history of the Five Nations, for the 1840s and 1850s were decades of constant threat to Indian sovereignty and unresolved differences within several nations. It was an era that intensified internal animosities. Rather than golden, it was a foreboding period, foreshadowing the greatest tragedy to befall the Five Nations since Columbus sailed west.

The day Abraham Lincoln assumed the presidency, the Confederate Congress adopted a resolution granting Confederate president Jefferson Davis authority to negotiate alliances with the residents of Indian Territory. The governments of Texas and Arkansas were already coercing their Native American neighbors to join the South. In May 1861 Indian Territory was incorporated in a Confederate military district. Rebel agents began raising troops in the nations of the Five Nations, and the Confederate Congress formally annexed their land.[11]

The Union reacted to the situation in Indian Territory with less urgency. Faced with an imminent threat to Washington, Lincoln had little time to ponder the fate of Native Americans. It was May before William G. Coffin of Indiana was appointed to head the Southern Superintendency, which administered Indian Territory. Finding suitable candidates to serve as agents for the Five Nations was not completed until 1862.[12]

The delay made little difference. At the beginning of the Civil War, U.S. troops garrisoned three Indian Territory posts—Fort Arbuckle, Fort Washita, and Fort Cobb. In May of 1861, when Confederate troops from Texas and Arkansas invaded Indian Territory, Union forces withdrew to Kansas, offering little resistance. Their departure and the termination of annuity payments by the U.S. government persuaded many leaders of the Five Nations the federal government had deserted them. Without military protection, Indian Bureau officials appointed by Lincoln could get no closer to their charges than Kansas. Union promises to dispatch troops to recover Indian Territory were sent to the Five Nations in a letter dated May 11, 1861. Since the message could not be delivered nor the promises fulfilled, Confederate agents experienced little difficulty in undermining the commitment of the nations to the Union.[13]

Albert Pike, a longtime Arkansas resident born in New England, was sent by the Confederacy to conclude treaties with the denizens of Indian Territory. He first called on the Cherokees in June 1861. John Ross, the seventy-one-year-old Cherokee chief, believed neutrality in the dispute between the states would serve the best interest of the Indians, but secessionists in Arkansas informed him that they preferred "an open enemy to a doubtful friend." Ross's rival Stand Watie, leader of the mixed-bloods, favored alliance with the Confederacy and had already raised troops for the South. Ross and the full-bloods rejected the proposed treaty although Stand Watie and his followers gave their full support to the South. Eventually, their dispute led the nations into a bloody intratribal civil war.[14]

Creeks, Choctaws, and Chickasaws met with Pike at North Fork Town. The Creeks were also divided, but mixed-bloods signed Pike's treaty on July 10. Full-blood leaders Opothleyahola and Oktarharsars Harjo (Sands) renounced the alliance and proclaimed neutrality. Two days after the Creeks signed, the Choctaws and Chickasaws concluded an alliance of their own with the South. On August 1, Pike negotiated a treaty with the Seminoles, who, like the Creeks, were divided over whether to join the Rebels.[15]

On August 10, 1861, while Pike was negotiating with the Plains Indians, a Confederate army defeated Union forces in southwestern Missouri at Wilson's Creek, compelling John Ross to sign a treaty with the South in October 1861. The Confederate-Indian treaties all guaranteed that the nations could govern themselves as long as they chose, promised to protect Indian Territory and pay annuity obligations, recognized slavery, gave all nations representation in the Confederate Congress, and authorized the Indians to raise military forces to defend their nations. Although the treaties seemed generous and offered assurance of Indian sovereignty, in transmitting the documents to Richmond, Pike informed Jefferson Davis, "The concessions made the Indians are really far more for *our* benefit than for *theirs*; and that it is *we*, a thousand times more than they, who are interested to have this country, the finest, in my opinion, on the continent, opened to settlement and formed into a State."[16]

The Five Nations raised four regiments and a few other units. Douglas Cooper, longtime Choctaw agent, organized and led a Choctaw-Chickasaw regiment, and the groups formed a separate battalion. Two regiments were raised by Cherokees. Stand Watie commanded a force of mixed-bloods, and John Drew recruited a regiment of full-bloods loyal to Ross. The Creeks mustered a regiment under the leadership of Daniel McIntosh, and they and the Seminoles formed a battalion led by Chilly McIntosh and John Jumper. The Five Nations mustered more than five thousand men initially. More would volunteer later.[17]

Opposition to alliance with the South was most pronounced among the Creeks. Opothleyahola and Oktarharsars Harjo, leaders of the neutral faction, wrote President Lincoln in mid-August urging him to honor the government's promise to protect the Creeks. It took more than a month for their letter to reach Washington. By then, Union defeats in Virginia and Missouri had dashed hope of federal assistance to those who favored neutrality in Indian Territory.[18]

A band of about five thousand of Opothleyahola's followers, mostly Creek and Seminole, established a camp near the junction of the Deep Fork and the North Fork of the Canadian River. They wanted to be left alone to live in peace, but leaders of the Confederacy in Indian Territory decided to move against those who would not support them. Warned of the Rebel operation, Opothleyahola's neutral Indians fled north, slowed by women, children, and baggage. Overtaken by the Confederate forces, they fought a series of defensive encounters from November 19 to December 26. In the final engagement, casualties were heavy. The survivors fled to Kansas through a bitter sleet storm. Many died of exposure; others had hands and feet amputated because of acute frostbite. Those who reached Kansas were no longer neutral; many sought vengeance.[19]

Their desire for revenge turned Indian Territory into the bloodiest theater of the Civil War. While the battles there were insignificant compared to Bull Run, Chancellorsville, or Gettysburg, proportionally no state experienced more damage or suffered heavier casualties than Indian Territory. Annie Eliza Hendrix, born in 1852 near Tahlequah, was the daughter and sister of Cherokees who fought for the North. She insisted that no nation had ever been as divided as the Cherokees. "The entire nation became almost deserted, as the Confederate faction moved their families south to the Choctaw Nation and those who supported the Union cause moved north to Kansas and a very few families remained at their homes in the war-torn nation."[20]

Edwin C. McReynolds, author of a history of the Seminoles, called the Civil War "the greatest misfortune of all for the Indians of the Five Tribes." Confederate colonel William Penn Adair, after whom Oklahoma humorist Will Rogers was named, claimed, "During the four years of the war ... the Cherokees, Creeks, and Seminoles lost all their property of every description" and received no remuneration from the government. The loss of life was more catastrophic; the number of Cherokee citizens declined from twenty-five thousand to thirteen thousand and the other nations suffered substantial reductions in population.[21]

More than fifty years after the war, Henry Falconer, a mixed-blood Choctaw, claimed neither states' rights nor the issue of slavery was as important as the Southern claim that the Union would not honor its commitments to Indians. Equally persuasive was the promise that the government in Richmond would not only assume those obligations but also offer better terms than the treaties made by Indian leaders with Washington. "It was these promises," Falconer suggested, "that actuated most of, though not all, the Choctaw people to cast their lot with the cause of the South." Annie Eliza Hendrix emphasized that the withdrawal of Federal soldiers "left the nation practically in the hands of the slave owners and all who were advancing the cause of the Confederacy." She also mentioned the "smoldering hatred existing between two political factions" since the Indian removal. She continued, "When the Civil War broke out, it only afforded an opportunity for the fire of this old feud to burst forth in all its fury."[22]

Animosities dating from removal influenced the decision of factions in other nations to take part in the conflict. Jake Simmons, a Creek of Indian, black, and white ancestry, was born in a refugee camp near Fort Washita while his father fought with a Confederate Creek regiment. He suggested the Creeks did not want to get involved in the white man's civil war, but "most of the Chiefs or Agents were southern men and through Albert Pike, Confederate Commissioner, made a treaty with one faction of the Creeks to fight with the South." James Scott, a Creek who was about ten when the war began, did not comprehend the meaning of war until "the many ruthless raids and destroying of homes by the McIntosh Creeks convinced me that there was discord. This destruction was heaped on the Muskogees [Creeks] who were remaining loyal to Opuithli Yahola."[23]

Before the Confederate campaign that drove Opothleyahola from Indian Territory, Albert Pike had been appointed commander of the Department of Indian Territory with the rank of brigadier general. He ordered the construction of Cantonment Davis across the Arkansas River from Fort Gibson, where he established his headquarters after his return to Indian Territory in February of 1862.[24] Since the beginning of the war, the South had encountered little effective opposition in Indian Territory, but the tide of battle was about to turn.

For more than six months the federal government had made no effort to support the loyal members of the Five Nations or to oppose Confederate troops occupying their territory. By December 3, 1861, however, Abraham Lincoln in his first annual message to Congress reported, "It is believed that upon the repossession of the country by the Federal forces the Indians will readily cease all hostile demonstrations and resume their former relations to the Government." A Federal victory at the Battle of Pea Ridge in early March of 1862 did not produce mass defection within the Five Nations, but it had consequences for their citizens. Although the treaties of alliance stipulated that Indian troops would not be ordered beyond the limits of Indian Country, Pike was instructed to lead his men into Arkansas. The employment of Native American troops by the South resolved a controversy over their enlistment in the Union army.[25]

The aftermath of the Confederate reversal produced friction between Pike and his superiors, who ordered him to move troops stationed in Indian Territory into Arkansas. General Pike, fuming over lack of support from Richmond and orders he felt infringed on his authority, resigned in frustration and was replaced by Douglas Cooper, who was promoted to general and given command of Native forces in Indian Territory in July.[26]

During a Union invasion several months after the Battle of Pea Ridge, John Ross let it be known that he was anxious to be "captured" and thereby honorably released from his oath to the Confederacy. When a Union patrol reached Park Hill, Ross surrendered willingly. His friend

Evan Jones, a Baptist missionary who accompanied the Federal invading force, gave Ross a letter from Superintendent William G. Coffin assuring the residents of Indian Territory of the U.S. government's continued interest. Neither Coffin nor the commissioner of Indian affairs considered the Cherokees' alliance with the South an act of betrayal. Both viewed it as the only recourse left to a people abandoned by the federal government. Lincoln's secretary of the interior had publicly supported this view in his first annual report to the president, but Lincoln reserved judgment.[27]

Confronted with the Union invasion force, nearly fifteen hundred soldiers of John Drew's regiment laid down their arms. Many enlisted in the Northern army and were mustered into a Union Indian regiment commanded by Maj. William A. Phillips, a Kansas abolitionist and newspaperman soon promoted to colonel. His regiment joined two other Indian units raised in Kansas from Opothleyahola's followers, but ultimately, lack of support and Rebel pressure compelled the three Native American regiments to withdraw to Baxter Springs in southeastern Kansas. Their departure enabled Confederate troops to reoccupy the Cherokee Nation.[28]

Paroled by his captors, Cherokee chief John Ross accompanied the withdrawing Union troops. By September 12, 1862, the Cherokee leader had made his way to Washington, where he met with the president, who promised a "careful investigation" of Ross's charge that the federal government had failed to protect the Cherokees. If that investigation was conducted, Lincoln never announced its results, lending credence to the charge of Kansas political leaders that the Five Nations had betrayed the Union. This claim became the primary justification for forcing the Indians to surrender almost half of their land after the war. Ross also urged the president to provide protection for the lives and property of his people and to issue a proclamation to restore the confidence of the Cherokees in the federal government. Lincoln promised to do all that he could to ensure that "the Cherokee country may not again be over-run by the enemy." It was a promise that was not kept; after Ross left the Cherokee Nation, the Confederates not only reoccupied it but also elected Stand Watie chief of the Cherokees.[29]

Although Lincoln drafted a proclamation addressed to the Five Nations admitting that the outbreak of the Civil War had prevented the North from honoring its commitments to the people of Indian Territory, for some reason, perhaps pressure from Kansas senators James Lane and Samuel Pomeroy, he never issued it. The president did address the subject in December in his second annual message to Congress when he noted a "spirit of insubordination" among the "Indian tribes upon our frontiers." Concerning Indian Territory, Lincoln added, "The tribes occupying the Indian country south of Kansas renounced their allegiance to the United States and entered into treaties with the insurgents. Those who remained loyal to the United States were driven from the country. The chief of the Cherokees has visited this city for the purpose of restoring the former relations of the tribe with the United States. He alleges that they were constrained by superior force to enter into treaties with the insurgents, and that the United States neglected to furnish the protection which their treaty stipulations require."[30] The president never said if he accepted Ross's interpretation of the reason the Cherokees allied with the Confederacy.

In the fall of 1862 Confederate reversals made it clear that its forces could not protect northern Indian Territory.[31] In February of 1863 Cherokees loyal to John Ross redeemed his promise to President Lincoln by gathering at Cowskin Prairie in the northeastern part of their nation and repudiating the Confederate alliance. They denounced the Watie government, proclaimed Ross their chief, and abolished slavery.

Subsequent Union military action resulted in a permanent reoccupation of much of the Cherokee Nation by midsummer and made it difficult for the Confederates to maintain an effective fighting force in the field. The victorious Union commander announced that Indian Territory was "now open to the settlement of the Kansas Indians."[32] While the claim was premature, it was what Kansas politicians, agitating for the removal of Indians from their state, wanted to hear.

The wives and families of Indian soldiers in the Five Nations suffered from the war as much as, perhaps more than, the combatants did. The pro-Southern family of Ella Robinson, who was sixteen in 1863, remained in its home at Webber's Falls after the Union occupied Fort Gibson and defeated the Rebels at Honey Springs. The teenager recalled, "In April of '63, Kansas troops commanded by Colonel Phillips had moved into the Territory and burned and robbed as they went." Although she could hear the artillery fire from the Battle of Honey Springs in July of 1863, her family had avoided the ever-widening path of destruction. That changed after the battle when black troops from Fort Gibson swooped down, "taking everything they wanted and destroying the things they couldn't take." Although they shredded bedding and clothing and took all the family's food, they left the house intact. Later that day, however, "another detachment of Union soldiers came with Colonel Phillips himself in charge and set fire to the house and burned it to the ground," Robinson reported. The family moved into a vacant house, "but in a few days Union troops set fire to the little village, and burned the whole place out." Robinson's family abandoned the Cherokee Nation and fled to Texas.[33]

For the last two years of the war, Confederate operations in Indian Territory were usually restricted to guerilla tactics or periodic thrusts into Union territory. Many partisan leaders were no better than thieves and murderers. For example, William Quantrill, who had a commission in the Confederate army, was more interested in looting than in Southern independence. When forced out of Missouri, he moved into Indian Territory, where he preyed on the families of Rebel and Union soldiers indiscriminately. Quantrill was the most notorious guerilla, but renegades, outcasts, and deserters from both sides terrorized residents of the territory.[34]

Aminda Hanley, whose father served in the Confederate army in Indian Territory, recalled, "During the Civil War the Pin Indians [also known as Keetoowahs] professed to be Union loyalists. In fact, and in light of their operations they were a well organized band of ruthless brigands and plunderers imposing their outrageous depredations upon any and all who happened to be assailable." She accused them of invading "the homes of helpless women and children," where "they robbed, stole and looted promiscuously and murdered deliberately when it appeared expedient to them." She continued, "Those whom the Pin Indians regarded as enemies, if apprehended, usually suffered torture or death or both."[35]

Late in 1863 Lincoln issued a Proclamation of Amnesty and Reconstruction, which did not mention Indian Territory, but the president extended terms to the Indians similar to those offered residents of states that seceded. In February 1864 Colonel Phillips, who commanded Union forces at Fort Gibson, led a Union column from the post to persuade the leaders of the Five Nations to disavow their treaties with the South. Blue-clad soldiers distributed Lincoln's amnesty proclamation, which offered full pardons and restoration of all property rights except slaves to most citizens. Many Rebel families longed for peace, but tribal leaders rejected Lincoln's offer. Phillips's superior, Gen. Samuel Curtis, feared efforts to woo Rebel Indians might undercut plans to force them to surrender territory for the relocation of Kansas Indians. He warned Phillips "to avoid any and all conclusions against our Government as to future rights of Indians who made war upon us." Phillips assured Curtis that he had no intention of promising Rebel Indians full restoration of their property. A Kansan who shared the desire to rid his state of Indians, he suggested that their land would make a "fair State" for "a loyal population."[36]

In 1863, after their long exile in Kansas, refugee Indians followed the Union invading forces in hope of returning to their homes, but Confederate raids compelled them to squat in squalid conditions around Fort Gibson. Although the Union could not adequately feed or protect returning refugees from the Rebels, in 1864 Congress authorized funds to move the remaining displaced Indians from Kansas. They reached Indian Territory too late to plant crops and joined those who left Kansas earlier, cowering around Fort Gibson. Rations for the sixteen thousand

Indians camped near the post, inadequate before the arrival of the 1864 exiles, were stretched thinner by Rebel raids and corrupt and inefficient federal officials.[37]

From the time of the 1862 Union invasion of the Cherokee Nation, pro-Confederate families had fled their homes for safety in the Choctaw and Chickasaw Nations or in Texas. Subsequent Northern occupation of the Cherokee Nation and incursions below the Arkansas River sent more Cherokees, as well as Creeks and members of other groups, south in quest of safety from marauding Yankees. Although received more hospitably than Northern refugees in Kansas, Rebel families fleeing south suffered from a shortage of food, clothing, and other necessities of life.[38]

Northern soldiers occupied the Cherokee Nation and Fort Smith until the end of the war, but Confederates constantly threatened Union supply lines. In June of 1864 Stand Watie captured the *J. R. Williams*, a Union steamboat, carrying $120,000 worth of goods up the Arkansas to Fort Gibson. In September, at the second Battle of Cabin Creek, Watie and a Texas general captured a Union wagon train carrying supplies valued at $1,500,000. These successes hampered Union operations but could not drive the Northern troops from Indian Territory.[39]

No major engagements were fought in Indian Territory after the capture of the Union supply wagons in September, but raids and partisan activity on both sides kept many in refugee camps and made life difficult for those who remained in their homes. Oce Gourd related the experiences of his grandfather, John Rattlinggourd, a member of the Union Indian brigade during the Civil War, who was shot in the abdomen by a band of Confederate partisans while he was at home on furlough. Only the determination of his wife, who refused to allow the assailants into her home, prevented them from finishing the job. Attacks by partisans on both sides occurred so often that visiting home on leave was considered dangerous for soldiers of both sides.[40]

By 1865 the Southern cause was hopeless. At a council at Camp Napoleon on the plains of southwestern Indian Territory in May, representatives of Indian nations at war with the Union learned of the surrender of Robert E. Lee. Realizing they must negotiate with Union officials, the delegates agreed to present a united front against Northern demands. Lincoln had never announced his plans for the restoration of relations with the Five Nations, and his assassination left that decision to others. Senator James Harlan of Iowa, whom Lincoln nominated as secretary of the interior shortly before his death, accused the Indians of "flagrant violation of treaties which had been observed by us with scrupulous good faith" and waging an "unprovoked war upon us." His interpretation of the Indians' conduct reflected the views of the senators from Kansas and provided justification for Harlan's demand that the Five Nations surrender a portion of their land within Indian Territory to "Indians now residing on reservations elsewhere" and accept "the ultimate establishment of civil government, subject to the supervision of the United States."[41]

Harlan's harsh terms reflected the need to justify the expropriation of the tribal land rather than a desire to punish Indians for disloyalty, for Harlan was fully aware of the hardships experienced by the residents of the Five Nations. In his annual report for 1865 he wrote, "The country within the Indian territory has been laid waste, vast amounts of property destroyed, and the inhabitants reduced from a prosperous condition to such extreme destitution that thousands of them must inevitably perish during the present winter, unless timely provisions be made by this government for their relief."[42]

The suffering of the Indians continued after the surrender of Gen. Stand Watie and other Indian commanders in June and July 1865. The quest for revenge in several nations prevented some refugees from returning to their homes and prolonged conditions that had impoverished those who had not fled. Indians who had remained loyal to the Union as well as those who swore allegiance to the South faced several more years of privation. Just before he was shot by John Wilkes Booth, the president said he opposed harsh treatment of the South.[43]

Had Lincoln lived, the nation's reunification might have been less traumatic. For Indian Territory, however, the bullet that ended the president's life probably made little difference. Senators Lane, Pomeroy, and others who favored forcing the nations to surrender land represented the views of many Americans. Although Lincoln favored compassionate peace terms, he was also a shrewd politician reluctant to fight battles he could not win. What Lincoln would have done, however, is moot, for he was dead by the time Stand Watie surrendered, and the Radical Republicans would soon secure control of the Reconstruction of the South.

In most of the South Reconstruction was demeaning; for some members of the Five Nations it was brutal. In parts of Indian Territory the killing continued. The capitulation of the Confederate Indians did not halt the quest for vengeance, nor did it immediately end the destitution that marked the war years. Sallie Manus, a Cherokee teenager, recalled, "Conditions following the War were absolutely indescribable, no law, no respect, life worth nothing, property rights wiped away, no food or clothing."[44]

In addition to the devastation and internal dissention, other factors slowed recovery. After the war men, hardened by the brutality of combat and unable to return to the mundane routine of civilian life, were attracted to Indian Territory, where legal jurisdiction was murky. The rule of law in Indian Territory had been undermined by four years in which rifles and sabers had replaced courts and reason in the settlement of disputes. Whatever stability the prewar tribal governments possessed was weakened by the turmoil in Indian Territory from 1861 to 1865 and the heavy loss of life, including key leaders. The end of slavery forced the Five Nations to allow whites into their nations to replace former slaves, who now had land of their own and could not be forced into sharecropping as were blacks in the states of the former Confederacy. These outsiders undermined the solidarity of the nations.

Perhaps the most debilitating condition facing the Indians as they sought to reestablish themselves and their governments was the belief that their days as an independent people were numbered. In his annual report for 1870, the Cherokee agent reported, "If asked why their high schools are not reestablished, . . . the reply inevitably comes: 'We expect to have our lands taken away; and what's the use of all that, when our doom as a nation is sealed?' "[45]

Summoned to a council at Fort Smith in early September of 1865 by agents of the victorious Union, delegates from the Five Nations were stunned by accusations and demands made by federal agents. The Indians were informed that by betraying the United States and by forming alliances with the Confederacy, they had forfeited their annuities and land. Tribal representatives were told the president was willing to negotiate new treaties if they agreed to certain conditions. The most significant of these included the freeing of all slaves, who must be incorporated into the nation as citizens with full rights, the establishment of a single Indian territorial government, and the forfeiture of large tracts of land for the resettlement of Indians from Kansas and elsewhere. Pleading a lack of authority to make the commitment, the delegates avoided reaching agreements with the federal commissioners. The strategy only delayed the inevitable. The next year, negotiations resumed in Washington, where the full influence of the government could be exerted on one or two groups at a time.[46]

In Washington DC in the summer of 1866, all of the Five Nations negotiated separate treaties with the United States except the Choctaws and Chickasaws, who signed a single document. Federal officials got almost everything they desired, although Indian delegates proved skillful in delaying the government's ultimate goal of dissolving the Indian nations and opening tribal lands. Negotiated separately, the treaties were similar; all abolished slavery and compelled the nations to treat former slaves more generously than any states that seceded. All nations pledged to establish an intertribal council, which many considered a first step toward a territorial government; all agreed to grant railroads the right to lay tracks across their nations. Bowing to the demands of Kansans, each group agreed to give up land, some in Kansas but most in what would become western Oklahoma, a name suggested by Allen Wright, a Choctaw delegate.[47]

In 1871 Congress passed a law that declared, "Hereafter no Indian nation or tribe within the territory of the United States shall be acknowledged or recognized as an independent nation, tribe, or power with whom the United States may contract by treaty."[48] The legislation dashed the claim of Native Americans to sovereignty. Six years later Reconstruction ended in the South, and the sovereignty of the states that had left the Union was restored. In Indian Territory, once the sovereignty of the Indian nations had been repudiated, events moved inexorably toward its opening to white settlement and the liquidation of tribal government. In the South defeat in the Civil War and humiliation during Reconstruction were followed by redemption and resurrection. In the Five Nations those traumatic eras foreshadowed a determined effort by American policy makers to eradicate Indian tradition and abolish tribal existence.

NOTES

1. Angie Debo, *A History of the Indians of the United States*, 9th printing (Norman: University of Oklahoma Press, 1986), 128; Wilma Mankiller and Michael Wallis, *Mankiller: A Chief and Her People* (New York: St. Martin's, 1993), 123.
2. Brad Agnew, *Fort Gibson: Terminal on the Trail of Tears* (Norman: University of Oklahoma Press, 1980), 185–204; Angie Debo, *The Road to Disappearance: A History of the Creek Indians* (Norman: University of Oklahoma Press, 1941), 88–112; Edwin C. McReynolds, *The Seminoles* (Norman: University of Oklahoma Press, 1957), 289–92; Kenneth W. Porter, "Billy Bowlegs (Holata Micco) in the Civil War (Part II)," *Florida Historical Quarterly* 45 (April 1967): 391–92; Jeffrey L. Fortney, Jr., "Slaves and Slaveholders in the Choctaw Nation: 1830–1866" (master's thesis, University of North Texas, 2009), 58–67, UNT Digital Library, http://digital.library.unt.edu/ark:/67531/metadc28371/.
3. Francis Paul Prucha, *The Great Father: The United States Government and the American Indians*, 2 vols. (Lincoln: University of Nebraska Press, 1984), 1:288; Arrell Morgan Gibson, *Oklahoma: A History of Five Centuries*, 2nd ed. (Norman: University of Oklahoma Press, 1981), 90–97; William G. McLoughlin, *After the Trail of Tears: The Cherokees' Struggle for Sovereignty, 1839–1880* (Chapel Hill: University of North Carolina Press, 1993), 88–89 and 94–95; *The Constitution and Laws of the Cherokee Nation: Passed at Tahlequah, Cherokee Nation, 1839–51* (Tahlequah, Cherokee Nation: Cherokee Nation, 1852), 59–60; S. A. Worcester to S. B. Treat, June 5, 1854, in ABCFM (Papers of the American

Board of Commissioners for Foreign Missions), quoted in McLoughlin, *After the Trail of Tears*, in ABCFM (Papers of the American Board of Commissioners for Foreign Missions).92–94.
4. Debo, *Road to Disappearance*, 118; Edward Everett Dale and Gene Aldrich, *History of Oklahoma*, 4th ed. (Edmond OK: Thompson Book and Supply, 1978), 144; McLoughlin, *After the Trail of Tears*, 136–40; Morris L. Wardell, *A Political History of the Cherokee Nation, 1838–1907* (Norman: University of Oklahoma Press, 1977), 118; Michael Welsh, "The Missionary Spirit: Protestantism among the Oklahoma Seminoles, 1842–1885," *Chronicles of Oklahoma* 61 (Spring 1983): 35–38.
5. Charles J. Kappler, comp. and ed., *Indian Affairs: Laws and Treaties*, 7 vols. (Washington DC: Government Printing Office, 1904–71), 2:442, online facsimile at http://digital.library.okstate.edu/kappler/index.htm; Annie Heloise Abel, *The American Indian as Slaveholder and Secessionist* (Lincoln: University of Nebraska Press, 1992), 28; Edward Everett Dale, *The Range Cattle Industry: Ranching on the Great Plains from 1865 to 1925* (Norman: University of Oklahoma Press, 1930), 8; McLoughlin, *After the Trail of Tears*, 112–13; George Manypenny to Robert McClelland, October 31, 1854, *Report Books of the Office of Indian Affairs, 1838–1885*, Microcopy 348, reel 8, 81; Debo, *Road to Disappearance*, 140–41.
6. McLoughlin, *After the Trail of Tears*, 116–17; J. Sullivan Cowden to President Franklin Pierce, April, 17, 1853, Letters Received by the Office of Indian Affairs, 1824–81, Microcopy 234, reel 96, 118–23; George Butler to Elias Rector, September 8, 1857, *Annual Report of the Commission of Indian Affairs for 1857*, 211–12; George Butler to Charles Mix, March 15, 1858, M-234, reel 98, 769; Kappler, *Indian Affairs: Laws and Treaties*, 2:442; *Cherokee Advocate* (Tahlequah, Cherokee Nation), February 20, 1845, 3; Roy Gittinger, *The Formation of the State of Oklahoma, 1803–1906* (Norman: University of Oklahoma Press, 1939), 33–34, 54–62.
7. Gittinger, *The Formation of the State of Oklahoma*, 33–34, 54–62; Wardell, *Political History of the Cherokee Nation*, 104–7; John Ross, Annual Message, October 2, 1854, in John Ross, *The Papers of Chief John Ross*, ed. Gary E. Moulton, 2 vols. (Norman: University of Oklahoma Press, 1984), 2:388–89.
8. James Buchanan: "First Annual Message to Congress on the State of the Union," December 8, 1857. Online by Gerhard Peters and John T. Woolley, American Presidency Project, http://www.presidency.ucsb.edu/ws/?pid=29498; Gittinger, *Formation of the State of Oklahoma*, 66; Abel, *American Indian as Slaveholder and Secessionist*, 58.
9. Wardell, *Political History of the Cherokee Nation*, 118; William G. McLoughlin, *Champions of the Cherokees: Evan and John B. Jones* (Princeton NJ: Princeton University Press, 1990), 345–45; Albert Pike to D. N. Cooley, February 17, 1866, in *The Cherokee Question*, a pamphlet published by the Department of the

Interior, Office of Indian Affairs, Washington, DC, June 15, 1866. To ANDREW JOHNSON, President of the United States: reprinted in Joseph Thoburn, ed., "The Cherokee Question," *Chronicles of Oklahoma* 2 (June 1924): 172–80.

10. McLoughlin, *Champions of the Cherokees*, 343, 364–65.

11. Abel, *American Indian as Slaveholder and Secessionist*, 63–125, 129; S. David Buice, "The Civil War and the Five Civilized Tribes: A Study in Federal Indian Relations" (PhD diss., University of Oklahoma, 1970), 27–29. Historical interpretation of the events leading the Five Nations into the Civil War has not evolved significantly in the past century. In *The Five Civilized Tribes*, Grant Foreman quotes an 1857 speech in which Cherokee chief John Ross cites "evidence of progress by the Cherokee people ... of the most cheering kind [415]."

This and similar reports justify widespread accounts in the historical literature of the return of prosperity throughout the land of the Five Nations following removal and provide support to the claims of Mankiller and others of a "Golden Age." Those who promoted this view were certainly aware of fissures within the tribes mentioned by Annie Heloise Abel in the first volume of *The American Indian as a Slaveholder and Secessionist*. She wrote, "In point of fact, during all the years between the various dates of Indian removal and the breaking out of the Civil War, the Indian country was constantly beset by difficulties. Some of the difficulties were incident to removal or to disturbances within the tribes but most of them were incident to changes and to political complications in the white man's country [25–27]."

Almost a century later Clarissa W. Confer, in *The Cherokee Nation in the Civil War* (Norman: University of Oklahoma Press, 2007), mentioned that "the Cherokee people had made great strides after removal [41]" but noted a "façade of unity [43]" that crumbled in 1861 because of "hostility from the 'Treaty Party' adherents [49]." Most accounts of the antebellum years in Indian Territory comment on the strides made between the arrival of the nations and the beginning of the Civil War. They also suggest lingering intratribal friction and continued white pressure.

12. Harry Kelsey, "William P. Dole and Mr. Lincoln's Indian Policy," *Journal of the West* 10 (July 1971): 484–92; Abel, *American Indian as Slaveholder and Secessionist*, 182–85; Buice, "Civil War," 31–32.

13. Muriel H. Wright, "Lieutenant Averell's Ride at the Outbreak of the Civil War," *Chronicles of Oklahoma* 39 (Spring 1961): 2–4, 11–14; Gittinger, *Formation of Oklahoma*, 68; Debo, *Road to Disappearance*, 143–44; William P. Dole to the Chiefs of the Five Civilized Tribes, May 11, 1861, *Report to the Commissioner of Indian Affairs for the Year l861*, 21.

14. Gary E. Moulton, *John Ross: Cherokee Chief* (Athens: University of Georgia Press, 1978), 167–78; Robert Lipscomb Duncan, *Reluctant General: The Life and Times of Albert Pike* (New York: E. P. Dutton, 1961), 172–75; *Message of*

the President and the Report of Albert Pike, Commissioner of the Confederate States to the Indian Nations West of Arkansas, of the Results of His Mission (Richmond VA: Enquirer Books and Job Press, 1861), 10; Lee David Benton, "On the Border of Indian Territory: The Oklahoma Adventure of William Quesenbury," *Chronicles of Oklahoma* 62 (Summer 1984): 142–43.

15. *Report of Albert Pike*, 18–20; Debo, *Road to Disappearance*, 144–47.
16. Debo, *History of the Indians*, 172; University of Nebraska–Lincoln, Center for Digital Research in the Humanities, "As Long as Grass Shall Grow and Water Run: The Treaties Formed by the Confederate States of America and the Tribes in Indian Territory, 1861," http://csaindiantreaties.unl.edu/csa_treaties.html.
17. Annie Heloise Abel, *The American Indian in the Civil War, 1862–1865* (Cleveland OH: Arthur H. Clark, 1919), 24–25; Paul Thomas Fisher, "Confederate Empire and the Indian Treaties: Pike, McCulloch, and the Five Civilized Tribes, 1861–1862" (master's thesis, [Baylor University], 2011), 79, BEARDocs, Baylor University Libraries, https://beardocs.baylor.edu/xmlui/bitstream/handle/2104/8133/Paul_Fisher_masters.pdf?sequence=1.
18. Debo, *Road to Disappearance*, 147–49.
19. Report of Col. Douglas H Cooper, First Choctaw and Chickasaw Regiment, commanding Indian Department, of operations November 19, 1861–January 4, 1862, January 29, 1862, *United States War Department: The War of the Rebellion: A Compilation of the Official Records of the Union and Confederate Armies*, 4 series, 128 vols. (Washington DC: Government Printing Office, 1880–1901), ser. 1, 8:5–14, facsimile at http://cdl.library.cornell.edu/moa/browse.monographs/waro.html (hereafter cited as *Official Records*); Jay Monaghan, *Civil War on the Western Border, 1845–1865* (Boston: Little, Brown, 1955), 225; Edmund J. Danziger, Jr., "The Office of Indian Affairs and the Problem of Civil War Indian Refugees in Kansas," *Kansas Historical Quarterly* 35 (Autumn 1969): 261–62; A. B. Campbell to James K. Barnes, February 5, 1862, and George W. Collamore to William P. Dole, April 21, 1862, *Annual Report of the Commissioner of Indian Affairs, for the Year 1862*, 151–52 and 155–58, facsimile at http://digital.library.wisc.edu/1711.dl/History.AnnRep62.
20. McReynolds, *The Seminoles*, 289; Interview with Annie Elize [Eliza] Hendrix of Tahlequah, Indian-Pioneer History Collection, 41:61–62, Western History Collections, University of Oklahoma, Norman OK, facsimile at http://digital.libraries.ou.edu/whc/pioneer (hereafter cited as Indian-Pioneer History).
21. McReynolds, *Seminoles*, 289; Colonel William Penn Adair, "The Indian Territory in 1878," *Chronicles of Oklahoma* 4 (September 1926): 265.
22. Life and Reminiscences of Henry I. and his wife, Ida L. Falconer, Indian-Pioneer History, 29:14–15; Hendrix, Indian-Pioneer History, 41:61–62.
23. Interview with Mr. Jake Simmons as given to L. W. Wilson, Indian Pioneer History, 83: 201–2; Interview of James Scott, Indian-Pioneer History, 81:78.

24. Duncan, *Reluctant General*, 184; Special Orders No. 234, *Official Records*, ser. 1, 8:690; Grant Foreman, "Fort Davis," *Chronicles of Oklahoma* 17 (June 1939): 148; Brig. Gen. Albert Pike to Capt. D. H. Maury, March 14, 1862, *Official Records*, ser. 1, 8:286–92.
25. Abraham Lincoln: "First Annual Message," December 3, 1861, online by Gerhard Peters and John T. Woolley, American Presidency Project, http://www.presidency.ucsb.edu/ws/?pid=29502; Roy A. Clifford, "The Indian Regiments in the Battle of Pea Ridge," *Chronicles of Oklahoma* 25 (Winter 1947–48): 314–22; Duncan, *Reluctant General*, 200–201 and 209; David A. Nichols, *Lincoln and the Indians: Civil War Policy and Politics* (Columbia: University of Missouri Press, 1978), 47–48.
26. Thomas W. Kremm and Diane Neal, "Crisis of Command: The Hindman/Pike Controversy over the Defense of the Tran-Mississippi District," *Chronicles of Oklahoma* 70 (Spring 1992): 26–28 and 33–36; Wright, "General Douglas H. Cooper, C.S.A.," *Chronicles of Oklahoma* 17 (June 1939): 167–69.
27. Moulton, *John Ross*, 174–75; Annie Heloise Abel, *The American Indian as a Participant in the Civil War* (Cleveland, Ohio: Arthur H. Clark Co., 1919), 121–22, Online facsimile at: http://books.google.com/books?id=AKoWAAA AYAAJ&printsec=frontcover&dq=Abel,+The+American+Indian+as+a+Part icipant&source=bl&ots=ZqWUBJHM2t&sig=-9wg8Ud_z4dLT8E2JUN_1FZ Z5TM&hl=en&sa=X&ei=7KEVUOmfHKT1ogHE_YC4CA&ved=0CDAQ6 AEwAA#v=onepage&q=Abel%2C%20The%20American%20Indian%20as%20 a%20Participant&f=false; Buice, "Civil War," 96.
28. Colonel Wm. Weer to Captain Thomas Moonlight, July 12, 1862, *Official Records*, ser. 1, 13:487–88; Gary N. Heath, "The First Federal Invasion of Indian Territory," *Chronicles of Oklahoma* 44 (Winter 1966-67): 417–19; Wiley Britton, *The Union Infantry Brigade in the Civil War* (Kansas City MO: Franklin Hudson, 1922), 309–12, facsimile at http://ia700209.us.archive.org/7/items/unionindi anbrigoobritrich/unionindianbrigoobritrich.pdf.
29. James G. Blunt, "General Blunt's Account of His Civil War Experiences," *Kansas Historical Quarterly* 1 (May 1932): 223–24; Moulton, *John Ross*, 174–75; John Ross to Abraham Lincoln, September 16, 1862, in Ross, *Papers*, 2:516–18; "A. Lincoln to John Ross, September 25, 1862," Gilder Lehrman Institute of American History, https://www.gilderlehrman.org/collections/d5aec6b3-1acd -437b-8c55-412615822256?back=/mweb/search%3fneedle%3d%2526fields%3dall%2 526era6%3dCivil%2bWar%2band%2bReconstruction%252c%2b1861-1877%2526 theme2%3dAmerican%2bIndian%2bHistory; Major General T. C. Hindman to General S. Cooper, June 19, 1863, *Official Records*, ser. 1, 13:42.
30. Buice, "Civil War," 124; Abraham Lincoln: "Second Annual Message," December 1, 1862, online by Gerhard Peters and John T. Woolley, American Presidency Project, http://www.presidency.ucsb.edu/ws/?pid=29503.

31. Blunt, "General Blunt's Account," 228, 232–33; Colonel Wm. A. Phillips to Major General Curtis, January 19, 1863, *Official Records*, ser. 1, vol. 22, pt. 2: 61–62.
32. Blunt, "General Blunt's Account," 239, 243–45; Britton, *Union Infantry Brigade*, 259–65, 268–85, and 287–96; Jas. G. Blunt to John M. Schofield, September 11, 1863, *Official Records*, ser. 1, vol. 22, pt. 2: 525–26.
33. Life and Experiences of a Cherokee Indian Woman, Indian-Pioneer History, 77:113–16; Carolyn Thomas Foreman, "A Cherokee Pioneer," *Chronicles of Oklahoma* 7 (December 1929): 364–74.
34. A Biographical Sketch of Mrs. Christine Bates, Indian-Pioneer History, 6:33; LeRoy Fischer and Lary C. Rampp, "Quantrill's Civil War Operations in Indian Territory," *Chronicles of Oklahoma* 46 (Summer 1968): 168–81.
35. Interview with Mrs. Aminda Latta Hanley, Indian-Pioneer History, 38:185–86; Wilfred Knight, *Red Fox: Stand Watie's Civil War Years in Indian Territory* (Glendale CA: Arthur H. Clark, 1988), 185–86.
36. Proclamation of Amnesty and Reconstruction, December 8, 1863, By the President of the United States of America, in Roy P. Basler, *The Collected Works of Abraham Lincoln*, 9 vols. (New Brunswick NJ: Rutgers University Press, 1953–1955), repr. at http://quod.lib.umich.edu/l/lincoln/lincoln7/1:79?rgn=div 1;view=fulltext; Angie Debo, *The Rise and Fall of the Choctaw Republic*, 2nd ed. (Norman: University of Oklahoma Press, 1961), 83; Major General S. R. Curtis to Col. William A. Phillips, February 11, 1864, *Official Records*, ser. 1, vol. 34, pt. 2: 301–2; Wm. A. Phillips to Major General Curtis, February 29, 1864, *Official Records*, ser. 1, vol. 34, pt. 2: 467–68.
37. Danziger, "The Office of Indian Affairs and the Problem of Civil War Indian Refugees in Kansas," 266–72; Abraham Lincoln's endorsement on a letter of Acting Secretary of the Interior William T. Otto enclosing a letter of William P. Dole, October 1, 1864, Basler, *Collected Works of Abraham Lincoln*, http://quod.lib.umich.edu/l/lincoln/lincoln8/1:81?rgn=div1;view=fulltext; Dean Banks, "Civil War Refugees from Indian Territory, in the North, 1861–1864," *Chronicles of Oklahoma* 41 (August 1963): 293–98.
38. LeRoy H. Fischer and William L. McMurry, "Confederate Refugees from Indian Territory," *Chronicles of Oklahoma* 67 (Winter 1979–80): 462.
39. Keun Sang Lee, "The Capture of the *J. R. Williams*," *Chronicles of Oklahoma* 60 (Spring 1982): 22–33; Marvin J. Hancock, "The Second Battle of Cabin Creek, 1864," *Chronicles of Oklahoma* 39 (Winter 1961–62): 414–26.
40. Interview with Oce R. Gourd, Indian-Pioneer History, 35:105–8.
41. Debo, *Road to Disappearance*, 164–65; Wardell, *Political History of the Cherokee Nation*, 170; Extract from the report of the secretary of the interior relative to the report of the commissioner of Indian affairs, *Annual Report of the Commissioner of Indian Affairs for the Year 1865* (Washington DC: Government Printing Office, 1865), iii.

42. *Annual Report of the Commissioner of Indian Affairs for the Year 1865*, iii.
43. M. Thomas Bailey, *Reconstruction in Indian Territory: A Story of Avarice, Discrimination, and Opportunism* (Port Washington NY: Kennikat, 1972), 41–46; Kenny Franks, *Stand Watie and the Agony of the Cherokee Nation* (Memphis TN: Memphis State University Press, 1979), 180; Benjamin P. Thomas, *Abraham Lincoln* (New York: Alfred A. Knopf, 1952), 517.
44. Interview with Sallie Manus, Indian-Pioneer History, 60:297.
45. Jno. N. Craig to the Commissioner of Indian Affairs, September 30, 1870, *Annual Report of the Commissioner of Indian Affairs for the Year 1870* (Washington DC: Government Printing Office, 1870), 285.
46. Debo, *Rise and Fall of the Choctaw Republic*, 84–87; David Buice, "Prelude to Fort Smith: Congress and the Five Civilized Tribes," *Red River Valley Historical Review* 7 (Summer 1982): 15–17; Annie Heloise Abel, *The American Indian and the End of the Confederacy, 1863–1866* (Cleveland OH: Arthur H. Clark, 1925), 173–218; Bailey, *Reconstruction in Indian Territory*, 192–93; Joseph B. Thoburn, "The Cherokee Question," *Chronicles of Oklahoma* 2 (June 1924): 141–46.
47. Kappler, *Indian Affairs*, 2:945; Debo, *History of the Indians*, 182–83; Bailey, *Reconstruction in Indian Territory*, 194–201. The desire of white settlers and railroad promoters for Indian land has been traced to the antebellum years and widely documented. In 1976 H. Craig Miner in *The Corporation and the Indian: Tribal Sovereignty and Industrial Civilization in Indian Territory 1865 to 1907* (Norman: University of Oklahoma Press, 1976), examined the growing pressure to open Indian land in the larger context of the burgeoning influence of corporate America. Almost twenty years later Jeffrey Burton broadened the account of the Indians' loss of sovereignty in *Indian Territory and the United States 1866–1906: Courts, Government, and the Movement for Oklahoma Statehood* (Norman: University of Oklahoma Press, 1995). In 2000 Murray R. Wickett provided even more insight into this crucial transitional period in his *Contested Territory: Whites, Native Americans and African Americans in Oklahoma, 1865–1907* (Baton Rouge: Louisiana State University Press, 2000). These studies and others exploring the era do not change the essential outline of its history, but they do provide a more nuanced understanding of it.
48. Wardell, *Political History of the Cherokee Nation*, 291; 25 U.S.C. Section 71.

4 "The Most Destitute" People in Indian Territory

The Wichita Agency Tribes and the Civil War

F. Todd Smith

Although the Native Americans who resided in the Wichita Agency—people from the Wichita, Caddo, Tonkawa, and Penateka Comanche tribes—lived in the westernmost part of Indian Territory, they suffered as much, if not more so, during the Civil War than the indigenous peoples in the eastern section of the province whose lands were located much nearer the fighting. Just two years after Texan citizens forced the various tribes to cross north of the Red River to find refuge at the newly created Wichita Agency, the outbreak of the Civil War caused these Indians to lose the much-needed protection and support of the federal government. By 1862 most of the Wichita Agency Indians had fled to Kansas, where they spent the remainder of the war in a destitute state, almost wholly dependent on the unorganized Union forces there to provide them with the most basic needs. By the time the Indians were allowed to return to the Wichita Agency in fall 1867, approximately one-third of the tribesmen had perished despite having avoided, for the most part, any battles between the Union and Confederate forces.

Whereas the Wichitas, Caddos, Tonkawas, and Penateka Comanches did not come under the supervision of the federal government at the Wichita Agency until summer 1859, all of the tribes were very familiar with the region, located in the southwestern quarter of Indian Territory.

In fact, some members of the Wichita tribe had resided in the area for three decades. The Wichitas were Caddoan-speaking agriculturalists who had lived in fixed villages on the eastern margins of the Great Plains between the Red and Arkansas Rivers before moving to Texas in the eighteenth century in order to gain easier access to French trade from Louisiana. The numerous, hostile Anglos—English-speaking Protestants—who migrated to the province from the United States following Mexican independence, however, quickly drove the Wichitas from their Central Texas villages, causing one group, the Taovayas, to cross the Red River and take refuge near the Wichita Mountains, while the Kichais, Wacos, and Tawakonis moved their towns northwestward, farther up the Brazos River.[1]

A closely related tribe, the Caddos, joined with the Wichitas soon after the Texas Revolution. Previously, the Caddos had lived in numerous farming villages located between the Trinity and Red Rivers, along the Louisiana-Texas frontier. Although the Caddos allied themselves with the United States following the Louisiana Purchase, Anglo immigration into the region following the War of 1812 forced one group, the Kadohadachos, to sign a treaty with the United States in 1835 in which they agreed to move to Mexican Texas to reside with the other two remaining Caddo groups, the Nadacos and the Hainais. The Texas Revolution and subsequent Anglo hostility, however, forced the Caddos, united under the leadership of Iesh, the Nadaco chief, to flee westward, where they established villages along the Brazos River near their Wichita brethren. Nearly two hundred Kadohadachos chose not to move to Texas and separated from the rest of the Caddos, ultimately settling in Indian Territory along the Washita River near Fort Arbuckle. This group, known as the Whitebead Caddos, was led by a chief named Showetat, who began calling himself George Washington in order to demonstrate his allegiance to the United States.[2]

Following the Mexican War, Anglos in Texas began to overrun the Wichita and Caddo villages, forcing state officials to grant land to the federal government in 1854 for the establishment of the Brazos Reserve, located about fifty miles west of Fort Worth. By 1859 450 Caddos lived on the reservation alongside 375 Wacos and Tawakonis. Eight hundred other Wichitas, however, did not trust the Texans and chose to remain north of the Red River in Indian Territory, where they settled among the Kichai and Taovaya villages, now located in the Washita Valley near the Whitebead Caddos. Unwisely, the federal government also placed the remaining 250 Tonkawa Indians on the Brazos Reserve. Unlike the Caddos and Wichitas, the Tonkawas did not raise crops and had recently made a portion of their living by serving as auxiliaries to the same Texas Rangers who had previously driven the Caddoan-speakers from their villages. Another nomadic, equestrian group, the Penateka Comanches, received their own reservation, located thirty miles west of the Brazos Reserve. About four hundred starving Penatekas, under the leadership of Chief Ketumse, reluctantly settled on the Comanche Reserve in order to obtain federal government rations, as the dwindling herds of buffalo no longer provided them with enough to eat.[3]

Federal Indian agents, led by Robert S. Neighbors, oversaw both reserves. Over the course of five years, the agents introduced cattle, chickens, and hogs to the receptive farmers of the Wichitas and Caddos, who also began to send their children to a school located on the Brazos Reserve. The agents had much less success with the nonagricultural Tonkawas and Penateka Comanches. Warriors from all three Brazos Reserve tribes also joined with Texas Rangers and troops from the U.S. Second Cavalry to attack nonreserve Comanches who raided the ever-encroaching settlements of the Anglo Texans, as well as the Caddo and Wichita ranches. Despite the assistance of the Brazos Reserve tribes, Texan settlers were alarmed by the numerous Indians in their midst and, under the leadership of John R. Baylor, attacked the Brazos Agency headquarters in May 1859 while the warriors were once again involved in a campaign, under the direction of Maj. Earl Van Dorn, against the hostile Comanches.[4]

Realizing the Texans would never allow the Indians to remain on the reserves in peace, the federal government arranged for their removal to Indian Territory. The United States obtained land for them in the so-called Leased District, territory obtained from the Choctaws and Chickasaws, located between the Red and the Canadian Rivers and the ninety-eighth and one hundredth meridians. Under the protection of Federal troops led by Maj. George Thomas, in August 1859 the Wichitas, Caddos, Tonkawas, and Penateka Comanches moved to the Leased District, where they were joined by the Taovayas, Kichais, and Whitebead Caddos. After turning over responsibility for the Brazos and Comanche Reserve Indians to their new agent, Samuel Blain, Neighbors returned to Texas, where hostile citizens assassinated him soon thereafter for his pro-Indian stance.[5]

Despite the Texan hostility, the various tribes were eager to begin settlement of what had been promised to be their permanent homes. Upon receiving jurisdiction of the Indians, Agent Blain decided to construct his headquarters—named the Wichita Agency—four miles upstream from the junction of Sugar Creek and the Washita River. The Indians, however, refused to disperse for their newly chosen homes until they were guaranteed military protection, as hostile Comanches and Kiowas were "still hovering" around the agency and threatening the newcomers. Fortunately, the tribes did not have long to wait for the military; on October 1, 1859, Maj. William H. Emory established a post called Fort Cobb about three miles west of the Wichita Agency. Two companies of the First Cavalry and one company of the First Infantry occupied Fort Cobb.[6]

With the troops in place, the Indians felt secure enough to take up residence at their villages, all located from three to ten miles from the agency. The Wichitas formed two separate villages in the Washita Valley near Fort Cobb; Chief Isadowa's Taovayas settled in one, while the Kichais joined Acaquash's Wacos and Ocherash's Tawakonis in the other. The Caddo tribes moved to their chosen site near the mouth of Sugar Creek and began constructing shelters for the winters. The chiefs of the three bands—Iesh of the Nadacos and Hainais, Tinah of the Kadohadachos, and George Washington of the Whitebeads—had log cabins built for them, while the other tribal members lived in "picket houses" covered with grass. By January 1860 the Caddos were "comfortably situated" and had "gone foremost" among the agency tribes in building houses. By September 1860 they had constructed eighty-two picket houses, while all the other tribes continued to live in grass houses or tepees.[7]

None of the Wichita Agency tribes was able to raise crops the first winter and were thus wholly dependent upon the rations provided by the federal government. However, Indian Territory superintendent Elias Rector believed that the object of the Wichita agent was to "teach these Indians to become tillers of the soil and raisers of stock, and to supplement themselves without expense to the government, and this within the briefest period practicable." In view of this policy, Agent Blain held a meeting with the various tribal headmen in January 1860 and "advised them to prepare for farming" because he did not believe that the government would continue to issue rations after the current year ended.[8]

The chiefs understood Blain's message and over the next few months "gave substantial evidence of their willingness to labor for their own support." The tribes immediately began fashioning oak rails for fences and soon thereafter had built many "horse lots and cowpens." Agent Blain had a blacksmith's shop and woodwork shop constructed, and the Indians kept the employees busy throughout the winter by having them repair wagons and plows for their spring planting. The agent procured seed corn and seed sweet potatoes so that the tribes could plant their fields in April. The Wichitas and Caddos, as usual, were very industrious and planted their crops in the traditional method—dividing them into many "different fields or patches"—with some having "tolerably good fences." As a counterpoint, the Tonkawas planted only a few acres, and the Penateka Comanches none. Unfortunately, all the tribes' corn crop failed from exposure to excessive heat and drought. As a result, the federal government was forced to renew the contract to provide rations to the Wichita Agency tribes for the following year.[9]

Drought was not the only problem the Wichita Agency Indians had to contend with. Their former enemies—hostile Comanches and Kiowas along with Texas citizens—continued to hound them north of the Red River. In October 1860 the newly appointed Wichita agent, Matthew Leeper, reported that there were large numbers of "wild Indians ... in or near the border" of the agency, who threatened that they intended to "overwhelm the reserve this winter." The Comanches and Kiowas lived up to their word by attacking the Caddo settlements in December, killing and scalping a Kadohadacho man on Sugar Creek, eight miles from the agency headquarters. The following month, Comanche and Kiowa attacks south of the Red River in Jack County caused the Texans to suspect the Wichita Agency Indians yet again. Leeper responded to the Texan charges by complaining that the agency Indians were placed "between two fires; denounced from Texas and attacked by wild Indians as well."[10]

A third fire was added in spring 1861 with the outbreak of the Civil War, placing the Wichita Agency Indians between the Confederate and Union armies. On March 18 the newly promoted lieutenant colonel Emory was ordered to abandon Fort Cobb and report to Fort Washita, downstream from the Wichita Agency, where all Union troops in Indian Territory were being concentrated. Emory was ordered to notify the Indians of his withdrawal so that they "may have a chance to move temporarily to the vicinity" of Fort Washita. The Wichita Agency tribes, however, were in the midst of planting their crops for the year and did not wish to be forced to move from their new homes once again. Upon the "earnest appeal" of Agent Leeper, who believed that "disastrous results would follow" the removal of the troops, Emory authorized two companies of cavalry to remain at Fort Cobb to protect the agency tribes from the Kiowas and the Comanches.[11] By the time Colonel Emory reached Fort Washita with his command, however, Confederate forces from Texas were already headed north and were threatening Indian Territory's southernmost military posts. In view of the superior number of enemy troops in the vicinity of Fort Washita, the colonel abandoned it to the Confederates on April 16 and started back to the aid of Forts Arbuckle and Cobb. En route to Fort Arbuckle, however, Colonel Emory received new orders directing all Union troops in Indian Territory to retreat north to Kansas. On May 3 Emory relieved the troops at Fort Arbuckle and sent orders ahead to Fort Cobb commanding the two remaining companies to leave the post and meet him on the road to Fort Leavenworth, Kansas. They abandoned Fort Cobb on May 9, and Texas troops, under the command of Col. William C. Young, occupied the post the following day.[12]

The Wichita Agency tribes now found themselves at the mercy of their old enemies from Texas. They agreed to enter into a temporary peace treaty with Colonel Young "on the condition that the Confederacy issue them supplies and protect them as had been done by the United States government." However, many of the Reserve Indians, fearful of the Texans' motives, abandoned their homes and fields and took refuge elsewhere in Indian Territory.[13]

The Confederates immediately took steps to solidify their position in Indian Territory. Gen. Albert Pike, appointed by President Jefferson Davis as Confederate commissioner to all of Indian Territory tribes, wrote Leeper on May 26 and asked him to stay on as Wichita agent for the new government. He instructed Leeper to gather the agency Indians—many now off the reserve—and inform them that the Confederacy would "comply with arrangements made by the United States." Pike also told Leeper to warn the Texans not to do any harm to the Wichita Agency tribes. Furthermore, Pike instructed Charles B. Johnson, contracted by the Union to feed the Indians, to continue to do so as under the conditions of his previous contract. General Pike then traveled to Indian Territory to make treaties with the numerous tribes that had settled there. In his treaties with the Choctaws and Chickasaws, Pike included a provision authorizing the Confederate government to use the Leased District as a reservation home for the Wichita Agency Indians.[14]

On August 1, 1861, the Wichita, Caddo, Tonkawa, and Penateka Comanche headmen—many of whom had only recently returned to their villages—met General Pike, accompanied by Confederate soldiers and sixty Creek and Seminole warriors, at the Wichita Agency. He distributed two thousand dollars' worth of presents to the tribes and promised to give them more when the council closed. During the next few days Pike set forth the terms of the proposed Confederate agreement, which was finally signed by the headmen of all the Wichita Agency tribes on August 12. Basically, the treaty was a restatement of the treaties with the United States. The tribes agreed to "place themselves under the laws and protection of the Confederate States of America in peace and war forever." The Indians retained the right to stay in the Leased District, where the Confederate government would supply them with agricultural implements, stock, and seed. The tribes were promised rations "for such time as may be necessary to enable them to feed themselves." The treaty also asserted that all hostilities between Texas and the tribes were ended and "to be forgotten and forgiven on both sides." The Wichita Agency tribes really had no option but to sign the treaty. The Union troops were gone, and the Confederates obviously were in possession of Indian Territory. The tribes retained the same agent, while the new government made the same pledges as the United States and backed its claim with presents. When the Confederate Congress ratified the treaty in December 1861, the Wichita Agency tribes yet again had a new "father."[15]

The Wichita Agency Indians' relationship with the Confederacy, however, proved to be short-lived. It quickly broke down for various reasons, and the tribes were left to meet the hazards of the Civil War—except for minor assistance from the Union—on their own. In the first place, none of the tribes trusted the Rebels to protect them from the Texans as the federal government at least had attempted to do. Second, the Confederates were unable to provide the Indians of the Wichita Agency with sufficient military protection from the Kiowas and Comanches. The Texan troops under Colonel Young soon abandoned the area. To serve as their replacements, the Confederacy enlisted about thirty agency Indians into the army to guard the reserve.[16]

These events did not inspire confidence among the Indians of the Wichita Agency. Small groups abandoned the reserve during winter 1861 to join other refugee tribes who had gathered at the Neosho River in southeastern Kansas, still held by the Union. Among these refugees were twenty Caddos, five Taovayas, and eighty-three Kichais. U.S. officials appointed E. H. Carruth as agent to these tribes, and in April 1862 he sent a request to the Wichita Agency asking the Indians to cooperate with a Union expedition, which planned to drive the Confederates out of Indian Territory. The arrival of Confederate troops to occupy Fort Cobb in May, however, did not allow the tribes to respond to Carruth. Because these troops were from Texas, they only served to frighten the Wichita Agency Indians even further. The Texans collected and guarded supplies during the summer but eventually abandoned the fort in August.[17]

That summer the Wichita Agency tribes suffered a serious blow with the death of one of their leading spokesmen, Iesh. The esteemed Nadaco chief had led the Caddos through the troubled times that had followed the Texas Revolution, and whatever small successes the tribe had enjoyed since then were largely a result of his firm guidance. The present confusing state of affairs demanded quality leadership, but no one, neither Kadohadacho chief Tinah nor any of the Wichita headmen, proved up to the task. Once again the Indians' corn crop failed from excessive drought, and though rations continued to be delivered, the tribes were said to be "suffering." Without Iesh present to guide them, about half of the Caddo people, along with many members of the Wichita tribes, panicked and fled from the agency.[18]

Some of the refugees joined a group of Indians—Shawnees, Delawares, Osages, Seminoles, and Cherokees—who had been armed by the Union forces and were on their way to destroy the Wichita Agency. On the evening of October 23 the group attacked the agency, burned it to the ground, and killed four white employees. Agent Leeper was first reported killed, but a friendly Comanche had provided him with a horse upon which he fled to safety in Texas. During the burning of the agency, the Indians heard a rumor claiming that the Tonkawas had killed a Kadohadacho boy. The Caddoan-speaking tribes of the reserve had never been close to the Tonkawas, despite having lived on the same reservation for six years. The Tonkawas spoke a different language, were not as agriculturally advanced, and had always been on relatively friendly terms with the Texans. In addition they were the only tribe at the Wichita Agency that had remained unshakably loyal to the Confederacy; none of the Tonkawas had fled to Kansas. The morning after Fort Cobb was destroyed, an infuriated mob of Kadohadacho warriors pursued the Tonkawas, who had already fled toward Fort Arbuckle. The attackers overtook the Tonkawas, and in a running fight that lasted nearly all day, they killed almost half of the fleeing tribe. Only about 140 Tonkawas, "in a most miserable and destitute condition," were able to gain the refuge of Fort Arbuckle. Eventually, the Tonkawa survivors made their way south of the Red River, where they helped the Texans protect the undermanned frontier during the remainder of the Civil War.[19]

The destruction of the Wichita Agency and the attack upon the Tonkawas caused the remaining Penateka Comanches, Wichitas, and Caddos—except for George Washington's band of Whitebeads—to abandon Indian Territory, despite the orders of the Confederates that they remain. Deprived of the unity provided by Iesh's leadership, the Caddo tribes splintered. By December the Hainais and the Nadacos—with the death of Iesh these two tribes collectively became known as the Hainais—arrived in Woodson County, Kansas, and settled, along with the four Wichita tribes, near the Verdigris and Fall Rivers. At nearby Belmont, Agent Carruth had established a temporary agency and supply depot for the refugees. The Kadohadachos, however, chose to remain aloof from the whites and wintered with the Penateka Comanches on the Arkansas River far to the west of the temporary agency.[20]

In May 1863 Agent Carruth began making arrangements to hold a council for all of the Indians belonging to the Wichita Agency. He sent a contingent of Taovayas, Hainais, Wacos, and Tawakonis to the Arkansas River to request that the Kadohadacho and Penateka

Comanche headmen attend the council. On June 8 Tinah and the new Penateka chief, Toshaway, arrived at the council grounds on Fall River and received presents from the agent. Carruth invited the two tribes to move to Woodson County with the other agency Indians so that they could receive clothes and rations from the government. Both tribes refused, insisting that they receive their supplies at the mouth of the Little Arkansas River, site of present Wichita, Kansas. They told Carruth that "we do not want to live near the whites, because of troubles between them and us in regard to ponies, timber fields, [and] green corn." The Wichita agent was forced to agree with their sentiments and acceded to their wishes. For the rest of the year, both the Kadohadachos and Penateka Comanches continued to live apart from their brethren.[21]

All of the Wichita Agency Indians supplemented the slight Union rations by entering the booming, uncontrolled cattle trade that had developed in Kansas. With the Civil War raging, there was a great demand for beef, and many whites in Kansas were offering high prices for cattle. At first the Indians were content to return to the environs of the Wichita Agency and round up their own cattle to sell. Increasingly, however, the whites offered the tribes "liberal sums of money" to go south into the abandoned Creek and Cherokee lands and drive in that cattle as well. Although some of the headmen tried to prevent this cattle rustling, a "good many" tribal members went ahead and participated in it.[22]

Milo Gookins, who was appointed Wichita agent following the death of Carruth, noted that most of the Indians of his agency "seem to have plenty of money, the proceeds mostly, I suppose, from the cattle trade." Unfortunately, the moneyed Indians attracted many opportunists, and the Wichitas and Caddos were plagued by swarms of whites who sold them whiskey, stole their horses, and "cheat[ed] and rob[bed] them of everything they have worth stealing." By late 1863, when intensely cold weather swept through Kansas, many of the Indians were left with "an insufficient supply of clothing, blankets, and shelter." The shipment of these articles did not arrive until January 12, 1864; by then many had already died from exposure, and others were severely weakened. At this point, a smallpox epidemic swept through the area and killed many of the infirm.[23]

Once the weather warmed in April, the Wichitas and Caddos abandoned Woodson County for the healthier regions to the west. They settled along with the Kadohadachos—the Penatekas having returned to Indian Territory, where they joined the Whitebead Caddos on the Washita River near Fort Arbuckle—in present Cowley County, Kansas, at the confluence of the Walnut and Arkansas Rivers. They told newly appointed southern superintendent W. G. Coffin that they preferred to "subsist on buffalo and antelope" rather than on government rations. Before they left, however, Coffin gave the tribes a "liberal amount" of flour and ammunition, and from April to October the Wichitas and Caddos were not supplied by the government at all.[24]

At first, all went well in their new villages except for the problem of the "vicious... vagabonds of whites" who followed the tribes hoping to rob and cheat them. The headmen complained to Agent Gookins about these "bad white men" who created "much trouble and difficulty." Superintendent Coffin gave Gookins full authority to "expel and drive out of the country" every white person found in the area without a legitimate reason to be there. In case they refused his orders, Gookins was to call on the nearest military post for assistance.[25]

In October Agent Gookins was able to resume the provisioning—albeit slight—of the Wichita Agency tribes located in Cowley County. On October 14 Gookins held a council with seventy headmen of the Caddo and Wichita tribes. Since the Kadohadacho chief, Tinah, had yet to return from a hunt, Nadaco leader Jim Pock Mark, "an intelligent man, spoke at considerable length" for the Caddos and the Wichitas. He stated that since they had left the Wichita Agency for Kansas, the tribes had not had an agent to advise them "and often did not know what to do." He complained of the "bad white men" who hounded them and stole their horses, and he asked Gookins to keep them away from the Indian camps, "and then there would be no trouble." Gookins reported that all of the headmen "express a strong wish, and seemed to expect, that the government would do something for them." As a result, the tribal headmen addressed a memorial to President Abraham Lincoln, "our great Father . . . and say to him that we are his friends, and friends to the Government, and to all white men who do right by us." They complained that they had been driven off their lands and had suffered greatly because they had been unable to raise crops or kill enough game, did not have adequate clothing or shelter, and had been decimated by disease. The headmen concluded that "we have always been told by our white Father that [the whites] would help us when we needed help, and we need it now very much and we hope that you will tell our Agent to give us bread for our women and children and clothing before the next snow falls. We hope our white fathers will not forget their red children when they are suffering." Three Caddos and seven Wichitas placed their marks on the document.[26]

Unfortunately, the federal government did not answer the Caddo and Wichita plea. After receiving Gookins's report of the council, Superintendent Coffin informed the agent that he did not have enough supplies to go around, and therefore he had to support the "more destitute" Indians who lived in the Cherokee Nation. Coffin felt these Indians were more needy because of their proximity to "robbers, thieves, and rebels," while the Wichita Agency Indians were safe out on the frontier. The Wichitas and Caddos, however, felt they were not far enough away from the whites and moved their villages farther west to winter at the mouth of the Little Arkansas River. Unfortunately, the tribes' suffering only increased at their new homes. Realizing that something needed to be done to help the ailing Indians, Agent Gookins obtained a "very limited and very inadequate supply" of food for them. This consisted of just less than two ounces of flour and "just enough sugar and coffee for them to quarrel over, but not enough to do them any good." Gookins also arranged for the tribes to receive a shipment of clothing, but winter was nearly over when it finally arrived on February 14, 1865.[27]

The Indians attempted to supplement the government rations in various ways. They continued their involvement in the cattle trade, but Gookins reported that by April 1865 they had completely run out of stock and had no money left. By hunting buffalo and other game the Indians were also able "partially to supply themselves with provisions and to keep up considerable traffic in robes, skins, furs, and tallow." Game, however, was becoming increasingly scarce because of constant white encroachment; in fact, by fall 1865 the buffalo range was a full one hundred miles west of the Wichita and Caddo camps.[28]

Agent Gookins also took great pains to get the Indians to raise their own crops for the first time since they had abandoned Indian Territory. On February 16, 1865, he wrote Superintendent Coffin to ask for agricultural supplies. Receiving no reply, he traveled to Fort Leavenworth in March, only to find Coffin absent. Taking matters into his own hands, Gookins purchased nine hundred dollars' worth of seed and farming implements for the tribes and returned to the Little Arkansas. In April the Reserve tribes "went to work earnestly, fencing and preparing their grounds, and planting their fields and patches." The prospects for an abundant yield were good until July, when extremely high water flooded most of their fields.[29]

By the end of the year Gookins was forced to admit that the Indians under his care were "very poor." He warned that their numbers were "decreasing at a rapid rate" from the "extreme destitution to which they have been exposed." A census taken in September 1866 provides a rough estimate of the severity of the population decline. Together, the four Wichita tribes numbered eight hundred members, down from about eleven hundred in 1859, nearly a 30 percent decline. Waco chief Acaquash, as well as Tawakoni chief Ocherash, were among the dead. Nearly one-fourth of the Kadohadachos and Hainais had died since the beginning of the Civil War; the Caddo population, excepting the two hundred or so Whitebeads—fell from nearly five hundred to just over three hundred fifty. Gookins reported that very often the headmen asked "when and where the Government will provide a permanent home for them." Because the Civil War had ended, both the Wichita Agent and the new southern superintendent, Elijah Sells, recommended that the Wichita Agency tribes be moved back to Indian Territory "where lands may be set apart for their permanent occupation."[30]

The federal government, however, took no action on these proposals during the following year. Once again Gookins encouraged the Indians to raise their own crops, and in April 1866 they began planting corn, pumpkins, and "garden vegetables." Their work was hampered, however, by having had no plows and only an "inadequate supply" of hoes. Although the tribes were busy in their fields, troubles occurred with the whites, whose numbers increased daily. Gookins reported that whiskey was prevalent in the camps and he was powerless to stop the "unprincipled white men" from carrying on this trade. Gookins did arrest and prosecute one trader in May, causing the others to be more cautious. Soon afterward, though, other whites stole horses from the Kadohadachos. In retaliation, a Kadohadacho band of warriors randomly stole horses from the first white man they encountered. Because of the growing tensions between the whites and the Indians, Gookins insisted to his superiors that the tribes be returned to Indian Territory "at the very earliest practicable period."[31]

By June the Wichitas and Caddos had successfully planted their crops, which appeared "to be doing quite well." The continued small amount of rations, however, caused many members to leave their crops and head west to hunt buffalo. This trek proved to be disastrous for the Wichita Agency tribes. While out on the plains the Indians met bands of Cheyennes and Arapahos, who refused to allow them to hunt and robbed them of what little they did have. The Wichitas and Caddos returned empty-handed to the Little Arkansas only to find that, yet again, high water had destroyed a good portion of their crop.[32]

Henry Shanklin, Agent Gookins's replacement, arrived at the camps soon after the hunting parties had returned from the plains. He found the Indians starving and in "utter destitution." Shanklin urgently sent a dispatch to Superintendent Sells stating that unless the Indians "receive immediate relief, starvation—actual starvation" would be the result. The Wichita agent complained that he was "besieged daily by old and young, entreating, begging, urging me to give them something to eat." He suggested that the Caddo and Wichita men return to the plains to hunt, but they refused out of fear of the hostile Indians. Superintendent Sells, in his annual report, stated that the Indians of the Wichita Agency were "probably the most destitute" of all the tribes in his care and warned that "unless some relief is furnished, they must suffer the horrors of both hunger and cold, as they are greatly in need of subsistence and clothing."[33]

This time the government responded. On August 3 rations finally arrived and were distributed to the Indians. Upon learning that the refugee Caddos were being fed, George Washington's Whitebeads abandoned Indian Territory and joined their brethren in Kansas. Three hundred Penateka Comanches followed them north soon thereafter. In September the government arranged for the Indians to receive daily rations, consisting of one pound of beef and either three-fourths of a pound of flour or one and a half pints of corn per person. Two months later Shanklin purchased two hundred dollars' worth of cooking utensils for the tribes. Unlike as in previous years, blankets, clothing, and socks arrived before the really cold weather had set in, and these goods were distributed to the Indians in early December.[34]

Meanwhile, plans were finally begun to move the refugee tribes back to the Leased District. On December 21, 1866, the southern superintendent informed the commissioner of Indian affairs that he would relocate the tribes in the following spring. Because the Indians had "but few ponies, and these generally in bad condition," he felt they would require one hundred two-horse team wagons to carry the Indians and their goods. On March 30, 1867, Agent Shanklin received instructions to move the tribes back to the old Wichita Agency on the Washita River and was forwarded ten thousand dollars to implement the move. J. J. Chollar was hired as special agent to "superintend and control the removal," and he began to collect the necessary wagons and supplies for the trip.[35]

It was quickly becoming imperative to move the refugee Indians from the area around the mouth of the Little Arkansas River. The land they occupied had been a part of territory reserved for the Osages, who had recently sold this land to the United States in order to move to Indian Territory. As a result, nearly one hundred white families had settled near the refugee Wichitas and Caddos by June. The Osages, whom Shanklin characterized as being "miserable thieves," remained in the area, stealing livestock from the white settlers and blaming the refugee tribes for the thefts. In addition, the Osages attempted to exact rent in horses from the Wichita Agency Indians, who refused to pay. Thus, the Osages stole the refugees' horses, and in turn the Wichitas and Caddos retaliated by taking the Osage ponies. Shanklin feared that if the refugee Indians were not "removed at the earliest day [this] bitter feud . . . may terminate disastrously."[36]

Luckily, Special Agent Chollar arrived at the refugee camps in mid-June with eighty wagons. Unfortunately, the return trip to the Washita River did not go smoothly. At first, heavy rains and high water in the rivers held up the removal process. Shanklin procured a small boat, and an attempt was made to cross the swollen Arkansas River on June 24. One Indian drowned, causing the Wichita agent to suspend further attempts "until such times as the streams could be crossed with safety." Unhappy with this delay, the newly appointed southern superintendent, James Wortham, took charge of the removal process a few days later. Unfortunately, his accession did not improve matters. Cholera broke out in the Taovaya village, killing eighteen tribal members in five days. The sickness quickly spread to the nearby Waco, Tawakoni, and Kichai villages, and even more Wichitas died. Despite the epidemic, the Wichitas refused to abandon their villages on the grounds that they needed to mourn their dead. They also refused to abandon their fields, arguing that the Great Spirit would be offended if they did not harvest the corn they had planted in the spring. The Indian agents were helpless in dissuading the Wichitas from this belief, and the tribes remained in their villages.[37]

In the meantime most of the Caddos and Penateka Comanches, along with a few Delawares, decided to head to the Leased District on their own before the cholera could reach them. On July 1 the agents distributed rations, which were to be consumed en route, to the refugees. Tinah, as leader for the entire Caddo tribe, signed a receipt for rations to feed five hundred or so Caddos, and most of them began the trip south. The remaining Caddos and Delawares stayed behind, however, waiting to depart with Chollar and the wagons. On August 3 this group had just crossed to the south bank of the Arkansas River when cholera struck, and thirty-four Indians died on the way to the Wichita Agency, which was reached a few weeks later.[38]

The Wichitas did not begin their own troublesome trek to the Leased District until October 1. Along with Agent Shanklin, they crossed the Arkansas River, where they were supposed to meet the hired wagons, but only ten wagons showed up equipped "with poor mules and oxen that gave out." Although Shanklin was able to hire a few more wagons from local farmers, many of the Wichitas were forced to walk, causing one observer to lament that "it was a pitiful sight to see the women and children, old men and old women trudging along on foot, most of them barefooted and nearly naked." A prairie fire only added to the Wichitas' misery on October 24 as high winds fanned the flames and burned to death eighty-five of their hobbled horses. Fortunately, the rest of the trip was uneventful, and the Wichitas arrived at the Washita River in mid-November.[39]

Although all of the Wichita Agency Indians—except the Tonkawas, who remained in Texas until 1885 when they received a small reservation in Indian Territory—had returned to their homes by the end of 1867, their travails had not ended. Upon their arrival, the Indians were surprised to find out that the federal government had set aside all the land south of the Washita River in the Leased District—territory promised to the Wichitas, Caddos, and Penatekas in 1859—to the previously hostile Kiowas and Comanches, along with a few Apaches. Eventually, the three hundred remaining Penatekas joined the twenty-five hundred or so tribal members on the Kiowa, Comanche, and Apache Reservation, three million acres of land located between the Washita and Red Rivers. Nearly one hundred Delawares settled down with the six hundred Caddos and seven hundred Wichitas, who were forced to accept their reduced reservation of 720,000 acres, unilaterally defined by the federal government in 1872 as being bounded by the Washita and Canadian Rivers. The two reservations were administered separately until the federal government consolidated the Kiowa, Comanche, and Wichita Agency headquarters at Anadarko, located on the south bank of the Washita River in 1878. In 1901 the Indians of the Kiowa, Comanche, and Wichita Agency were forced to accept allotment, and their excess lands were opened up to white settlement.[40]

NOTES

1. For background on the Wichitas, see Elizabeth A. H. John, *Storms Brewed in Other Men's Worlds: The Confrontation of Indians, Spanish, and French in the Southwest, 1540–1795* (College Station: Texas A&M University Press, 1975); Gary Anderson, *The Indian Southwest, 1580–1830: Ethnogenesis and Reinvention* (Norman: University of Oklahoma Press, 1999); F. Todd Smith, *The Wichita Indians: Traders of Texas and the Southern Plains, 1540–1845* (College Station: Texas A&M University Press, 2000).
2. For background on the Caddos, see F. Todd Smith, *The Caddo Indians: Tribes at the Convergence of Empires, 1542–1854* (College Station: Texas A&M University Press, 1995); Cecile Elkins Carter, *Caddo Indians: Where We Come From* (Norman: University of Oklahoma Press, 1995); David LaVere, *The Caddo Chiefdoms: Caddo Economics and Politics, 700–1835* (Lincoln: University of Nebraska Press, 1998).
3. For background on Texas Indians following Mexican independence, see F. Todd Smith, *From Dominance to Disappearance: The Indians of Texas and the Near Southwest, 1786–1859* (Lincoln: University of Nebraska Press, 1995); Gary Anderson, *The Conquest of Texas: Ethnic Cleansing in the Promised Land, 1820–1875* (Norman: University of Oklahoma Press, 2005).
4. F. Todd Smith, *The Caddos, the Wichitas, and the United States, 1846–1901* (College Station: Texas A&M University Press, 1996): 39–69.
5. Smith, *Caddos, Wichitas, and the United States*, 70–78.
6. Muriel H. Wright, "A History of Fort Cobb," *Chronicles of Oklahoma* 34 (Spring 1956): 55–56; Robert S. Neighbors to A. B. Greenwood, September 3, 1859, *Senate Executive Document*, 36th Cong., 1st sess., doc. 2, 700.

7. Neighbors to Greenwood, September 3, 1859, *Senate Executive Document*, 36th Cong., 1st sess., doc. 2, 700; Samuel Blain to Greenwood, January 25, 1860, Letters received by the Office of Indian Affairs, Wichita Agency, 1857–1878, National Archives Microfilm Publications M-234, Rolls 928–33 (hereafter cited as WAL); Matthew Leeper to Elias Rector, September 26, 1860, WAL; Leeper to Rector, January 13, 1862, in Annie Heloise Abel, *The American Indian as Slaveholder and Secessionist* (Lincoln: University of Nebraska Press, 1992), 339–41.
8. Rector to Greenwood, February 15, 1859, WAL; Blain to Greenwood, March 31, 1859, WAL.
9. Rector to Greenwood, August 9, 1860, WAL; Rector to Charles E. Mix, September 10, 1860, WAL; Leeper to Rector, September 26, 1860, WAL.
10. Leeper to Rector, October 12, 1860, WAL; Leeper to Greenwood, January 19, 1861, WAL.
11. E. D. Townsend to Lt. Col. William H. Emory, March 18, 1861, *The War of the Rebellion: A Compilation of the Official Records of the Union and Confederate Armies*, 130 vols. (Washington DC: Government Printing Office, 1880), 1st ser., 1:658; Wright, "History of Fort Cobb," 57; Leeper to Emory, March 31, 1861, WAL; Emory to the commanding officer at Fort Cobb, April 10, 1861, *War of the Rebellion*, 1st ser., 1:663; Emory to Townsend, April 13, 1861, *War of the Rebellion*, 1st ser., 1:665.
12. Emory to Townsend, April 13, 1861, *War of the Rebellion*, 1st ser., 1:648; Wright, "History of Fort Cobb," 57–59.
13. Wright, "History of Fort Cobb," 59; Ariel Gibson, "Confederates on the Plains: The Pike Mission to the Wichita Agency," *Great Plains Journal* 4 (Fall 1964): 9, 14.
14. Albert Pike to Leeper, May 26, 1861, WAL; Pike to Robert Toombs, May 29, 1861, *War of the Rebellion*, 4th ser., 1:359–61; Gibson, "Confederates on the Plains," 9–10.
15. Gibson, "Confederates on the Plains," 10; Articles of a Convention, August 12, 1861, *War of the Rebellion*, 4th ser., 1:542–46; J. J. Hooper to President Jefferson Davis, December 24, 1861, *War of the Rebellion*, 4th ser., 1:813.
16. Wright, "History of Fort Cobb," 59; John Reed Swanton, *Source Material on the History and Ethnology of the Caddo Indians* (Washington DC: Government Printing Office, 1942), 116.
17. E. H. Carruth to William P. Dole, April 10, 1862, WAL; George W. Collamore to Dole, April 21, 1862, *Senate Executive Document*, 37th Cong., 3rd sess., doc. 1, 301.
18. Kenneth F. Neighbours, "José María: Anadarko Chief," *Chronicles of Oklahoma* 44 (Autumn 1966): 274; Wright, "History of Fort Cobb," 59.
19. S. S. Scott to James A. Seddon, January 12, 1863, *War of the Rebellion*, 4th ser., 2: 354–56; Jeanne V. Harmon, "Matthew Leeper, Confederate Agent at the Wichita

Agency, Indian Territory," *Chronicles of Oklahoma* 47 (Fall 1967): 249; Wright, "History of Fort Cobb," 61; Smith, *From Dominance to Disappearance*, 247.

20. Carruth to W. G. Coffin, September 6, 1863, *House Executive Document*, 38th Cong., 1st sess., doc. 1, 304; Coffin to Dole, September 24, 1863, *House Executive Document*, 38th Cong., 1st sess., doc. 1, 295.
21. Carruth to Coffin, June 14, 1863, *House Executive Document*, 38th Cong., 1st sess., doc. 1, 326.
22. Milo Gookins to Coffin, October 20, 1864, *House Executive Document*, 38th Cong., 2nd sess., doc. 1, 465.
23. Coffin to Dole, September 24, 1864, *House Executive Document*, 38th Cong., 2nd sess., doc. 1, 449; Gookins to Coffin, October 11, 1864, WAL.
24. Coffin to Dole, September 24, 1864, *House Executive Document*, 38th Cong., 2nd sess., doc. 1, 449; Allan C. Ashcraft, ed., "Confederate Indian Department Conditions in August 1864," *Chronicles of Oklahoma* 41 (Autumn 1963): 280.
25. Coffin to Dole, September 24, 1864, *House Executive Document*, 38th Cong., 2nd sess., doc. 1, 449; Gookins to Coffin, October 20, 1864, *House Executive Document*, 38th Cong., 2nd sess., doc. 1, 463-64.
26. Memorial of the Chiefs and Headmen, October 14, 1864, WAL; Gookins to Coffin, October 17, 1864, WAL; Gookins to Coffin, October 20, 1864, *House Executive Document*, 38th Cong., 2nd sess., doc. 1, 463.
27. Coffin to Gookins, October 27, 1864, WAL; Gookins to Elijah Sells, September 18, 1865, *House Executive Document*, 39th Cong., 1st sess., doc. 1, 473-74; Gookins to D. N. Cooley, December 18, 1865, WAL.
28. Gookins to Dole, April 24, 1865, WAL; Gookins to Sells, September 18, 1865, *House Executive Document*, 39th Cong., 1st sess., doc. 1, 473.
29. Gookins to Dole, April 24, 1865, WAL; Gookins to Sells, September 18, 1865, *House Executive Document*, 39th Cong., 1st sess., doc. 1, 472-73.
30. Gookins to Sells, September 18, 1865, *House Executive Document*, 39th Cong., 1st sess., doc. 1, 472-73; Sells to Cooley, n.d., *House Executive Document*, 39th Cong., 1st sess., doc. 1, 443-44; Henry Shanklin to Sells, September 29, 1866, *House Executive Document*, 39th Cong., 2nd sess., doc. 1, 322.
31. Gookins to Cooley, March 29, 1866, WAL; Gookins to Cooley, May 2, 1866, WAL; Gookins to Cooley, May 10, 1866, WAL; Gookins to Cooley, June 2, 1866, WAL.
32. Gookins to Cooley, June 2, 1866, WAL; Henry Shanklin to Sells, July 13, 1866, WAL; Shanklin to Sells, July 13, 1866, WAL; Shanklin to Sells, September 29, 1866, *House Executive Document*, 39th Cong., 2nd sess., doc. 1, 322.
33. Shanklin to Sells, July 6, 1866, WAL; Shanklin to Sells, July 23, 1866, WAL; Sells to Cooley, September 30, 1866, *House Executive Document*, 39th Cong., 2nd sess., doc. 1, 322.
34. Statement of provisions, August 3, 1866, WAL; James McCullough to Cooley, September 21, 1866, WAL; Shanklin to William Byers, November 12, 1866, WAL; Byers to William Bogy, December 7, 1866, WAL.

35. Byers to Bogy, December 21, 1866, WAL; Shanklin to Colonel James Wortham, July 5, 1867, WAL.
36. Shanklin to Taylor, May 21, 1867, WAL; E. G. Ross to Taylor, May 28, 1867, WAL; Wortham to N. G. Taylor, October 21, 1867, *House Executive Document*, 40th Cong., 2nd sess., doc. 1, 316.
37. Shanklin to Wortham, July 5, 1867, WAL; Shanklin to Wortham, September 1, 1867, *House Executive Document*, 40th Cong., 2nd sess., doc. 1, 322.
38. Shanklin to Wortham, September 1, 1867, *House Executive Document*, 40th Cong., 2nd sess., doc. 1, 322; Statement of provisions issued to Indians from July 1–31, July 31, 1867, WAL; J. J. Chollar to Wortham, October 19, 1867, WAL.
39. Shanklin to Wortham, October 24, 1867, WAL; Philip McCaskin to Colonel Thomas Murphy, November 15, 1867, WAL; Shanklin to Colonel James Hotchiss, November 17, 1867, WAL.
40. Smith, *From Dominance to Disappearance*, 247–49.

5 Who Defines a Nation?

Reconstruction in Indian Territory

Christopher B. Bean

With the end of the Civil War, the U.S. government attempted to remake the Southern states in the image of the more republican, capitalistic North. Known as Reconstruction, this was a multifaceted process that involved reworked relationships between the federal government and the states, the states and their citizens, and former slaveholders and their former slaves. For the public at large, the government's role after the Civil War limited itself to the former Confederate states. Yet Reconstruction was in fact a national process, used for both opportunistic means and the beneficial redress of long-standing problems. Such a dichotomy, some might say contradiction, existed in the government's Reconstruction policies with the various Indian nations located in Indian Territory.

The purpose of this essay is to chronicle the major issues and events of the reconstruction process in Indian Territory.[1] Capitalizing on the war, the government used Reconstruction to reshape the relationship with indigenous peoples. Before the war, the Five Nations (Choctaw, Cherokee, Creek, Chickasaw, and Seminole) of Indian Territory were sovereign and retained meaningful independence with regard to tribal affairs and land. After the war, the government moved to end that sovereignty, bringing the peoples under complete congressional control. Beginning what would be called assimilation, the policy, which would continue for the next four decades and to a similar extent was attempted in the Southern states, had the ultimate objective of unifying the nation under similar values and institutions.

The need for any Reconstruction policy came about because of secession and war. Thinking the area indefensible, U.S. forces initially abandoned Indian Territory. This left the Indian habitants, with some more transient and dependent on governmental assistance than others, to the mercies of war. With few alternatives, a need for self-preservation, and at the mercy of the so-called white man's war, the various nations that had not followed the Federal withdrawal signed treaties with the newly created Confederate States of America—agreements, of course, that would greatly complicate relations between Indian nations and the U.S. government after the war. Federal forces began retaking the territory in 1862. By the summer of 1863 U.S. forces had retaken several key forts and had won decisive victories. By the last year of the war Confederate forces could only nip at Union interests with minor swipes of little strategic significance. Throughout the spring and summer of 1865 the last remaining Rebel forces surrendered.[2]

Even with Confederate forces still in the field, Indian nations began negotiations with U.S. officials in early summer. Viewing the area as "the gateway to the southwest" and desirous to open up the vast amounts of "unused" lands to white settlers, government officials were eager to begin negotiations toward a "new Indian policy in restoring political relations." Delegates (both Union and Confederate delegates and factions) from the Five Nations and various smaller nations, including but not limited to the Osage, Seneca, and Shawnee tribes, were present at Fort Smith, Arkansas. Newly appointed commissioner of Indian affairs Dennis Nelson Cooley met the various factions. Experienced in academics, business, and law, Cooley, however, had no experience in Indian affairs. What he lacked in indigenous knowledge, he compensated in loyalty and friendship to James Harlan, the new secretary of the interior. Desirous of a free hand with Indian affairs, Harlan wanted a sycophant, not a maverick.[3]

Harlan's plan for the Indian peoples quickly became apparent: "to provide for the consolidation of the Indian tribes, and to establish civil government in Indian Territory." With the opportunity presented by war, the interior secretary planned to alter existing agreements in order to free up land for white settlement. This in turn would consign the Indians to smaller, more manageable, and agriculturally friendlier reserves. Placed under a territorial, that is, white, American-styled government, the Indians would be moved one step closer to assimilation. As with the defeated Confederate states, the nations in Indian Territory were now at the mercy of the victorious Union, a Union filled with confidence that its vision for the future could be pressed upon previously resistant populations, Indian and non-Indian alike.[4]

With the meeting called to order, Cooley announced that the recent war had disrupted the previous relationship between the Indian peoples and the U.S. government. By signing treaties with the Confederacy, the tribes had "rightfully forfeited all annuities and interests in the lands in the Indian Territory." Thus, they had to sign new treaties of "peace and amity." The commissioner then requested each tribe to send a delegation (five members) to Washington to sign new agreements. Cooley informed them the new treaties had to include certain stipulations: a treaty of peace and friendship with the United States, other Indian nations, and intertribal factions; assistance in maintaining peace with Plains Indians; abolition of slavery, with all slaves being unconditionally freed and incorporated into the tribe or "suitably provided for"; each nation's setting land aside for the resettlement of Indians in Kansas; and preparation for the consolidation of all Indian nations in Indian Territory under one government. Despite reminders of loyalty and cries of unfairness from various loyal factions, raised points of concern about black colonization in their lands by unapologetic Choctaws and Chickasaws or the weak Seminoles, or sensitivity about accusations of disloyalty by the Senecas, Cooley informed them that such concerns would be taken under consideration and discussed in Washington.[5]

As with whites in the North and South, the cleavages within the Indian peoples borne out of the war did not suddenly disappear with the end of hostilities. Within the various nations arriving at Fort Smith were Union, or loyal, and Confederate, or Southern, factions, each struggling for supremacy over their respective members. Such fissures, of course, only further weakened Indian resistance and effectiveness in this different struggle. At a time when unity of purpose and thought was most needed, Indian groups were splintered, resulting in an all-too-familiar outcome.

Of the Five Nations, the Seminoles and Creeks, most stricken by the war, received the least favorable terms; the Choctaws and Chickasaws the most. Whether the Cherokee treaty was fair or not was a matter of perspective, with the loyal faction frustrated and disappointed and the Southern faction as pleased as any could be under the circumstances. Forfeiture of lands varied. The Seminoles lost about 90 percent of their two-million-acre reserve. The most unapologetic for their alliance with the Confederacy, the Choctaws and Chickasaws, lost no territory. The Cherokees sold the Neutral Lands (they retained the Cherokee Strip, however) for a fair market price of $1.25 an acre. The Creeks, however, got the short end of a deal in which the United States turned a handsome profit on cheaply purchased land. All the nations agreed to abolish slavery. All the peoples allocated lands (rights-of-way) for railroads. The status of freedpeople within the Indian societies, however, varied. The Seminoles, Creeks, and Cherokees were forced to grant citizenship and equality to their former slaves; the Choctaws and Chickasaws were not.[6]

More telling than the treaties was the variation that existed among the Five Nations' actions. Outside a few nonnegotiable mandates, such as emancipation and railroad rights-of-way, U.S. officials proved themselves willing to compromise. In other words, it was not guaranteed that the Seminoles and Creeks would be punitively punished, while the Choctaws and Chickasaws would "shirk their pound of flesh." Those who quickly ascertained governmental intentions, remained united, and, most important, embraced "white man's" customs, such as legal representation and lobbyists, retained remarkable agency. The examples of the fractured Creeks and united Choctaws and Chickasaws highlight the disparity in approaches and in results.

Divided by intratribal politics and weakened by the war, the Creeks arrived more suspicious of the opposition faction than resistant to U.S. intentions. Long before they began postwar negotiations, the Creek Nation was a "house divided." White encroachment threatened not only Creek ownership of the land but also their culture. Decades of Anglo-Indian interaction had resulted in a profound and ultimately disruptive dichotomy within Creek society, resulting in several internecine conflicts. The threat went well beyond the simple dispossession of land. For many, the very existence of Creek culture, way of life, and bloodline was at stake. In the words of one student of the Creek Nation, "Creek mestizos [biracial Creeks, or previously called "mixed bloods"] had a profound and disruptive impact on Creek society."[7]

Before the Southern Creek faction had even arrived in Washington, delegates of the loyal faction already had agreed to terms. Initially, government officials refused to recognize Southern faction delegates. They were also refused the draft the loyal faction agreed to. Only after repeated badgering did federal officials produce the document. Quite naturally, the Southern faction was "appalled." When the Southern faction approached the loyal faction with the offer of assistance, a united front against something that would be detrimental to the entire Creek people, the former were rebuffed. In fact, the loyal Creeks stood firm against the wishes of the Southern faction only on equality for the freedpeople, citing loyalty to those slaves who, like themselves, suffered at the hands of their disloyal faction. As noble a stance then as today, equality for the freedpeople, however, meant little to a people suffering from the war and who would suffer even more with the immense loss of land. This minor tactical win, against an opponent who shared far more in common than either would admit, resulted in an enormous strategic loss for both. What the Creeks needed—humility, insight, and unity—fell victim to bitterness and obtuseness. The gulf between the two was simply unbridgeable, and that resulted in a "punitive and confiscatory" treaty based on "ungenerous principles."[8]

Such a punitive treaty was not predetermined. The Indians, although "they" threw their lot in on the "losing" side, according to the U.S. government, hardly had to act defeated. As the Choctaw and Chickasaw Nations revealed, this meeting was as much negotiation as edict. The Choctaws and Chickasaws, unapologetic to the point of defiance, acknowledged the outcome of the war but refused to repudiate the principles that moved them to ally with the Confederacy. They were veterans of many negotiations. The Choctaws and Chickasaws, unlike the Creeks, had points they were willing to compromise and others not—in their case, they refused to cede any land east of 98 degrees longitude.

At the same time, the duo had the humility to offer concessions, the courage to demand compensation, and the intuition to seek compromise to nearly every stipulation by the government. Furthermore, the Choctaws and Chickasaws, employing public relations and the democratic process in a way the other nations failed to, retained the services of powerful, pro-Union attorneys, who proved "most helpful in obtaining a favorable treaty." Although the two nations had to cede land west of 98 degrees and, of course, emancipate their slaves, the United States compensated both groups for the land cession and did not require either to grant equality to freedpeople. Both nations also could purchase stock in the railroads that passed through their land reserves, a possible financial windfall denied the other nations. Plus, their negotiators successfully argued that previous treaties still bound the United States to obligations to the Choctaws and Chickasaws. This resulted in millions in previously owed monies. This development is an astounding fact when one remembers these two nations admitted to waging war against the United States. To say that the two negotiated the most lenient and favorable treaty would be an understatement. This leniency, of course, was borne of design, not luck.[9]

Like white society for the better part of three decades, the nations in Indian Territory also struggled with the "negro question." Problems arose not from the practice of slavery or even emancipation per se, but rather, quite ironically, from whether former slaves would be assimilated into the nations of their former masters. Reactions to such desires varied. For the Seminoles, who by the 1860s had a long history of intermarriage with blacks, assimilation was a relative formality. The Creeks and Cherokees, as with all other political questions at the time, were divided. Yet for the Choctaws and Chickasaws, who were considered the "most Southern" of the Indians, hostility marked the day. As one historian has stated, every nation experienced "difficulties ranging from minor to severe."[10]

How and why such difficulties arose goes beyond simple answers such as racism and political obtuseness. The answer, in fact, can be found in the intricacies of Reconstruction and the ongoing struggle for the past, present, and future of the respective Indian peoples. Conflict from "the freedman question" goes to the heart of tribal sovereignty, what defined freedom, and the Indians' sensitivity to cultural homogeneity. "The ideology of freedom was at once emancipatory and oppressive," notes historian Claudio Saunt. "In the name of freedom, the federal government fought to abolish tribal sovereignty, distribute Indian lands in severalty, and absorb Indians into the American republic."[11]

The meaning of freedom for the Creeks depended on the faction. Loyal Creeks vigorously fought for equality for former slaves, believing it a matter of honor and kinship. In fact, Oktarsars Harjo, the leader of the loyal faction, declared the "Colored-people residing among the Creek under their laws and usages were entitled to all the rights and privileges of full-blooded Indians of the Nation." In a twist of irony, considering that he was making an impassioned plea for inclusion based on a liberal definition of freedom, the chief further declared, "With them as with other Creek, no distinctions were to be based save those on the score of loyalty to the U.S. Government." In Harjo's eyes, the former slaves were more Creek than the Creeks who sided with the Confederacy.[12]

More so than the Creeks, the Cherokees struggled with the effects of emancipation. With a strong Southern tradition, the Cherokees resisted the altered relationship brought on by emancipation, acknowledging that blacks were still not their equal and remained beneath them. The Cherokee Treaty of 1866 required the nation to adopt and grant full equality to their former slaves. In order to qualify for adoption, however, the freedpeople had to return to the Cherokee Nation within six months of the agreement, a stipulation the Cherokees maximized to the fullest. In the summer and fall of 1866 several incidents of Cherokee hostility against returning freedpeople occurred near the Kansas and Arkansas borders. "This land is Cherokee land," one elderly Cherokee declared in congressional testimony that sheds insight on such actions. "You have millions of acres of land, why don't you send them out and settle them on it?" For years to come, former slaves in the Cherokee Nation remained in a sort of limbo. Despite congressional statutes and calls for leniency, the Cherokees continued to resist adoption of the "late comers."[13]

Of all the nations to resist equality for the freedpeople, none were more adamant than the Chickasaws and Choctaws. Unlike the other treaties, theirs did not mandate equality for former slaves. Instead, the Indians had the option to adopt the freedpeople and receive $300,000 for their expropriated lands or have the freedpeople removed by the United States at the end of two years. Both favored removal. The federal government, however, failed to act when the two-year period lapsed. For the next two decades, the Choctaw and Chickasaw freedpeople lived, worked, and tilled the land, "in spite of the insecurity of their lives." In the meantime, more and more freedpeople migrated to the region. In response, the Indians took matters into their own hands. They formed armed patrols in attempts to protect, which only concerned the government all the more. Both the Chickasaws and Choctaws, throughout the late 1860s and 1870s, continued to petition the U.S. government for fulfillment of the treaty of 1866 and remove the freedpeople. Each time the U.S. government ignored the petition.[14]

By the 1880s, however, attitudes began to change among Indians and freedpeople alike. The former slaves, who typically had been adamant about no adoption and governmental relocation, now desired adoption within the nations. Having put down roots, many naturally called the area home. In 1873, realizing that the government would never remove the freedpeople, the Cherokees passed a law adopting their former slaves. Although the law was presented to Congress, no action was taken. Rethinking their adoption stance, the Chickasaws would repudiate the adoption law of 1873 on two separate occasions: 1876 and 1885. The Choctaws' attitude also evolved. Initially adamantly opposed to adoption, by the early 1880s the Choctaws moved to adopt their freedpeople. Conflict continued until 1894 with the allotment of tribal land by the government, land the freedpeople were now entitled to despite Indian protests.[15]

Resistance to adoption by the southern faction of Creeks, Cherokees, Choctaws, and Chickasaws were caused by more than simple racism or unwillingness to accept slavery's demise. Issues such as sovereignty, nationalism, and self-preservation were more pressing. Indian leaders also feared, justifiably, that the federal government would use their lands as a depository for freedpeople. This scenario promised to overwhelm the nations with freedpeople, altering the balance of power within their societies. For example, had the Chickasaws fully adopted their former slaves, the black population would have far outnumbered the Indian population—something that happened by 1893. This would result in tribal suicide, since the Indians would "surrender all their own rights of property and political entity to be outnumbered and lose their identity in their own country." Thus, as one influential Chickasaw stated about the idea of an all-black community, they would "be anything but desirable neighbors as a separate community."[16]

With dwindling resources, one Cherokee expressed the sentiments of certainly many other non-Cherokee Indians as to why he objected to granting citizenship to freedpeople. "As much as we feel for the former slaves of Cherokee masters, we confess to feeling more for those Cherokees who did not own any slaves at all," he stated. The nations believed that they, not the U.S. government, should define what it meant to be

Indian. "In the name of freedom," notes historian Claudio Saunt, "the federal government fought to abolish tribal sovereignty, distribute Indian lands in severalty, and absorb Indians into the American republic." In order for the government to achieve assimilation, tribal sovereignty had to be destroyed.[17]

Even more threatening to tribal survival were railroads. In each of the treaties, the government forced the nations to permit railroads to build through the nations' respective lands. The Indians were not outright against the railroads. Prior to the war, several of the nations had "given a virtual blanket grant of right of way" to the industry. After the war, however, the Indian nations "had reasons to be concerned about the implications of that decision. Feelings about the railroads were mixed. Negatives had to be weighed against the positives. Their concern was one of who would control these gateways into their land. At the heart of the struggle was what the railroads brought with them, the by-products of "civilization" that historically have been the death of the indigenous ways of life and culture. With Reconstruction, the Indian peoples quickly realized "that the expansion of railroads was intimately related to the federal government's intention to create a new state out of Indian territory."[18]

Called progress by white America, the railroads spanned out across the vast western wilderness. Connecting markets to people, they also opened up previously uninhabited lands. The railroads had to negotiate directly with the Indian nations. This did not sit well with the railroad companies. They continually pressured Congress to "extinguish Indian title without tribal consent." Unfortunately, Indian concerns toward railroads through their lands contrasted governmental attitudes toward tribal sovereignty. Ely S. Parker, commissioner of Indian affairs and a member of the Seneca Nation, believed that the Indian nations doubted Indian sovereignty. "The Indian tribes of the United States are not sovereign nations," he declared, "capable of making treaties, as none of them have an organized government of such inherent strength as would secure a faithful obedience of its people in the observance of compacts of this character.... The only title the law concedes to them to the lands they occupy or claim is a mere possessory one." He further added that Indian peoples, because the U.S. government negotiated treaties for land cessions, "have become falsely impressed with the notion of national independence." On the advice of Parker, Congress passed a law that ended the government practice of making treaties with Indian peoples (it, however, did not abrogate previous treaties).[19]

With the Panic of 1873, an economic downturn that left numerous railroads bankrupt, railroad enthusiasm for Indian Territory dampened. It simply was not worth the trouble for uncertain profits. By the early 1880s, however, economic prosperity renewed interest in the region. This renewed effort by the railroad interests finally paid dividends. Citing the law that no longer mandated the United States to negotiate treaties with the Indian peoples, Congress granted a right of way to several railroad companies. This was justified under congressional power of eminent domain. The nations were now powerless to prevent and control railroad access to their lands. For all intents and purposes, this act allowed Congress to control Indian Territory with little interference from the Indian nations. A new era had begun.[20]

It was not long before the Indian nations felt the consequences of the railroads. Timber was indiscriminately felled, land cleared and spoiled, and Indian livestock stolen. "The building of the railroad," according to historian Angie Debo, "intensified the greed of every predatory interest that was watching the Indian Territory." Laborers who built the railroads, entrepreneurs who sought business opportunities, land speculators, and whiskey peddlers, gamblers, prostitutes, and horse thieves also characterized this influx of people. To be sure, this milieu included those who sought an honest living and a piece of the American dream as well as those with nefarious intentions who hoped to steal their piece of the American dream. Collectively, these elements brought what white society called civilization, or what one Indian observer called "strings of little houses."[21]

To the citizens of the Indian nations, whites' desires were not limited to money, resources, or even land. More insidious and, some believed, threatening were those who desired Indian women. Intermarriage, previously a way to bridge the cultural gap between white and Indian and a fact of life within various Indian nations, now posed a serious threat to tribal sovereignty and existence. Through marriage, white men also gained access to the nation's resources. Furthermore, white men fostered within these bonds of matrimony economic interests, such as coal and railroads, bringing transformative change to the indigenous people's interests and cultures. Intermarriage also changed the people's complexion, and not just politically. Such amalgamation raised fears of Indian extinction. One concerned Choctaw reported, "The Indians who inhabit the Territory are civilized and have adopted many of the customs and ways of their white brethren. They wear 'store clothes,' attend places of religious worship, and by intermarriage the old type of the aboriginal Indian is fast disappearing among the living. A genuine full-blood Indian will soon be a curiosity in the Indian Territory, and will be looked on as a relic of an extinct species."[22]

Fearing this influx of non-Indians, different values, and the white man's "road to disappearance," a governor of one of the Five Nations in 1874 embodied the sentiments of many when he stated, "For God [sic] sake, when we bought this country, we did not buy white men with it."[23]

Within the primary struggle between the Indian nations and the U.S. government was a secondary one. This one, however, was between two opposing factions of Indians: progressives and traditionalists. Often of mixed blood, Christian, educated, entrepreneurial, and accepting of Anglo-Saxon culture, progressives believed that "some adaptation of Anglo-American ways was necessary to protect Indian sovereignty." Accused of selling out, these people actually believed their course to be the only one for the Indian. They had read the tea leaves and understood "the white road" was not only the present but also the future. "They believed," according to historian Joyce Ann Kievit, "that through making selective changes, their nation could endure."[24]

Unlike the progressives, traditionalists remained "more Indian" in thought and action. Generally thought of as "full-bloods," they dressed in traditional clothing, lived in traditional housing, and farmed in the traditional way. They did not embrace white ways, resisting what they considered cultural heresy. They, instead, selectively chose certain elements from white society and culture, melding those elements to traditional Indian ways. For example, many traditionalists adopted Christianity but infused elements of indigenous religions. Traditionalists were not opposed to education per se. They simply wanted their children schooled "in their native language, not English."[25]

In one form or another, this struggle existed among all the Indian peoples. These divisions within Indian society manifested themselves in the debates concerning treaty negotiations and ratification, education and schools, railroads through Indian Territory, and intratribal elections. Nevertheless, despite all the disagreement, the competing sides agreed on one thing: Indian sovereignty must be preserved. This unanimity, as well as continued division, was on display with the creation of a consolidated Indian government in 1870. Under the treaties signed in 1866, the U.S. government required the formation of a consolidated government. Concerns and fears initially inhibited the conference at Okmulgee in the Creek Nation. Although the Cherokees, Creeks, Seminoles, and a few smaller nations attended, the Choctaws and Chickasaws were noticeably absent, disagreeing with the participants' policies on freedpeople and resisting allotment of their land. Informed that they would be subject to the authority of the new government whether in attendance or not, the absentees ultimately decided to attend.[26]

After several meetings and lengthy deliberations, the council finally drafted a constitution. Patterned on the U.S. Constitution, the Okmulgee government consisted of three branches of government, with a popularly elected governor, tribal courts, and a bicameral General Assembly proportioned along the lines of the House of Representatives and Senate, with one by population and the other equal representation. When the draft constitution was presented to eligible voters within each of the Indian nations, many refused to ratify it. Those peoples with a small population, such as the Chickasaws and Seminoles, opposed the document, fearing the power of more populous nations. The Cherokees refused ratification because they feared their consent would be misinterpreted as desiring a territorial government. They suspected that for any territorial government created, "Congress would assume power to modify the territorial government as they saw fit . . . and formulate a territorial government to detribalize the Indians and allot their land." The Creeks and Choctaws also shared this concern but understood that the Indian nations needed a united front to resist congressional machinations. As a result, the constitution did not receive the mandatory votes for passage.[27]

Throughout the 1870s the council continued to meet, drafting another constitution in 1875. Only one Indian nation ratified this document. By this time, an alliance between progressives and traditionalists had formed "to protect themselves from infringements" from Congress. In the words of one historian, the Indian peoples had developed "a sense of pan-Indian identity." In fact, this renewed sense of nationalism resulted in Indians thinking of and referring to themselves as "the red race." What appeared to be a sense of racial solidarity against white threats to sovereignty in reality only further divided Indian peoples. Up to this time progressives controlled the political process, comprising the vast majority of delegates to the Okmulgee conference and past treaty delegations. Angry, fearful, and frustrated, traditionalists, who always formed the largest portion of the Indian populations, asserted their power and gained leadership and control of the Creek, Cherokee, and Choctaw Nations. This resurgence in traditionalist power in the 1870s can best be explained by one Cherokee chief. "All experience has proven," he concluded, "that Indians (the weaker party) perish when commingled indiscriminately with the whites." Unfortunately, this intratribal struggle would continue for years, sometimes resulting in bloodshed, and continuing to undermine the already weaker party in the defense of tribal sovereignty.[28]

While the Five Nations experienced a changing association with the United States, other Indian peoples struggled to begin anew. Among those affected by the disruptions of war and impositions of Reconstruction were those peoples of the Wichita Agency in southwest Indian Territory. Driven from Texas in 1859, the Caddos, Wichitas, Tonkawas, and Penateka Comanches relocated on federal lands in Indian Territory. No sooner had these people settled in a new home than the Civil War erupted. After Arkansas joined Texas in seceding from the Union, federal officials deemed Indian Territory indefensible and ordered U.S. forces to evacuate to Kansas. The Wichita Agency Indians, as well as those of the Five Nations, were essentially abandoned to their own fate. Materially weak and with a sense of abandonment, the Wichita Agency Indians had little choice but to come to agreement with the Confederacy—primarily out of self-preservation. This alliance, however, soon deteriorated, partly because the Confederacy never lived up to its treaty promises and partly because conditions worsened for those at the agency. Thoughts of relocating to Kansas began to circulate. Any doubts were removed in October 1862, when Union-allied Indians attacked and burned the Wichita Agency.[29]

With the defeat of the Confederacy, the Wichita Agency Indians returned to southwest Indian Territory in late 1867. The lands that the Wichita Agency Indians returned to, however, were being reorganized. As a result of the Medicine Lodge Treaty, the Comanches and Kiowas received parts of the lands previously reserved to the Caddos and Wichitas. The Caddos and Wichitas not only disliked the Comanches and Kiowas but had assisted the U.S. government in fighting against them for the previous decade. Disrupted by the war, the government's policy of "civilizing" was begun anew, this time "reinvigorated by a new crusading zeal, influenced by Christian humanitarianism." Indian policy was now to be turned over to Quakers, Baptists, and Catholics instead of the military. The Wichita Agency Indians, it was hoped, would be taught the "arts of civilization." Known as "Peace Policy," this policy was ultimately doomed to fail. Instead of focusing on the more sedentary, agricultural Caddos and Wichitas, the government's policy of "civilizing" focused on the nomadic, warlike Plains Indians. The Kiowas and Comanches, disgruntled with reservation life and protected by naïve religious figures, resumed raiding into Texas. After their raids, they would retreat to the safety of the reservation. This charade continued until highly publicized raids and the Red River War brought reconstruction efforts on the Wichita Agency to an abrupt end. The government abandoned its "Peace Policy" toward the Wichita Agency Indians and forced them into the allotment system.[30]

Unlike the process in the former Confederate states, a hard end date does not exist for Reconstruction in Indian Territory. Does it end in the mid-1870s with the end of "Peace Process," or does it end in the late 1880s with the allotment process, or does it end in the first decade of the twentieth century with the end of sovereign tribal nations? More important than when Reconstruction ended were the intent and outcome of the process. Confident and with a renewed sense of mission following victory, the U.S. government used the opportunity of the Civil War to bring the nations under congressional control and within American society. Vital to these goals was ending tribal sovereignty. The Chickasaws and Choctaws spoke with one voice, discerning white intentions and thus reconciling themselves to white ways. These two nations came out of the Reconstruction process relatively unchanged, and in some ways actually benefited. Those nations that remained fractured and failed to reconcile their loss of sovereignty fared worse. The Creeks, Seminoles, and Cherokees faced persistent schisms within their societies and continued to struggle against U.S. attempts at "civilizing." They continued to hold on to traditions the dominant white society had already deemed counterproductive. Thus, the government saw more need to "reconstruct" (and in this sense, through punitive measures) the Creeks, Seminoles, and Cherokees compared with the already relatively "reconstructed" Chickasaws and Choctaws.

Through the treaties of 1866, federal officials forced from the Indian nations land cessions, emancipation, access to railroads, and consolidation. Like in the former Confederacy, northern officials and humanitarians imposed their vision of prosperity, hoping to eliminate those elements of primitivism holding back the "red race" from "civilization" and "prosperity." At the same time that they struggled to preserve sovereignty against the intrigues of the United States, certain nations endeavored to define the membership of their respective nations. Resistance to granting freedpeople citizenship went beyond simple racism. At the heart of the issue was what it meant to be a nation—whether a nation could determine its own citizenry. Although implementation and resistance varied, the Reconstruction process brought fundamental change to the relationship between the government and its Indian wards and presaged a policy a generation later that proved more transformative and disruptive to Indian ways of life than any government action since forced relocation.

NOTES

1. Since M. Thomas Bailey's pivotal work *Reconstruction in Indian Territory: Story of Avarice, Discrimination, and Opportunism*, the field of Reconstruction in Indian Territory has greatly expanded beyond the standard story of "avarice, discrimination, and opportunism." More nuanced and in-depth studies have gone beyond the simple dichotomy of a morality play, with whites portraying the bad and Indians the good. This historiography has shown Indian societies to be hardly monolithic, even lacking consensus in their definition of what it meant to be Indian. Recent work has examined the inner conflicts within Indian societies, uncovering "avarice, discrimination, and opportunism" in peoples previously considered to be powerless victims. For these studies, see David A. Chang, *The Color of the Land: Race, Nation, and the Politics of Landownership in Oklahoma, 1832–1929* (Chapel Hill: University of North Carolina Press, 2010); Claudio Saunt, *A New Order of Things: Property, Power, and the Transformation of the Creek Indians, 1733–1816* (Cambridge: Cambridge University Press, 1999); Daniel F. Littlefield, *Africans and Seminoles: From Removal to Emancipation* (Jackson: University Press of Mississippi, 2001); and Fay A. Yarbrough, *Race and the Cherokee Nation: Sovereignty in the Nineteenth Century* (Philadelphia: University of Pennsylvania Press, 2008).

2. For more extensive studies on the Civil War in Indian Territory besides the previous essays in this work, see Laurence M. Hauptman, *Between Two Fires: American Indians in the Civil War* (New York: Free Press, 1995); W. Craig

Gaines, *The Confederate Cherokees: John Drew's Regiment of Mounted Rifles* (Baton Rouge: Louisiana State University Press, 1989); Christine Schultz White and Benton R. White, *Now the Wolf Has Come: The Creek Nation in the Civil War* (College Station: Texas A&M University Press, 1996); Edmund J. Danziger, "The Office of Indian Affairs and the Problem of Civil War Indian Refugees in Kansas," *Kansas Historical Quarterly* 35 (1969): 257–75; Frank Cunningham, *General Stand Watie's Confederate Indians* (Norman: University of Oklahoma Press, 1998); Clarissa Confer, *The Cherokee Nation in the Civil War* (Norman: University of Oklahoma Press, 2007); Richard S. Brownlee, *Gray Ghosts of the Confederacy: Guerrilla Warfare in the West, 1861–1865* (Baton Rouge: Louisiana State University Press, 1958); Whit Edwards, *"The Prairie Was on Fire": Eyewitness Accounts of the Civil War in the Indian Territory* (Oklahoma City: Oklahoma Historical Society, 2001): LeRoy H. Fischer, ed., *The Civil War Era in Indian Territory* (Los Angeles: Lorrin L. Morrison, 1974); Lary C. Rampp and Donald L. Rampp, *The Civil War in the Indian Territory* (Austin: Presidial, 1975); Alvin M. Josephy, Jr., *The Civil War in the American West* (New York: Vintage, 1991); George H. Shirk, "Indian Territory Command in the Civil War," *Chronicles of Oklahoma* 45 (Winter 1967): 464–71; Carolynn Ross Johnston, "'The Panther's Scream Is Often Heard': Cherokee Women in Indian Territory during the Civil War," *Chronicles of Oklahoma* 78 (Spring 2000): 84–107; Ohland Morton, "Confederate Government Relations with the Five Civilized Tribes," *Chronicles of Oklahoma* 31 (Summer 1953): 189–203; Dean Banks, "Civil War Refugees from Indian Territory in the North, 1861–1864," *Chronicles of Oklahoma* 41 (Autumn 1963): 286–98; Allen C. Ashcraft, "Confederate Indian Department Conditions in August 1864," *Chronicles of Oklahoma* 41 (Autumn 1963): 270–85; Ohland Morton, "The Confederate States Government and the Five Civilized Tribes," *Chronicles of Oklahoma* 31 (Autumn 1953): 299–322; Walter Lee Brown, *A Life of Albert Pike* (Fayetteville: University of Arkansas Press, 1997); Dean Trickett, "The Civil War in the Indian Territory," *Chronicles of Oklahoma* 18 (December 1940): 266–80; Gary E. Moulton, *John Ross, Cherokee Chief* (Athens: University of Georgia Press, 1978); and Fred Hood, "Twilight of the Confederacy in Indian Territory," *Chronicles of Oklahoma* 41 (Winter 1963–64): 424–41.

3. Bailey, *Reconstruction in Indian Territory*, 66; Gary L. Roberts, "Dennis Nelson Cooley," in *The Commissioners of Indian Affairs*, ed. Robert M. Kvasnicka and Herman J. Viola (Lincoln: University of Nebraska Press, 1979), 99–100.
4. Roberts, "Dennis Nelson Cooley," 99; Joyce Ann Kievit, "Trail of Tears to Veil of Tears: The Impact of Removal on Reconstruction" (PhD diss., University of Houston, 2002), 130; Bailey, *Reconstruction in Indian Territory*, 58–59.
5. Kievit, "Trail of Tears to Veil of Tears," 131–43; Bailey, *Reconstruction in Indian Territory*, 63–65. There were seven stipulations: (1) each tribe must enter into a

treaty for permanent peace and amity among themselves as nations and with the United States; (2) the nations settled in Indian Territory were to agree, at the call of U.S. authorities, to assist in compelling the tribes of the plains to keep peace; (3) slavery must be abolished and measures taken to incorporate the slaves into the societies, with their civil rights guaranteed; (4) a general stipulation that slavery was henceforth abolished and involuntary servitude would never again exist in the tribes or Nation, except in punishment of crime, must be incorporated in the new treaties; (5) a part of Indian Territory would be set aside to be purchased for the use of Indians from Kansas or elsewhere, as the government might desire to colonize therein; (6) the policy of the government to unite all of the Indian nations of the region into one consolidated government should be accepted; and (7) no white persons except government employees or officers or employees of internal improvement companies authorized by the government would be permitted to reside among the Indians unless adopted by the several Nations.

6. For the specifics, which also included compensation for losses of property of persons loyal to the United States during the war, U.S. military occupation of the area, and increased federal jurisdiction within the territory, such as courts, of the treaties, see vol. 2 of Charles J. Kappler, ed., *Indian Affairs: Laws and Treaties* (New York: AMS, 1971); Harry Henslick, "The Seminole Treaty of 1866," *Chronicles of Oklahoma* 48 (Autumn 1970): 280–94; Gail Balman, "The Creek Treaty of 1866," *Chronicles of Oklahoma* 48 (Autumn 1970): 184–96; Marion Ray McCullar, "The Choctaw-Chickasaw Reconstruction Treaty of 1866," *Journal of the West* 12 (July 1973): 462–70; Paul F. Lambert, "The Cherokee Reconstruction Treaty of 1866," *Journal of the West* 12 (July 1973): 471–89; and Francis Paul Prucha, *American Indian Treaties: The History of a Political Anomaly* (Berkeley: University of California Press, 1994).

7. For a detailed examination of the schisms within Creek society caused by the interaction of Creek and Anglo societies, see Saunt, *New Order of Things*, quotation: 2; and Chang, *Color of the Land*, esp. chap. 1.

8. Kievit, "Trail of Tears to Veil of Tears," 152; Bailey, *Reconstruction in Indian Territory*, 75–76. For the divisions within the Creek Nation during the Civil War and Reconstruction, see Angie Debo, *The Road to Disappearance: A History of the Creek Indians* (Norman: University of Oklahoma Press, 1941), esp. chaps. 5 and 6. The quotes came from pp. 171–72; Ohland Morton, "Reconstruction in the Creek Nation," *Chronicles of Oklahoma* 9 (June 1931): 170–90; and Bernice Carter Benson, "The Creek Nation during the Reconstruction Period" (master's thesis, Oklahoma Agricultural and Mechanical College, 1937).

9. Kievit, "Trail of Tears to Veil of Tears," 148–51. For the Choctaw and Chickasaw approach to the negotiations and specifics of the treaty, see Clara Sue Kidwell, *The Choctaws in Oklahoma: From Tribe to Nation, 1855–1870* (Norman: University

of Oklahoma Press, 2007), esp. chap. 6; and Lewis Anthony Kensell, "Phases of Reconstruction in the Choctaw Nation, 1865–1870," *Chronicles of Oklahoma* 47 (Summer 1969): 138–53.

10. Walt Wilson, "Freedmen in Indian Territory during Reconstruction," *Chronicles of Oklahoma* 49 (Summer 1971): 237. For Seminole relations toward slaves and slavery and reaction to emancipation and assimilation, see Littlefield, *Africans and Seminoles*; Kevin Mulroy, *The Seminole Freedmen: A History* (Norman: University of Oklahoma Press, 2007); Edwin C. McReynolds, *The Seminoles* (Norman: University of Oklahoma Press, 1947); and Jane F. Lancaster, *Removal Aftershock: The Seminoles' Struggles to Survive in the West, 1836–1866* (Knoxville: University of Tennessee Press, 1994). For Creek relations toward slaves and slavery and reaction to emancipation and assimilation, see Annie Heloise Abel, *The American Indian under Reconstruction* (Cleveland OH: A. H. Clark, 1925); Donald A. Grinde and Quintard Taylor, "Red vs. Black: Conflict and Accommodation in the Post Civil War Indian Territory," *American Indian Quarterly* 10 (Summer 1984): 211–89; Debo, *Road to Disappearance*; Sigmund E. Sameth, "Creek Negroes: A Study of Race Relations" (master's thesis, University of Oklahoma, 1940); Thomas F. Andrews, "Freedmen in Indian Territory: A Post-Civil War Dilemma," *Journal of the West* 4 (July 1965); Benson, "Creek Nation during the Reconstruction Period"; and Morton, "Reconstruction in the Creek Nation." For the Cherokee relations toward slaves and slavery and reaction to emancipation and assimilation, see Hanna R. Warren, "Reconstruction in the Cherokee Nation," *Chronicles of Oklahoma* 54 (Summer 1976): 180–89; Tim Gammon, "Black Freedmen and the Cherokee Nation," *Journal of American Studies* 11 (December 1977): 357–64; and Gary R. Kremer, "For Justice and a Fee: James Milton Turner and the Cherokee Freedmen," *Chronicles of Oklahoma* 58 (Winter 1980): 376–91. For Choctaw and Chickasaw relations toward slaves and slavery and reaction to emancipation and assimilation, see Daniel F. Littlefield, Jr., *The Chickasaw Freedmen: A People without a Country* (Westport CT: Greenwood, 1980); Kidwell, *Choctaws in Oklahoma*; Angie Debo, *And Still the Waters Run: The Betrayal of the Five Civilized Tribes* (Princeton NJ: Princeton University Press, 1972); and Parthena Louis James, "Reconstruction in the Chickasaw Nation: The Freedmen Problem," *Chronicles of Oklahoma* 45 (Spring 1967): 44–57.

11. Claudio Saunt, "The Paradox of Freedom: Tribal Sovereignty and Emancipation during the Reconstruction of Indian Territory," *Journal of Southern History* 40 (January 2004): 93.

12. Wilson, "Freedmen in Indian Territory during Reconstruction," 237–38; Saunt, "Paradox of Freedom," 83–84.

13. Saunt, "Paradox of Freedom," 87–88; Kievit, "Trail of Tears to Veil of Tears," 177–78; Warren, "Reconstruction in the Cherokee Nation," 185; Saunt, "Paradox

of Freedom," 88–89; Wilson, "Freedmen in Indian Territory," 238; William G. McLoughlin, *After the Trail of Tears: The Cherokees' Struggle for Sovereignty, 1839–1880* (Chapel Hill: University of North Carolina Press, 1993), 251–54, 281–84, 291–93, 354–59. For the struggles in Cherokee society concerning slavery, see Theda Perdue, *Slavery and the Evolution of Cherokee Society, 1540–1866* (Knoxville: University of Tennessee Press, 1979); Yarbrough, *Race and the Cherokee Nation*; and Celia E. Naylor, *African Cherokees in Indian Territory: From Chattel to Citizens* (Chapel Hill: University of North Carolina Press, 2007).

14. Angie Debo, *The Rise and Fall of the Choctaw Republic* (Norman: University of Oklahoma Press, 1961), 100–103; Kensell, "Phases of Reconstruction in the Choctaw Nation," 1149–51; Wilson, "Freedmen in Indian Territory during Reconstruction," 240; Parthena Louise James, "Reconstruction in the Chickasaw Nation, 1865–1877" (master's thesis, Oklahoma State University, 1963), 38; Arrell M. Gibson, *The Chickasaws* (Norman: University of Oklahoma Press, 1971), 291.

15. Debo, *Rise and Fall of the Choctaw Republic*, 104–5; James, "Reconstruction in the Chickasaw Nation: The Freedmen Problem," 48–56; Gibson, *Chickasaws*, 292, 295, 302–6.

16. James, "Reconstruction in the Chickasaw Nation, 1865–1877," 33; Wilson, "Freedmen in Indian Territory during Reconstruction," 240–22; Kievit, "Trail of Tears to Veil of Tears," 188; Saunt, "Paradox of Freedom," 93; James, "Reconstruction in the Chickasaw Nation: The Freedmen Problem," 53.

17. Kievit, "Trail of Tears to Veil of Tears," 188; Saunt, "Paradox of Freedom," 93. For the government's attempt to end tribal sovereignty in the name of freedom and assimilation, see Henry E. Fritz, *The Movement for Indian Assimilation, 1860–1890* (Philadelphia: University of Pennsylvania Press, 1963); Robert Winston Mardock, *The Reformers and the American Indian* (Columbia: University of Missouri Press, 1971); Francis Paul Prucha, *American Indian Policy in Crisis: Christian Reformers and the Indian, 1865–1900* (Norman: University of Oklahoma Press, 1976); and Frederick E. Hoxie, *A Final Promise: The Campaign to Assimilate the Indians, 1880–1920* (Lincoln: University of Nebraska Press, 1984).

18. Kidwell, *Choctaws in Oklahoma*, 88; Wade D. Foster, "The Federal Government and the Five Civilized Tribes during Reconstruction" (master's thesis, Oklahoma State University, 1956), 53; McLoughlin, *After the Trail of Tears*, 271. For a more detailed account of the relationship between the Indian peoples, the government, and the railroads and the effects of that relationship, both beneficial and detrimental to the Indian peoples, see Will Roger Todd, "Federal Policy Relating to the Lands of Five Civilized Tribes, 1865–1900" (master's thesis, Oklahoma State University, 1957), esp. chaps. 3 and 4. For Indian concerns about economic prosperity on tribal sovereignty, see H. Craig Miner, *The*

Corporation and the Indian: Tribal Sovereignty and Industrial Civilization in Indian Territory, 1865–1907 (Columbia: University of Missouri Press, 1976). It must be noted that the Seminole Nation evaded the problems of the railroads longer than any of the other Five Nations, since the first railroad did not come into that people's land until 1895. (See Bailey, *Reconstruction in Indian Territory*, 97).

19. Kidwell, *Choctaws in Oklahoma*, 91–92.
20. Foster, "Federal Government and the Five Civilized Tribes," 53–63; Bailey, *Reconstruction in Indian Territory*, 136–38.
21. Debo, *Road to Disappearance*, 199–201; McLoughlin, *After the Trail of Tears*, 273; Bailey, *Reconstruction in Indian Territory*, 170; Kievit, "From Trail of Tears to Veil of Tears," 227–34.
22. Kidwell, *Choctaws in Oklahoma*, 102–3.
23. Kidwell, *Choctaws in Oklahoma*, 87.
24. Kievit, "From Trail of Tears to Veil of Tears," 211–12.
25. Kievit, "From Trail of Tears to Veil of Tears," 212–13.
26. Kievit, "From Trail of Tears to Veil of Tears," 213, 239; Debo, *The Rise and Fall of the Choctaw Republic*, 214.
27. Kievit, "From Trail of Tears to Veil of Tears," 240–41; McLoughlin, *After the Trail of Tears*, 275; Curtis L. Nolen, "The Okmulgee Constitution: A Step towards Indian Self-Determination," *Chronicles of Oklahoma* 58 (Fall 1980): 264–81; Debo, *Road to Disappearance*, 207.
28. Kievit, "From Trail of Tears to Veil of Tears," 241; McLoughlin, *After the Trail of Tears*, 341; Morris L. Wardell, *A Political History of the Cherokee Nation, 1838–1907* (Norman: University of Oklahoma Press, 1977), 210.
29. F. Todd Smith, *The Caddos, the Wichitas, and the United States, 1846–1901* (College Station: Texas A&M University Press, 1996), 73–87; Ariel Gibson, "Confederates on the Plains: The Pike Mission to the Wichita Agency," *Great Plains Journal* 4 (Fall 1964): 7–16; Jeanne V. Harmon, "Matthew Leeper, Confederate Agent at the Wichita Agency, Indian Territory," *Chronicles of Oklahoma* 47 (Fall 1967): 242–57.
30. Smith, *Caddos, Wichitas, and the United States*, 95–116; Aubrey Steele, "The Beginning of Quaker Administration of Indian Affairs in Oklahoma," *Chronicles of Oklahoma* 17 (December 1939): 364–92. For a more detailed account of the "Peace Policy" in Indian Territory, see Thomas C. Battey, *The Life and Adventures of a Quaker among the Indians* (Williamstown MA: Corner House, 1972); Josiah Butler, "Pioneer School Teaching at the Comanche-Kiowa Agency School, 1870–1873: Being the Reminiscences of the First Teacher," *Chronicles of Oklahoma* 6 (December 1928): 482–528; and William T. Hagan, *United States–Comanche Relations: The Reservation Years* (Norman: University of Oklahoma Press, 1990).

6 "We Had a Lot of Trouble Getting Things Settled after the War"

The Freedpeople's Civil Wars

Linda W. Reese

Two civil wars occurred in nineteenth-century Indian Territory. One involved military engagements of Indian rebellion against the U.S. government, and the other, confrontations between Indians and freedpeople for equality. Each war had undefined battlefields and shifting alliances. A Union cavalry ambush of a small Confederate Indian detachment at Old Boggy Depot, Choctaw Nation, on April 24, 1865, ended the Civil War in Indian Territory. When the last shots died down, the smell of gunpowder lingered in the air along with the hollow understanding of defeat. Although divided in their sympathies between the North and the South, factional leadership in all of the Five Nations, Cherokee, Choctaw, Chickasaw, Seminole, and Muscogee Creek, had wagered autonomy and continued control of their lands on the success of the Confederacy. Now they faced harsh penalties from the federal government that would ultimately extinguish Indian Territory and lead to the creation of the state of Oklahoma.[1]

Negotiation of the individual peace treaties initially took place at Fort Smith, Arkansas, in September 1865 but were finalized and signed in Washington DC in 1866. The stipulations that applied to the Five Nations' former slaves would have repercussions well beyond the Reconstruction years. Contention between the descendants of the freedpeople and the

Five Nations over the validity of their rights outlined in these treaties endures in twenty-first-century courts. In effect, the second civil war, legal confrontations, remains active today. This essay, however, covers only the period 1865 until 1889, when the Unassigned Lands were opened to non-Indian settlement and the demise of Indian Territory became imminent.[2]

Indian Territory slavery had been as diverse as the terrain, the makeup of the tribal population, and the personalities of individual slaveholders. In general, Indian traditionalists pursued smaller subsistence farming that required little additional labor beyond family, and more acculturated Indian planters of mixed ancestry operated large acreages tied into the commerce of the United States. Therefore, this group bought, sold, and traded in large numbers of enslaved people. Some slaveholders practiced the Southern model of bondage, while others allowed a more independent, tributary form. The Cherokees were less likely to intermarry with enslaved people than the Muscogee Creek and Seminole Indians. The Choctaws and the Chickasaws rarely pursued formal marriage alliances with their enslaved people. There were obvious exceptions to each of these generalizations over time, and it should not be inferred that tribal slavery was more benign than Southern slavery. In addition to the corrosive nature of ownership in human property, the Works Progress Administration (WPA) Slave Narratives from Oklahoma, collected in the 1930s, speak to horrendous acts of abuse and violence occurring under slavery. In 1860 there were approximately eighty-four hundred people enslaved by the Five Nations in Indian Territory, and perhaps as many as one thousand free blacks. The circumstances of their lives grew far worse during and after the Civil War.[3]

War came to Indian Territory in the fall of 1861 through a Confederate attack on the civilian followers of loyal Creek chief Opothleyahola. They were fleeing north to Union-held Kansas in an attempt to reach safety. His camp included Creek slaves, runaway slaves from other tribal groups, free blacks, loyal Cherokees, Seminoles, and frightened family groups, including white men married to Indian women from other tribes. After twice failing to defeat them, on December 26, 1861, Indian Confederate troops caught them, forcing the retreating families to abandon all of their supplies. Many died along the way, and those who reached Kansas arrived debilitated from injuries, frostbite, hunger, disease, and exhaustion. They remained there huddled in poorly supplied encampments until Federal troops led a return to Indian Territory in 1863.

Following the initial battles, a mass exodus out of Indian Territory continued. The war scattered families, destroyed property, and irreparably altered the life in these Indian-held lands. With the exception of those men who chose to stand and fight, Five Nations members with Southern sympathies packed up what belongings they could load onto wagons and headed for Texas. Those families who remained loyal to the United States followed the same pattern but escaped mainly to Kansas. The destiny of the enslaved people became terrifying. Some ran away, some were taken away with their slaveholders, many were rapidly sold to slave dealers, and the infirm and some trusted individuals were left behind to guard the homesteads in the absence of the Indian members.[4]

A number of enslaved men joined military service. Whether by command or loyalty, some, like Henry Clay and Henry Henderson, hauled supplies or fought for the Confederacy. "I use[d] to be a fighting man and a strong southern soldier, until the Yanks captured me," Henderson reported in a WPA interview. Others, like Charley Nave and Buck Bushyhead, joined Union forces and returned to fight in Indian Territory. Between 1863 and 1865, the First and Second Colored Volunteers Regiments, recruited in Kansas and commanded by Colonel James M. Williams, fought alongside Union Indian Home Guard Regiments and white troops inflicting significant damage on Confederate forces. Their operations deep into Confederate Indian Territory and confrontations at Cabin Creek and Honey Springs in 1863 contributed to the failure of the Confederate forces to hold Indian Territory.[5]

The destruction of property during the war was enormous. The animosities between the two sides ran deeper than the collision over slaveholding. Among some Native Americans the war was a reenactment of old blood feuds dating back to preremoval days. Confederate Cherokee officer Stand Watie, long an enemy of Principal Chief John Ross, burned the chief's beautiful home known as "Rose Cottage" as a visible statement of long-held grievances against his family. For others the war represented a cultural divide between assimilation to a white, Christian, capitalist mindset and the retention of Native beliefs and traditions. For others it was a contest for leadership, wealth, and power. Both armies survived on what they could bring in, buy, or steal. The end result was devastation across the territory.

Hardest hit were the lands of the Cherokees, Creeks, and Seminoles. Oklahoma historian Arrell M. Gibson described Indian Territory in 1865 as a "melancholy wasteland." Substantial herds of livestock had been confiscated by both sides. Homes, fences, and farm buildings lay in ruins, and fields were covered by weeds and brush. Anything of value had been stolen or destroyed. When the fighting ended, all inhabitants suffered the consequences of this desolation.[6]

The Federal peace treaty–negotiating delegates arrived at Fort Smith, Arkansas, the first week in September 1865. Initially, delegates from the Five Nations represented only the parties that had remained loyal, and they were caught by surprise at the demands the federal agents laid out for them. Led by Commissioner of Indian Affairs Dennis Cooley, seven stipulations were announced at this time: The first and second called for peace among themselves and with the United States, and aid in compelling peace from the Plains tribes. Conditions five, six, and seven demanded portions of their lands to be set aside for other tribes to be settled upon, required the consolidation of Indian Territory under one government, and forbade any white residents in Indian Territory unless incorporated into a tribe. Items two and three dealt specifically with the former slaves. Slavery in Indian Territory was to be abolished, and "measures must be taken ... for their incorporation in the tribes on an equal footing with the original members, or suitably provided for."[7]

It was too soon even for the loyalist Indian representatives present to come to general agreement, especially about the incorporation of their enslaved people as citizens. They did ask for a modification of issue number seven. They requested an addendum that read, "Also, no person of African descent except our former slaves, or free persons of color who are now, or have been, residents of the territory, will be permitted to reside in the territory, unless formally incorporated with some tribe."[8]

The Unionist representatives fervently denied Cooley's assertions that placed singular responsibility on the Five Nations for the abrogation of earlier treaties, and loss of their lands and annuities, based on their collusion with an enemy of the United States. When some of the secessionist Indian representatives arrived on the fifth day of the proceedings, they too made their case claiming that Federal abandonment in the midst of war had been the deciding factor. The meetings ended with a signed peace agreement with the United States, but the members of the Five Nations present claimed that they did not have treaty-making authority, they needed to consider several of these demands, and they needed to confer with a united tribal leadership. The commission adjourned on September 21, 1865.[9]

President Lincoln's Emancipation Proclamation in 1863 had granted freedom to American slaves in territories in rebellion, although many Indian Territory slaves remained ignorant of their freedom until the end of the war, and some as late as 1867. It would not be until passage in 1868 of the Fourteenth Amendment to the Constitution, which defined citizenship, that African Americans gained nominal citizenship rights in the United States. The peace treaties with the Five Nations, however, provided not only for the abolition of slavery but for the incorporation of their freedpeople as citizens of their Indian groups with full rights and benefits. The Cherokee Nation had already set a preliminary example for this in February 1863. Principal Chief John Ross had been removed by federal authorities from Indian Territory, and Acting Chief Thomas Pegg assembled a wartime council at Cowskin Prairie. They enacted legislation declaring all "Negro and other slaves" to be "forever free" effective June 25, 1863. These words entitled the Cherokee freedpeople to use of the Cherokee common land.[10]

The federal imposition on all of the Indian groups, however, completely ignored traditional tribal designation of citizenship along matrilineal clan lines and demanded citizenship for all of the freedpeople. Some questions arise from this decision. Were these provisions included as a reward for the military aid provided by the black soldiers of Indian Territory? Were government officials worried about a return of numerous free blacks to U.S. lands? Was the government attempting to maintain control over Indian freedpeople or to protect them from harm? More than likely, these measures were both a projection of postwar U.S. racial policy and a portent of future incorporation of these Indian-held lands into the corpus of the United States. Thus began a long and sometimes brutal conflict in Indian Territory among the Indian peoples, the federal government, and the freedpeople over the extent of those citizenship rights.

When the representatives of the Five Nations journeyed to Washington DC in January 1866, they were far better prepared to negotiate their positions. This time the leading men of the Indian nations, many university educated, had formulated responses. All of the Five Nations had written constitutions and formed governments similar in nature to the United States before the Civil War, and they believed that they had standing as nations.[11]

The chief federal diplomats were Secretary of the Interior James Harlan, Commissioner Dennis Cooley, and Superintendent of Indian Affairs Elijah Sells. In each tribe both the previous Union and Confederate Indian leaders and their advocates petitioned the government. Federal negotiators generally worked with the more receptive Union factions. There were no delegates officially representing the interests of the freedmen, but decisions about their future became the most important of the proceedings. Former slaves from the Creek and Seminole Nations acted as interpreters, and when the factions returned home, Confederate

Indians believed they had deliberately influenced the proceedings in favor of freedpeople's interests. By mid-August 1866 the Reconstruction treaties, similar in outline to the Fort Smith stipulations but also including a provision for the construction of north–south and east–west railroads through the territory, were concluded.[12]

The fate of the Indian Territory freedpeople became the pivotal factor in the dissolution of a homeland for the Five Nations and their former slaves. While all of the Five Nations agreed to the abolition of slavery, they had very different interpretations on adoption, citizenship, and rights for the freedpeople. One of the ideas that had been circulated, but later discounted, was the removal of the former slaves of the Five Nations to segregated areas such as the Canadian District of the Cherokees and an area that had been forfeited as a result of the war just west of the Seminole lands. Both areas represented regions of contention. Rapidly, the former Seminole lands became known as the "unassigned lands," the objective of land-hungry Americans.[13]

As negotiation of the treaties took place in Washington DC conditions in Indian Territory grew ominous for the freedpeople. Union soldier Buck Bushyhead, along with ten other freedpeople, wrote as early as October 1865 to the Fort Smith, Arkansas, Freedmen's Bureau about their concerns. "Our dear ones are still held and tyrannized ever in a most cruel manner, by their former masters," they wrote. "Since the right of property in our race has been abolished by the U.S. Government the masters have become brutal in their treatment of our color." The Confederate refugees returned to their homes and faced the utter ruin of their life's work. The Canadian District began to fill up with Confederate Cherokees. They learned that their holdings had been confiscated during the war. In many cases they found freedpeople living on and cultivating their lands. Violence quickly erupted. The members of Eliza Daniel Strout's family returned to their Cherokee lands to find "negroes who had been freed in our absence" living in their house. Eliza's brothers forcefully bargained "some little trifle" to get them to leave. When the black family departed, they took three horses belonging to the Daniel family. Eliza's brothers tracked them down, recovered the horses, and "sent the negroes on the road to where all horse thieves went in those days," she said. Such vigilante action became common and carried few penalties.[14]

When these kinds of reports reached Secretary of the Interior James Harlan, he sent Maj. Gen. John B. Sanborn to Indian Territory. Sanborn, a Minnesota attorney and politician, had served with Gen. Henry Halleck and Gen. Ulysses S. Grant in the Mississippi campaigns. Sanborn was to acquaint himself with the condition of the freedpeople and the "state of feeling, relations, prejudices or difficulties existing between them and their former masters." His initial reports in 1866 expressed the circumstances he found in each nation. Seminole and Creek freedpeople experienced some hostility but little else, and the Cherokees wanted their former slaves removed. There were, however, particular problems in the Choctaw and Chickasaw lands. Sanborn wrote that former slaves were being "shot down like dogs," driven from their homes, some still held in bondage, and all had no rights in these two nations. He believed that federal supervision was necessary to rectify these issues, and he requested that a military force be posted to these lands.[15]

The post-treaty circumstances for the freedpeople in each of the Five Nations would follow patterns similar to those outlined by Sanborn. Their future depended on how each Indian government interpreted acceptance of the original Fort Smith demand, "on an equal footing with the original members." The returning Cherokees did not believe the actions taken by their wartime government qualified their former slaves for citizenship rights, only freedom and use of common land. Their treaty placed a time restriction on admission of the freedpeople. They must have been in the country at the time of the war or return to Cherokee lands no later than June 19, 1866. The Cherokee constitution was amended forthwith guaranteeing citizenship based on this date. The precipitous deadline placed an enormous hardship on the freedpeople who had been dislocated north and south during the war. Destitution, lack of transportation, scattering of families, death of mothers and fathers, and the retention in bondage by some slaveholders made this time limit impossible for all to meet. Agents to the Cherokees during this time, William B. Davis and John N. Craig, believed the deadline too restrictive and exercised leniency toward the returning free blacks and freedpeople. This continued even after Cherokee courts, established to pass judgment on individual freedpeople citizenship, limited the certification of many of those making their way back to Cherokee lands.[16]

While Cherokee relationships and internal politics continued to be strained for some time because of Civil War allegiances, they became moderately civil with regard to the former slaves. Many of the freedpeople at that time were less interested in Cherokee politics than in establishing themselves and their families on sustainable farms and businesses. During this period they voted in parties representing both Union and Confederate factions, but only one freedperson, Joseph Brown, was elected to the National Council.[17]

The dispersal of Cherokee money created more conflict. In 1883 the Cherokee government sold land west of the nation to the federal government for the sum of $300,000. This money was supposed to be allocated on a per capita basis. The Cherokee legislature, however, placed a restriction, "by Cherokee blood" basis, on the distribution of funds. This second civil war on behalf of freedpeople required not guns, but expert legal representation. Former slave, Missouri attorney, and America's first black diplomat James Milton Turner took up the cause of the black Cherokees. First he organized the Association of Cherokee Freedmen, and then he proceeded to represent them through lengthy appeals to President Grover Cleveland and the Office of Indian Affairs. Finally, in 1888 Congress passed a bill allocating $75,000, charged to the Cherokee government, to be issued to the freedpeople for their share of the land sale. In this way Congress authenticated the provisions of the 1866 treaty with regard to the freedpeople and intended that they be carried out.[18]

Post-treaty relations between the Seminole and Muscogee Creek peoples and their former slaves have most often been held up as the most positive examples of cooperation in postwar Indian Territory. Most scholars maintain that the wider practice of intermarriage with their slaves accounted for this. Historian Kevin Mulroy, however, in his study of the Seminoles, asserts that cultural factors had far more influence. He suggests that the Seminoles at this time were far less acculturated and capitalist oriented than the other Indian nations and that their historical pattern of separate Indian and black townships reduced conflict. Their prolonged wars with the United States, brutal removal, and contentious settlement on Creek lands made them more eager for peace. Mulroy believes that the subsequent growth in the population of Seminole freedpeople resulted mainly from intermarriage with Creek freedpeople.[19]

The loyal Seminoles along with freedpeople interpreters Robert Johnson and Harry Island negotiated the 1866 peace treaty. At first the Confederate Seminoles rejected the incorporation of the freedpeople, stating that "it shocks the lesson we have learned for long years from the white man as to the negro's inferiority." They also objected to receiving only fifteen cents per acre for ceding their entire domain in exchange for a smaller area for which they paid fifty cents per acre. With government urging and additional funds made available to rebuild, both sides came together and agreed to all of the treaty terms.[20]

The Seminoles followed through with their commitment. Freedmen participated immediately in the political life of the nation. The Seminole National Council, its legislative body, included three representatives each from their fourteen towns. By 1875 the two freedpeople towns sent six representatives to the National Council. The freedpeople prospered economically, culturally, and socially. As former Confederate Seminole leader Heniha Mikko stated in 1885, "Our people in the past have seen enough turmoil and strife and greatly desire peace. We are enlarging our farms, our stock is increasing, our people are more industrious and prosperous."[21]

The Creek Nation had a more difficult time in moving forward. When the Creeks formulated a constitution in 1824, they included penalties for intermarriage with "Negroes" by either sex as well as a rule against slaves holding property. They did, however, include a provision for emancipation. In Indian Territory the Creeks still retained a division in their economic production: the Lower Creeks pursued large-scale plantation agriculture and a Southern model of slaveholding, and the Upper Creeks lived in separate towns from their slaves and practiced a more tributary form of slavery. The nation developed as a people of mixed Indian, white, and black ancestry. By 1858 Creek law declared that children born of Creek mothers and black fathers were considered members of the nation. With the Civil War looming, however, the Creeks passed much more stringent laws to control both free blacks and slaves.[22]

The Civil War opened again old preremoval divisions, and both sides were prepared to fight. These fierce antagonisms fueled the brutality of the war and the animosities that lingered after the peace treaty. Opothleyoholo had promised the slaves their freedom if they joined him. The alliance of Creek slaves and free black men with the loyal Creeks gave them an advantage during and after the war. At the September meetings, three factions represented the Creeks: the loyal Creeks, the Southern Creeks, and the African Creeks. The African Creek delegates included Ketch Barnett, Tobe McIntosh, Scipio Barnett, Jack Brown, and Cow Tom. The loyal Creeks did not object to abolishing slavery and incorporating the freedpeople. Their main objections were to any colonization of non-Creek freedpeople and to the creation of a consolidated territory. The Southern Creeks agreed to emancipation but nothing else, stating, "We cannot believe the government desires us to do more than it has seen fit thus far to do." They suggested that the government ought to reimburse them for their losses (in the slaves) and consider letting them become a separate tribe. In the end they signed only a preliminary peace agreement.[23]

The Creek delegation to Washington DC included Oktarharsars Harjo (Sands), the newly elected Creek chief, and Cowetta Micco and Cotchoche, with freedperson Harry Island as interpreter. By February 1866 the Southern Creeks decided they should attend as well, and sent D. N. McIntosh and James M. C. Smith. When the final draft appeared on March 6, the McIntosh group protested the proceedings and the treaty, especially the rights of the freedpeople. With regard to the freedpeople, the McIntosh group maintained that "we believe that our ancient care and kindness ought to be a sure guarantee that their interests and welfare will be safe." Officials as high as President Andrew Johnson urged compromise, but the loyal Creek delegates held firm claiming their exclusive right to negotiate, and the treaty remained as written. The Creek freedpeople had won full membership in the Creek Nation including rights to land, monies, and protection of the laws.[24]

The 1866 treaty included a one-year time frame for the return of the freedpeople to the nation, and like the Cherokees, this created a hardship for many, especially those still in unreconstructed Texas after the war. The Creek Agency west of Fort Gibson became an expanding area of settlement, but Creek freedpeople hurried back across the nation to establish themselves on lands not already taken. They quickly set to work clearing fields, establishing businesses, and building schools and communities. In 1867 the Creeks adopted a new constitution and formed a new government in Okmulgee with Sands as principal chief. Forty-seven Creek towns including the three African Creek towns, Arkansas Colored, North Fork Colored, and Canadian Colored sent representatives and elected Lighthorse (police force) Companies. The African Creeks remained a significant presence in Creek national politics.[25]

Distribution of Creek Nation funds created controversy in 1867. Samuel Checote, chief of the Southern Creeks during the Civil War, had written to Commissioner of Indian Affairs Lewis V. Bogy that the treaty did not authorize equal payment for recently sold Creek lands to the freedpeople. Bogy ordered the exclusion of the former slaves. The African Creeks protested to James Harlan, now serving on the Senate Subcommittee on Indian Appropriations, and Washington agreed that the freedpeople should receive their share. Checote's followers tried again through their National Council to deprive the freedpeople of a full share, but finally in 1869 the freedpeople received payment.[26]

Election of a Creek principal chief in 1867 nearly led to violence. Checote insisted that rather than following the traditional pattern of Creek voting by numbers on the grounds, members should vote on paper ballots. Inasmuch as most of the Creeks were illiterate at this time, it was no surprise that Checote won the election. In spite of protests, the federal government recognized Checote as chief. By 1869 the animosity between the Sands and Checote factions had reached a high point. When Sands sent his Lighthorse to arrest some of the Checote followers, rumors spread of an overthrow. Creek agent Franklin A. Fields ordered U.S. troops from Fort Gibson into the nation, and violence was averted.[27]

The elections throughout the 1870s and 1880s continued to provoke objections and armed protests from the Loyal Party and their African Creek followers. The Checotes (Constitutional Party) pushed through a series of laws meant to establish control over the African Creek towns in the name of "law and order." They impeached the loyal elected chief, Lochar Harjo, in 1875, but under the leadership of Ward Coachman relations with the African Creeks became more settled. Coachman actively worked to include the rights of the freedpeople in the nation's politics. A series of armed skirmishes between loyal and Constitutional factions known as the "Green Peach War" unsettled the Creeks in 1881, but larger issues became important. The need for farm laborers and the construction of railroads through Creek lands in the 1870s and 1880s had far more impact than the fading Civil War memories. Black and white railroad construction workers who created temporary towns and landless farmers from other states invaded Creek lands for employment and a fresh start. Stemming the flow of intruders became the chief occupation of Creek leadership.[28]

The Choctaw and Chickasaw Nations represented the major resistance against government interference in their relationships with their former slaves. Because these nations were larger, wealthier, and more acculturated than the other nations, in neither group was intermarriage as prevalent as in the other three. At the time of the Civil War, together they held more than thirty-three hundred enslaved people, nearly 40 percent of all slaves in Indian Territory. Many practiced large-scale cotton plantation agriculture and traded their crops for the finest American manufactured goods. After removal the Chickasaws lived originally on Choctaw lands, but in 1855 they received their own domain west of the Choctaws. Both established constitutional governments, progressive schools for their children, and Christian churches.[29]

Their acculturated lifestyle, level of white American intermarriage, extent of slaveholding, and geographic location next to Texas made their treaty alliances with the Confederacy predictable, and the majority of the Choctaws and Chickasaws supported the Southern side during the Civil War. When Washington DC peace treaty negotiations began in 1866, they were the most adamant in opposition to the acceptance of freedpeople into tribal membership. Choctaw and Chickasaw leadership claimed that Lincoln's Emancipation Proclamation and later the Thirteenth and Fourteenth Amendments to the Constitution did not apply to them since they were not citizens of the United States. Choctaw and Chickasaw commissioners and hired attorneys negotiated a joint treaty. They agreed to give up their lands west of the ninety-eighth meridian (the Leased District) for the sum of $300,000 that would be held in trust until other provisions were carried out. The Chickasaws were to receive one-quarter of this amount. They were exempted from adopting their freedmen as members of the nation and from granting them any share in *tribal* lands, monies, and annuities. They must grant to the freedmen forty acres of land and civil and political rights, including the vote. Negotiators argued for removal of the freedpeople to the Leased District they had given up, but this was never implemented. Unlike the treaties with the other Five Nations, this treaty granted amnesty to the Confederate Indians for actions both outside and inside their lands.[30]

Persecution toward the former slaves was rampant in the Choctaw and Chickasaw Nations. After the Civil War the Chickasaw Nation refused to recognize Chickasaw-black intermarriage and deemed the children of such marriages "illegitimate." Freedmen from other tribes had to buy a permit to marry a Chickasaw freedwoman. The Choctaw government passed a law in 1885 making intermarriage with blacks a felony. Both nations passed "Black Codes" and used both violent and nonviolent means to force freedpeople out of their lands. Public whippings were common. Indian citizens and newly hired white "permit" workers frequently fenced off lands already improved by the freedpeople, cut down their trees, and lawlessly raided and burned down black settlements. Commissioner of Indian Affairs Edward P. Smith commented regarding Chickasaw freedpeople in 1874 that their farms "once well improved are not infrequently taken from them."[31]

The united Choctaw and Chickasaw treaty obligations, the issues of the trust fund, and the resilience of the freedpeople themselves played key roles in the ultimate fate of the freedpeople in their nations. In time Choctaws and Chickasaws chose different paths. Both areas experienced a widespread intrusion of black and white Americans seeking land and better circumstances westward or arriving as part of the railroad construction. Political party factions grew up in each nation that reflected either a passion to retain past values and ways of life or hopes for future economic development, to accept the freedpeople or to eject them from the nations. Many Choctaw and Chickasaw freedpeople steadfastly continued to remain on and develop the only land they had ever known against all resistance. While the Chickasaws continually demanded removal of the freedpeople to the Leased District, the Choctaws became concerned about the possibility of a large black colony near their lands. The Freedmen's Oklahoma Association, led by attorney J. Milton Turner, publicized after 1881 one-hundred-and-sixty-acre homesteads for all freedmen in the Leased District. Congress began to receive large numbers of petitions to settle on these lands.[32]

The freedpeople in these two nations remained in limbo for close to twenty years while the Chickasaws, the Choctaws, and the federal government wrangled over the implementation of the 1866 treaty provisions and the rights of the freedpeople. At the end of the two-year time frame for meeting the fulfillment of the treaty obligations, no progress had been made. Neither nation provided schools for the children of the freedpeople. At various times the government paid portions of the share of the trust fund to both the Choctaws and the Chickasaws. The Choctaws wavered back and forth until 1882 when congressional action forced a decision. Congress appropriated $10,000 of Choctaw and Chickasaw funds to support freedmen schools. If they followed through with adoption, the money would be reimbursed from the remaining trust fund. This action allowed the two nations to act separately regarding their freedpeople. In 1883 the Choctaw Nation formally adopted their freedpeople.[33]

The former slaves in the Chickasaw Nation faced the most difficult and uncertain circumstances. In 1866 the Chickasaw legislature voted to give up their $75,000 share of the trust fund in favor of the removal of the freedpeople to the Leased District. That same year Congress received a petition from a group of Chickasaw freedpeople requesting removal, claiming that their former Indian masters were different from whites in that they had "all the hatred and vindictiveness of their race toward a weaker race, who they formerly controlled and oppressed." By 1869 when no action had been taken, Chickasaw agent George Olmstead held a council of Choctaw and Chickasaw freedpeople attended by Chickasaw governor Cyrus Harris and Choctaw principal chief Allen Wright. By this point the freedpeople were determined to remain in their homeland.[34]

The Chickasaw freedpeople's status was complicated by two circumstances. Their legal position at that time was that of any other U.S. citizen resident in the Chickasaw Nation. Redress of their grievances could be gotten far across the territory only at the federal office in Fort Smith, Arkansas. The second issue was the arrival in the area of free blacks and former slaves from other tribes who were greatly resented by the Chickasaws. This second civil war over citizenship status and rights continued unabated. Both the federal government and the Chickasaws attempted to come to a settlement throughout the 1870s. Congress passed conflicting bills to extend the timeline for compliance, to remove the freedpeople, and later to force their adoption. The Chickasaw legislature passed legislation variously both to adopt the former slaves and to have them removed. In 1879 the U.S. Senate held an extensive investigation into the condition of the freedpeople that allowed the former slaves to testify about their circumstances, and the refusal of the Chickasaws to allow them citizenship rights or even safety. No action was forthcoming until 1882 when Congress forced the issue with the $10,000 charge for freedmen schools. The Chickasaws had already received approximately $55,000 of their share of the trust fund money. Even though the Choctaws chose adoption, the Chickasaws alerted the Department of the Interior that they refused to accept the freedpeople as citizens, "upon any terms or conditions whatever." This remained the final Chickasaw decision.[35]

In 1889 President Benjamin Harrison opened the famous "unassigned lands" in the heart of Indian Territory to American settlement. By 1890 the Indian Territory census reported 18,636 black residents and 50,055 Indians. These together were overwhelmed by a white population of 109,393. Autonomy over the spaces granted to the Five Nations following removal reached an end. The culmination of nearly twenty-five years of federal Indian policy following the Civil War, concerted and effective Indian resistance, and negotiation of the rights of the freedpeople resulted in the creation of Oklahoma Territory. The policy of allotment in severalty extended to the Five Nations led ultimately to the end of Indian Territory and to the creation of the state of Oklahoma.[36]

The enslaved people in Indian Territory had fought two civil wars. When violence erupted in their homelands, some of the men marched alongside their slaveholders to fight for the Confederacy, and many served in the ranks of the Union army volunteers. Their wives and children were scattered from Kansas to Texas in the midst of chaos and destruction, hunger, disease, and death. Following the military war they reunited to build for themselves farms and businesses in the same lands they had served before. The freedpeople found themselves caught in a second civil war for their rights as members of the Five Nations. Citizenship for the freedpeople became entangled in questions of race, culture, sovereignty, and money. This was a treacherous struggle between the powers of the federal government and the Indian governments, fought out legally in Washington DC but more intimately at home. That war came to a temporary end when statehood arrived in 1907.

NOTES

1. R. C. Smith, quoted in T. Lindsay Baker and Julie P. Baker, eds., *The WPA Slave Narratives* (Norman: University of Oklahoma Press, 1996), 402; Charles Robert Goins and Danney Goble, *Historical Atlas of Oklahoma*, 4th ed. (Norman: University of Oklahoma Press, 2006), 87. Although only a very small military aspect of the Civil War, Indian Territory represented an important bridge between the east and west that therefore made its control by the federal government a necessity.
2. Annie Heloise Abel, *The American Indian and the End of the Confederacy* (Lincoln: University of Nebraska Press, 1993), 173–218, 301–63 (repr., *The American Indian under Reconstruction*, Arthur H. Clark, 1925); see also Arrell Morgan Gibson, *Oklahoma, a History of Five Centuries* (Norman: University of Oklahoma Press, 1981), 117–42.
3. Michael F. Doran, "Negro Slaves of the Five Civilized Tribes," *Annals of the Association of American Geographers* 68 (September 1978): 335–50; 1860 Census, in Doran, "Negro Slaves of the Five Civilized Tribes," 347; Claudio Saunt asserts that the census figures undercounted the number of slaves in "The Paradox of Freedom: Tribal Sovereignty and Emancipation during the Reconstruction of Indian Territory," *Journal of Southern History* 1 (January 2004): n6; Monroe Billington, "Black Slavery in Indian Territory: The Ex-Slave Narratives," *Chronicles of Oklahoma* 60 (Spring 1982): 56–65; Baker and Baker, eds., *The WPA Oklahoma Slave Narratives*. Celia Naylor writes about the issue of a supposed benign Indian slavery. Her research "tells a painful story that speaks of the horror of bondage" and "shatters ideas of 'kind' Indian masters," in Celia E. Naylor, *African Cherokees in Indian Territory: From Chattel to Citizens* (Chapel Hill: University of North Carolina Press, 2008), 4. Fay A. Yarbrough also examines the issues of interracial sexual relations between American Indians and blacks, noting that some scholars see these frequently as "consensual." She believes that this "popular myth" of cultural affinity does not recognize "a more sinister side to their interaction," in Fay A. Yarbrough, *Race and the Cherokee Nation: Sovereignty in the Nineteenth Century* (Philadelphia: University of Pennsylvania Press, 2008), 2–3. Studies of comparisons among the Five Nations are needed to clarify these issues.
4. Mary Jane Warde, "Now the Wolf Has Come: The Civilian Civil War in Indian Territory," *Chronicles of Oklahoma* 71 (Spring 1993): 64–87; Dean Trickett, "Civil War in Indian Territory, 1861," *Chronicles of Oklahoma* 17 (September 1939):

315–27; Dan Banks, "Civil War Refugees from Indian Territory in the North, 1861–1864," *Chronicles of Oklahoma* 41 (Fall 1963): 286–98; Neeley B. Jackson, " Political and Economic History of the Negro in Indian Territory" (master's thesis, University of Oklahoma, 1960), 66–77; Allan C. Ashcraft, "Confederate Indian Department Conditions in August, 1864," *Chronicles of Oklahoma* 41 (Autumn 1963): 270–85.

5. Baker and Baker, *Oklahoma Slave Narratives*, 83, 194–95, 301; Angela Y. Walton-Raji, "The African–Native American Genealogy Blog," July 3, 2010, http://african-nativeamerican.blogspot.com/2010/07/earliestlist-of slaves-from-indian-html; Lary C. Rampp, "Negro Troop Activity in Indian Territory, 1863–1865," *Chronicles of Oklahoma* 47 (Spring 1969): 531–59.
6. Gibson, *Oklahoma*, 119, 131; Warde, "'Now the Wolf Has Come,'" 82–84; Walt Willson, "Freedmen in Indian Territory during Reconstruction," *Chronicles of Oklahoma* 49 (Summer 1971): 230–31.
7. Abel, *End of the Confederacy*, 183–84, 188–90.
8. Abel, *End of the Confederacy*, 191–92.
9. Abel, *End of the Confederacy*, 191–98.
10. David R. Wrone, ed., "The Cherokee Act of Emancipation," *Journal of Ethnic Studies* 1 (Fall 1973): 87–90.
11. Gibson, *Oklahoma*, 71–83. In 1831 U.S. Supreme Court Chief Justice John Marshall ruled that the Cherokee Nation was a "domestic dependent nation," similar in nature to a ward of the government, http://www.law.cornell.edu/supct/html/historics/ussc_cr_0030_0001_zs.html.
12. Abel, *End of the Confederacy*, 301–43; William D. Pennington, "Reconstruction Treaties," http://digital.library.okstate.edu/encyclopedia/entires/R/re001.html; Saunt, "Paradox of Freedom," 78–84; Willson, "Freedmen in Indian Territory," 232–37. For a discussion of the significance of the maintenance of gender roles, see Theda Perdue, *Cherokee Women: Gender and Culture change, 1700–1835* (Lincoln: University of Nebraska Press, 1999). Perdue argues that retaining traditional male and female gender roles enabled the Cherokees to thrive under pressure.
13. Willson, "Freedmen in Indian Territory," 234; Thomas F. Andrews, "Freedmen in Indian Territory: A Post–Civil War Dilemma," *Journal of the West* 4 (July 1965): 367–76; Saunt, "Paradox of Freedom," 76.
14. Walton-Raji, "African–Native American Genealogy Blog"; Eliza Daniel Strout, Indian-Pioneer Papers, Western History Collection, University of Oklahoma, Norman, Oklahoma, 88:181–82.
15. John B. Sanborn, "Hd. Quarters Commission for Regulating Relations between Freedmen of the Indian Territory and Their Former Masters," January 5 and January 8, 1866, http://freedmensbureau.com/arkansas/indianterritory.htm.
16. Treaty with the Cherokee, 1866, in *Indian Treaties, 1778–1883*, ed. Charles J. Kappler (New York: Oklahoma State University, 1972), 943–44; Morris R.

Wardell, *A Political History of the Cherokee Nation* (Norman: University of Oklahoma Press, 1938), 177–207; Hanna R. Warren, "Reconstruction in the Cherokee Nation," *Chronicles of Oklahoma* 45 (Summer 1967): 180–86; Bailey, *Reconstruction in Indian Territory*, 178–81; Sue Hammond, "Socioeconomic Reconstruction in the Cherokee Nation, 1865–1870," *Chronicles of Oklahoma* 56, no. 2 (1978): 158–70.

17. Donald A. Grinde and Quintard Taylor, "Red vs. Black: Conflict and Accommodation in the Post Civil War Indian Territory," *American Indian Quarterly* 10 (Summer 1984): 215.

18. Tim Gammon, "Black Freedmen and the Cherokee Nation," *Journal of American Studies* 11, no. 3 (1977): 357–64; Bailey, *Reconstruction in the Cherokee Nation*, 181–82; Daniel F. Littlefield, Jr., *The Cherokee Freedmen: From Emancipation to American Citizenship* (Westport CT: Greenwood, 1978), 49–74; V. A. Travis, "Life in the Cherokee Nation a Decade after the Civil War," *Chronicles of Oklahoma* 4 (March 1926): 16–30.

19. Kevin Mulroy, *The Seminole Freedmen: A History* (Norman: University of Oklahoma Press, 2007), 224–66. For a thorough challenge to all previous research on mixed relationships between the Seminoles and African Americans, see Susan A. Miller, "Seminoles and Africans under Seminole Law: Sources and Discourses of Tribal Sovereignty and 'Black Indian' Entitlement," *Wicazo Sa Review* (Spring 2005): 23–47.

20. Mulroy, *Seminole Freedmen*, 196–203; Daniel F. Littlefield, Jr., *Africans and Seminoles: From Removal to Emancipation* (Jackson: University Press of Mississippi), 180–96.

21. Mulroy, *Seminole Freedmen*, 203–23, Henniha Mikko quoted on 248; Grinde and Taylor, "Red vs. Black," 214–15; Edwin C. McReynolds, *The Seminoles* (Norman: University of Oklahoma Press, 1957), 313–30.

22. Janet Halliburton, "Black Slavery in the Creek Nation," *Chronicles of Oklahoma* 56 (Fall 1978): 303–11; Grant Foreman, *The Five Civilized Tribes* (Norman: University of Oklahoma Press), 213, 215–16; See also Daniel F. Littlefield, Jr., *Africans and Creeks: From the Colonial Period to the Civil War* (Westport CT: Greenwood, 1979); Mary Jane Warde, *George Washington Grayson and the Creek Nation, 1843–1920* (Norman: University of Oklahoma Press, 1999); Claudio Saunt, *Black, White, and Indian: Race and the Unmaking of an American Family* (New York: Oxford University Press, 2005); Angie Debo, *The Road to Disappearance: A History of the Creek Indians* (Norman: University of Oklahoma Press, 1941), 141–76.

23. Gary Zellar, "If I Ain't One, You Won't Find One Here: Race, Identity, Citizenship, and Land; The African Creek Experience in the Indian Territory and Oklahoma, 1830–1910" (PhD diss., University of Arkansas, 2003), 52–111, 112–17, D. N. McIntosh and R. S. Smith quoted, 116; Debo, *Road to Disappearance*, 177–213.

24. Zellar, "African Creek Experience," 125–30, McIntosh quoted, 129. See also Debo, *Road to Disappearance*, 214–48.
25. Zellar, "African Creek Experience," 131–48.
26. Zellar, "African Creek Experience," 148–50.
27. Zellar, "African Creek Experience," 150–61.
28. Zellar, "African Creek Experience," 161–69; Debo, *Road to Disappearance*, 249–84; John Bartlett Meserve, "Chief Isparhecher," *Chronicles of Oklahoma* 10, no. 1 (March 1932): 52–76.
29. Doran, "Negro Slaves," 347; Angie Debo, *The Rise and Fall of the Choctaw Republic* (Norman: University of Oklahoma Press, 1934; repr., 1961), 58–79; Clara Sue Kidwell, *The Choctaws in Oklahoma: From Tribe to Nation, 1855–1970* (Norman: University of Oklahoma Press, 2007), 3–40; Arrell M. Gibson, *The Chickasaws* (Norman: University of Oklahoma Press, 1971), 184–226; Grant Foreman, *The Five Civilized Tribes* (Norman: University of Oklahoma Press, 10th printing, 1989), 121–32.
30. Abel, *End of the Confederacy*, 329–37; Debo, *Rise and Fall of Choctaw Republic*, 88–90; Kidwell, *Choctaws*, 80–81; Wyatt F. Jeltz, "The Relations of Negroes and Choctaw and Chickasaw Indians," *Journal of Negro History* 33 (January 1948): 33–34.
31. Fifty-fourth Cong., 1st sess., Senate doc., 182, 110–11, Edward P. Smith quoted in Daniel F. Littlefield, Jr., *Chickasaw Freedmen: A People without a Country* (Westport CT: Greenwood, 1980), 80–81, 83, 92–94; Grinde and Taylor, "Red vs. Black," 217; J. H. Johnston, "Documentary Evidence of the Relations of Negroes and Indians, *Journal of Negro History* 14 (January 1929): 40–41.
32. Iwasaki Yoshitaka, "Freedmen in the Indian Territory after the Civil War: The Dual Approaches of the Choctaw and Chickasaw Nations," *Nanzan Review of American Studies* 30 (2008): 96–102.
33. Debo, *Rise and Fall of the Choctaw Republic*, 101–105; Yoshitaka, "Freedmen in Indian Territory," 102; Oliver Knight, "Fifty Years of Choctaw Law," *Chronicles of Oklahoma* 31, no. 1 (1953): 90–91.
34. One of the clearest explications of the freedmen issues in the Chickasaw Nation is found in Parthena Louise James, "Reconstruction in the Chickasaw Nation: The Freedmen Problem," *Chronicles of Oklahoma* 45 (1967): 44–57; Abel, *End of the Confederacy*, 330–35; Gibson, *Chickasaws*, 243–44.
35. James, "Reconstruction in the Chickasaw Nation," 48–53.
36. Grinde and Taylor, "Red vs. Black," 217.

7 Hearth and Home

Cherokee and Creek Women's Memories
of the Civil War in Indian Territory

Amanda Cobb-Greetham

> At last we got back home, but what a homecoming. Everything was so changed. The old chimney was standing as good as ever, but there was no house.
>
> Bettie Perdue Woodall (Cherokee)

Beginnings

In this chapter, I focus on memories of the U.S. Civil War in Indian Territory shared by Cherokee and Creek women of the Five Nations who were interviewed in the 1930s by Federal Writer's Project relief workers as part of the Works Progress Administration project S-149.[1] This joint project of the Oklahoma Historical Society and the University of Oklahoma culminated in over one hundred volumes now referred to as the Indian-Pioneer Papers. Among these memories is the poignant recollection of Bettie Perdue Woodall, quoted above.

Almost 150 years ago Bettie Perdue Woodall, like so many Cherokee refugees of the Civil War, returned to her home in Indian Territory. There she found a devastated landscape and only a chimney where her home had been; she was not alone. Too many of those who had sought refuge elsewhere during the storm of the Civil War returned home to find, as Woodall did, that "there was no house."

On the afternoon of May 20, 2013, one of the most powerful tornados in the history of the United States ripped through the Oklahoma landscape, leaving twenty-four people dead and hundreds of people's homes reduced to piles of rubble.

Although many decades separate these events, they are tangled in my memory and understanding.

I spent the morning of May 20, 2013 researching the Indian-Pioneer Papers. As I read the narratives of Cherokee and Creek women who shared their Civil War memories, I was particularly struck by the content of the narratives. By and large, the women interviewed did not focus at all on the grand narratives of the Civil War—battles won or lost, heroes and enemies, slavery and states' rights. They did share, though rarely at great length, some of the experiences of their fathers, husbands, and sons. They spent the most time, however, sharing the difficulty of daily life and the constant, frequently unfulfilled need for food, shelter, and safety. Their stories were stories of hearth and home, and in particular the displacement from and often complete loss of home. They often described the pain of leaving home and the landscape upon returning—offering difficult-to-imagine descriptions of the destruction and desolation left in the wake of war. I spent that afternoon underground in our own storm shelter in Norman, Oklahoma, coming out to find that for people just ten miles north—to use the words of Bettie Woodall—"everything had changed." My home was safe and secure, but others stepped out of underground shelters into the debris of their homes. Still others, who had taken shelter in offices or schools, returned to find nothing to return to.

Witnessing the homes demolished by the Moore tornado with my own eyes was shocking, sickening, and heartbreaking. Just minutes before the tornado I had been reading accounts of more than a century ago. Now, I could better imagine just what these American Indian women had witnessed on their homecoming and just why so many women devoted so much time to this topic in their interviews.

For me, these recounted events have fused with my own experience of a particular, and separate, time and event—a melding that illustrates the fluidity and complexity of the concepts of memory and narrative at work in this research.

Specifically, I consider the ways in which the Civil War memories of the Cherokee and Creek women included in the Indian-Pioneer Papers Collection establish a narrative of continuing disaster, displacement, and the desire for and rebuilding of hearth and home. But first, let me place the Indian-Pioneer Papers in the context of recent scholarship on the Civil War in American memory and the Federal Writers' Project as an important producer of cultural heritage and collective memory.

The Civil War and Memory

In recent years a burgeoning of excellent scholarly work has concentrated on conceptions of collective and cultural memory. Marita Sturken, for example, in *Tangled Memories* defines cultural memory as a "field of cultural negotiation through which different stories vie for a place in history."[2] She notes that such shared memories occur "outside formal historical discourse" but are "entangled with cultural products and imbued with meaning." Through these shared memories, for example, we produce conceptions of "American" and "nation."[3]

Few events in U.S. history figure as prominently in American cultural memory as the Civil War. As Robert Penn Warren famously noted, "The Civil War is our *felt* history," and several scholars of memory have focused specifically on the ways in which Americans have felt, remembered, and commemorated the Civil War.[4] A few particularly noteworthy investigations include Caroline Janney's *Burying the Dead but Not the Past*, in which she examines how Virginia's Ladies' Memorial Association shaped the public rituals of Confederate memory in order to present the war and its outcome in a positive, deeply nostalgic light.[5] Others, like scholar Kirk Savage, have concentrated not on the rituals of memory, but on the way it figures in our public spaces through physical memorials and monuments. In *Standing Soldiers, Kneeling Slaves*, Savage explores how the history of slavery has been told and reshaped through sculptural monuments.[6] Arguably, the most influential study of the Civil War in American memory is David W. Blight's *Race and Reunion*. In this impressive, synthetic history, Blight contends that American memories of the Civil War fit within one of three overarching visions: (1) the reconciliationist vision, which primarily focused on the remembrance and honoring of the dead; (2) the white supremacist vision, which included terror and violence and a segregationist narrative; and (3) the emancipationist vision, which understood the liberation of African Americans to citizens as the complete reinvention of the republic. Blight goes on to assert that these visions collided and intermingled over time until the reconciliationist and white supremacist visions merged, ultimately overshadowing the emancipationist vision of the war in collective American memory.[7]

As powerful and persuasive as Blight's argument is, however, Jeff Fortney aptly notes in his noteworthy article "Lest We Remember: Civil War Memory and Commemoration among the Five Tribes" that these visions do not apply to the way the Five Nations have remembered the Civil War. According to Fortney, "By focusing on white and black, however, this model ignores the red element of the war. Consequently, not only does Blight exclude Native memories from his analysis, but he also presents interpretations that do not coincide with the Native experience."[8] Fortney continues this critique noting that "the models of reconciliation and white supremacy that shaped Civil War memory did not develop in Indian Territory, since there was no previous unity to reconcile."[9] Fortney indicates but stops just short of stating a critical point: Blight's tripartite model of the Civil War in American memory does not apply easily or well to Indian Territory because Indian Territory, while under the protection of the United States by treaties, was not actually part of the United States at that time. As many scholars have pointed out, the Civil War in Indian Territory is frequently overlooked. As a result, the specific experiences of the sovereign Indian nations and their citizens in Indian Territory are often subsumed into the larger American historical narrative of Union and Confederacy, thus effectively eliding tribal sovereignty and ignoring distinctive tribal histories and experiences. Importantly, Fortney contends that Natives practiced "self-silence" in regard to public Civil War commemoration. Instead, white settlers who arrived in Indian Territory after the Civil War led the charge for commemoration. In an effort to memorialize the war in Indian Territory and to honor their own ancestors, the white settlers succeeded in supplanting Native memories of the Civil War in Indian Territory with their own experiences and memories that they brought to Indian Territory. Fortney goes on to analyze the ways in which the United Daughters of the Confederacy aggressively worked in the years following Oklahoma statehood in 1907 to integrate Native Civil War memory into the dominant visions of American memory forwarded by Blight. Fortney's article effectively explains both the reason for "self-silence" and the process of "white-washing" public commemoration, but it ultimately succeeds as a study of commemoration among *Oklahomans* rather than among the citizens of the Five Nations per se. Furthermore, Fortney does not distinguish among "Native" memories and memories of the "Five Tribes," blurring the distinction between and among individual efforts toward commemoration, formal commemorative efforts by each individual tribal sovereign, and collective commemorative efforts by the Five Nations together.

Although I agree with Fortney that the Five Nations have not (either together or separately) commemorated their experiences, their citizens do hold and have shared memories of those experiences. Interestingly, if the history of the Civil War in Indian Territory is the history of the *United States Civil War* in Indian Territory, then the experiences of the citizens of the Five Nations in the U.S. Civil War were not *American* experiences. After all, citizens of the Five Nations were not U.S. citizens at the time of the war. Instead, their memories—as citizens of the Chickasaw, Choctaw, Cherokee, Creek, and Seminole Nations and only later as dual citizens of Oklahoma—offer a particularly distinctive perspective worth examination.

The Indian-Pioneer Papers Collection

I elected to study the Indian-Pioneer Papers Collection for a number of reasons. First, because of the self-silence and whitewashing process described by Fortney, very few examples of Five Nations' memory and commemoration exist. Oral history collections, however, do include the recollections of many tribal citizens, although by and large they are not indexed separately and are often mixed with oral histories of the general public. Second, that the interviews culminating in the Indian-Pioneer Papers were collected in the 1930s meant that some of the subjects would personally remember the Civil War as well as the stories shared by their parents and grandparents. Finally, I was interested not only in the scope and content of the Indian-Pioneer Papers but also in their cultural history and method of collection.

The Indian-Pioneer project was part of the Historical Records Survey directed by historian Grant Foreman as part of the Oklahoma branch of the Works Progress Administration's (WPA) Federal Writers' Project (FWP). The FWP, established in 1935, aimed to achieve two disparate goals: (1) to provide immediate employment for out-of-work Americans and (2) to redefine the popular understanding of American national identity based on the celebration of cultural pluralism and diversity. FWP units were established in every state. Oklahoma's branch elected to develop projects that would emphasize and further develop the state's identity as the home of pioneers. According to Foreman in his foreword to the papers, the goal of the project was to "collect from living witnesses vital facts and impressions of pioneer life in Oklahoma."[10] The papers exist at two locations: (1) the University of Oklahoma's Western History Collection, where they are called the Indian-Pioneer Papers Collection, and (2) the Oklahoma Historical Society, where they are called the Indian-Pioneer History or Grant Foreman Papers.

Consisting of approximately eighty thousand entries, the collection includes information gathered from over twenty-five thousand questionnaires and over eleven thousand individual interviews conducted by FWP relief workers.

Significantly, scholars have become increasingly interested in these oral histories as the field has embraced the examination of concepts of collective and cultural memory, the production of memory, and the processes of remembrance. The FWP oral histories are fascinating examples of such cultural production. FWP officials, wrestling with directives of romantic nationalism, cultural pluralism, and the celebration of both diversity and unity, believed that the oral histories allowed new voices—voices traditionally marginalized—to be heard by highlighting the life stories of "common" people of a variety of ethnicities and socioeconomic backgrounds.

Foreman seems to firmly believe that the Indian-Pioneer project allows new voices to be heard and clearly seeks to celebrate, deepen, and reinforce Oklahoma's pioneer identity. However, he does not clarify his definition of "pioneer" or explain who was selected to be interviewed or why. Although the papers came later to be called the "Indian-Pioneer" collection, only "Pioneers" are mentioned in the foreword. Foreman does not explain whether Indians and Pioneers were perceived of as separate categories of identity, and the papers are not organized or categorized separately into "Indians" and "Pioneers" and do not specify tribal affiliation in the index.

Another example of the papers as a producer of collective memory occurs in Foreman's description of the papers in the foreword. Foreman states that, taken together, the interviews "represent an accurate cross section of early *Oklahoma* life" [italics added].[11] Although many, if not the majority, of the interviews include accounts of events pre-statehood, ostensibly during the settlement of Indian Territory by "pioneers," Foreman does not note that the interviews also represent a cross-section of life in *Indian Territory*, which erases the distinct history of Indian Territory and histories of individual tribes and effectively replaces those histories by naming it Oklahoma history, thus extending the history of Oklahoma into its pre-statehood past.

Although the original vision and purpose of the Indian-Pioneer papers as well as the process by which the interviews were collected are worth further analysis, my primary interest in this chapter lies in the narratives themselves, specifically the narratives of women. Although I searched for interviews of women from all of the Five Nations, the bulk of the interviews I was able to find were of Cherokee and Creek women. This could be a result of the fact that the Civil War battles fought in Indian Territory occurred more within these nations' boundaries than within the others'. Furthermore, from a practical perspective, the FWP branch office was headquartered in Muskogee, the headquarters of the Creek Nation, and in close proximity to the Cherokee Nation, which presumably made subjects from these nations relatively easy to locate and interview.

Regardless, the narrative power of the interviews is undeniable, and in spite of the limitations posed by the collection processes, the Cherokee and Creek FWP interviewees are much more than mere informants. In the words of Jerrold Hirsch, they are, significantly, "narrators and historians, preservers and creators of memory."[12] As such, the memory created by the Cherokee and Creek women is a memory of hearth and home that describes the fear of decision making and disaster that followed, the shock and pain of displacement, and finally the emotion of returning home and the determination to rebuild.

Memories of Decision Making, Disaster, and Displacement

Indian Territory was not part of the United States at the time of the American Civil War, and none of the Five Nations had a direct stake in the conflict. Many of the women interviewed recalled their family's feelings that the war was not theirs to fight and that participating would be disastrous. As interviewee Elizabeth Watts (Cherokee) stated, "The Indians did not want to fight. They had had enough trouble."[13] But the clouds of the Civil War were gathering, and Indian Territory was threatened because of its strategic importance geographically. Indian families soon found out that staying out of the conflict would be as impossible as avoiding a natural disaster. Watts remembered, "They had to take one side or another and that caused much trouble."[14] Both the Union and Confederacy recognized the territory's importance; the Confederacy, however, moved more quickly, aggressively campaigning for alliances with the Five Nations, and from the perspectives of the interviewees, strong-arming their families and making life almost unbearable. Nancy Jane Rider (Cherokee) recalled, "Father did not believe in fighting and did not enlist on either side thinking that the trouble would soon be over."[15] Because troops in the area searched out able-bodied men, her father "with a few other men decided they would hide out until matters were settled; the result was that they remained in seclusion for the entire duration of the war."[16] Rider remembered the impact of this decision on her family, expressing, "This entailed a dreadful hardship on my mother as it was left to her to provide for her large family of nine children."[17]

Like Nancy Jane Rider, Bettie Perdue Woodall also remembered her father's desire to stay out of the war. Furthermore, because her father's health was failing, he was unable to fight. She recalled, "He had never been very strong.... Father ... didn't want to take sides either way. He was not able to fight and thought he would be better off to remain neutral. This didn't help much."[18] According to Woodall, Northern soldiers did not care about her father's fragile condition; she stated, "The Northern soldiers drove off all of our stock and actually drove off the last milk cow my mother was milking [for her husband]."[19] Woodall remembered her mother's anger and frustration vividly, noting, "It made her so furious that she threw the milk stool at them and told them to take that too."[20] Later Woodall's family was brutalized by others in the area. Woodall related, "Some of the neighborhood women told my mother that the Pins were going to burn our house that night and she carried my poor dying father in her arms, while I carried his feather bed and pillow to a cave near our place. . . . Sure enough that night our house and all we had burned to the ground."[21]

Many scholars have speculated on the reasons that each of the Five Nations allied with the Confederacy.[22] Members of the nations certainly remembered their forced removal at the hands of the federal government, an American ethnic cleansing of the southeastern states implemented just a generation before—and feared the Lincoln administration would now seek to open Indian Territory to white settlement, thus further displacing these already displaced peoples.[23] That the nations' homelands were in the South, that slavery was legal under tribal laws, and that some citizens of each group owned slaves likely also created cultural and economic sympathies. All of these reasons may have played some role in the decision-making process. At the same time, we know that all five nations, particularly the Cherokee and Creek, struggled internally with their decisions. We also know that the decision was not merely academic—the lives of tribal citizens were endangered. We can see from the memories of the women interviewed that in the days before the war officially started—regardless of any official decision by tribal governments—the homes of tribal citizens were literally being torn apart, their families fractured, and their lives dramatically and violently altered.

The official decisions of the tribal governments were made quickly. When the Union pulled out of Indian Territory in 1861, abandoning the area to the Confederacy once and for all, no "choice" remained; each of the five signed a treaty of alliance with the Confederacy.[24]

The families of tribal citizens now had their own decisions to make about how and where to make their homes during wartime. Staying in the area meant facing the threat of raiding parties. Many interviewees vividly remembered raiding parties emphasizing that formal alliances made no difference in the situation; while the men were fighting, the women and children were raided by bands of Northern soldiers, Southern soldiers, Pins, and outlaws. According to Elizabeth Watts, raiding parties would "go over the country, burning all the houses, cabins, barns, and cribs, and carrying all the beds and chairs away, and killing or driving away the cattle."[25]

Nancy Jane Rider, whose father was hiding in a cave nearby, remembers that her mother wanted to stay in the area to help her father and the other men. She recalled, "Mother always knew where they were and sent my oldest brother with food for them."[26] Staying in the area, however, proved difficult for her mother and the nine children. According to Rider, "we would have fared much better had we not been robbed regularly, first by the Northern Army, then by the Pin Indians. What the Federals left, the Pins did not."[27] She remembered that the deprivation became worse over time: "After we were stripped of everything . . . we children slept in our clothes on the bare cowhides. Mother would take her dress skirt off and wrap it around the baby and lie down on the floor to sleep. When the raids were made the solders took what could be of any use to them and destroyed the rest; ripping the feather beds open and scattering the feathers over the countryside."[28]

Elizabeth Watts remembered that her family, like Rider's family, stayed in the area but moved close to Fort Gibson because her father, who joined the Union in spite of the Cherokee alliance with the Confederacy, was stationed there. Despite their proximity to the fort, they were not protected. According to Watts, "one day four Southern soldiers came and took the food we had. Took out the feather bed and cut it open, let the feathers fly in the wind and used the tick for a saddle blanket."[29] She recalled how taking items in the home was not enough for the soldiers, noting, "As they went through the yard they took all our green onions. . . . Mother took her best dress and sat on it to hide it. They made her get up and they tore the dress into strings."[30]

Because raiding was so commonplace, most of the women and children left their homes and sought refuge north in Kansas or south near the Red River in the Choctaw and Chickasaw Nations or in Texas. Refugees from the Cherokee and Creek Nations flooded the Chickasaw and

Choctaw territories. The number of refugees in the Chickasaw Nation was actually greater than the number of Chickasaw citizens by 1864.[31]

Although refugee depots provided some rations, many interviewees remember having difficulty finding food. Agnes Kelley (Creek) remembered that "the women and children on both sides had a hard time.... They ate sand plums, squirrels and some of them had corn which was parched and pounded and made into coffee.... Some, a lot, of them took smallpox and got sick and died."[32]

Kelley's memories of deprivation and hardship reveal that those who sought refuge away from their homes may have escaped raiding but did not always find comfort or safety. The women's narratives illustrate that the individual decisions to leave home or stay home had little impact on the outcome. From the perspective of the women interviewees, tribal decisions to forge alliances were made by their governments. Decisions to fight or to flee were made by their fathers and husbands. Few women had the power to make to decisions about their fate during the war—the violence and destruction of the Civil War happened *to them*, almost like a natural disaster. They were not without agency, however. Their power lay in the decision to persevere, to provide shelter and security for their families, and as the following interviewees demonstrate, to find the strength to rebuild.

Memories of Homecoming and Homemaking

The images of homecoming shared by the interviewees are heartrending. As related by Elizabeth Watts, "Cherokee country was in complete desolation."[33] She goes on to paint a grim picture of the landscape: "Cattle and hogs had been eaten or driven off, and went wild in the wilderness and canebrakes. Orchards had died out and the clearings where crops once grew were growing up in weeds and sprouts."[34]

Perhaps the most striking image offered by several of the interviewees is the image of the lone chimney marking where a home had once stood. Movingly, Watts shared, "Homes and barns burned and the old fireplaces stood as monuments to mark the once happy homes of the

Cherokees."[35] Watts's memories of the lone fireplaces are especially telling. Seeing only a fireplace where a home had been must have been shocking, perhaps even more startling than finding nothing at all. The fireplace—the hearth—more than any feature of the house is the symbol of safety and security. A fireplace provides warmth, the ability to prepare food, and significantly, a place to gather together as a family and community. Furthermore, for the Five Nations, fire is an important cultural marker; the tribes' sacred fires, representative of the life of the people, were carried from the homelands to Indian Territory during the forced removal of the southeastern tribes. The "old fireplaces" that "stood as monuments" can be interpreted as monuments to the destruction and hardships the tribal citizens endured during the war. Alternately, the "old fireplaces" can be interpreted as the "old" or ongoing sense of family, hearth, and home shared by families, or even as the "old" fire of culture and tradition, thus making the fireplaces monuments to cultural continuance.

Interestingly, Watts prefaces her Civil War story with a narrative of the Trail of Tears: "Naturally, most of them did not want to leave and go out into the wilderness and start life anew. . . . They did not willingly want to do this."[36] She goes on to say, "The white people used all means to get the Indians out of Georgia . . . burned their homes and made life a torment to them."[37] Significantly, the language she used to describe the Civil War is remarkably similar: "The Indian did not want to fight . . . but they had to take one side or another. . . . Soldiers came and . . . simply stripped us of everything we had."[38] By using similar language, Watts draws a straight line between the advent of removal and the advent of the Civil War. She appears to perceive both events as moments in which the people did not want to leave or participate but were forced as others made their lives "a torment."[39]

Her vivid descriptions of the journey to Indian Territory and the blasted-out landscape following the Civil War are also directly related. Of the Trail of Tears, she stated, "This trail was more than tears. It was death, sorrow, hunger, exposure, and humiliation." However, she emphasizes in no uncertain terms, "They started all over again." Of the Civil War landscape, she sadly related, "Even the population was much decreased on account of . . . disease, hunger, and cold. The Cherokee Nation was almost wiped out." Again, however, she follows this comment with a firm assertion of perseverance, contending, "The Indians never knew anything but suffering, and with the tenacity of a bull dog, they never gave up. Once their cabins were built again, they started building rail fences, barns and cribs. Farming was started again with about as much difficulty as when they arrived here on the 'Trail of Tears.'"[40]

For Elizabeth Watts, the lone chimney—a symbol of the displacement caused by the Civil War—was part of a much longer narrative of the continuing displacement of her people at the hands of others. Although the continued suffering clearly angered her, her pride in the determination of the people of the Cherokee Nation was the outstanding feature of her narrative.

Like Watts, Bettie Perdue Woodall also shared a narrative of the lone chimney. She previously recounted the story of her mother carrying her dying father to a cave as the night her house and all they had burned to the ground. Arguably, her most emotional memories, however, are of her return home. She expressed, "At last we got back home, but what a homecoming. Everything was so changed. The old chimney was standing as good as ever, but there was no house."[41]

Woodall's narrative creates a memory of determination and resilience, sharing that on the night of their homecoming, "Mother cooked our supper on the old fireplace, standing all alone where we had left it."[42] For Woodall's family, the lone fireplace meant that they would share a hot meal that night, providing a hearth, if not actually a home. Nevertheless, Woodall remembered the scene without bitterness and even with some joy, recounting, "There was one of the sheds left standing so we made our beds there, and my how we did sleep. It was so good to be home." Woodall's last statement indicates that "home" does not refer only to a physical structure but to the sustenance of food, the safety of shelter, and the warmth of family.

At this point, Woodall's narrative turns into a story of rebuilding. She notes, "We had only been home a few days when some of the men of the neighborhood came in and built us a new log house. Since the fireplace was already standing, the house was ready to live in that night, and how proud we were of it."[43] Woodall constructs a memory of community and the willingness of members of the community to help each other. She recalled, "Some of the men's wives . . . brought great baskets of food. They gave us most of the cooking utensils they had brought along."[44] Her memory reveals the desire of members of the community to stick together and their willingness to give or share possessions that they in all likelihood needed themselves.

Watts's narrative merges her story of the Civil War with a story of removal. Woodall, too, begins her narrative with an account of removal, stating, "My mother told me about many of the hardships and privations she and the women suffered while on the way from Georgia. Some of them were almost unbelievable, yet I know they are true."[45] From this story, Woodall turns to the Civil War but ultimately ends with a story of Oklahoma statehood. Her memory of the log cabin built around the lone chimney is followed by the memory of her first home after marriage, then later her family's move to a larger, "nice two-story house." She expressed, "We were living easy when Statehood came. With all that things changed." Woodall explained changes in the landscape, noting, "It was hard to get used to little farms, wire fences, and the awful roads fenced on either side."[46] Taken together, Woodall creates a narrative of homes left, homes built, and homes made by family even if no house existed.

The narratives constructed by Elizabeth Watts and Bettie Perdue Woodall do not fit easily into the original vision of the FWP project, through which Grant Foreman hoped to embrace and solidify a collective cultural memory among Oklahomans as "pioneers." Instead, Watts, Woodall, and other like them create a distinctly nationalist memory of Cherokee women in Indian Territory. Unlike "pioneers" who are known for willingly leaving a home to "settle" an area perceived as new or unexplored, the southeastern tribes did not move—during the removal era, during the Civil War era, or during the statehood era—by choice. This lack of choice does not erase either tribal or individual agency, however. It would have been easy, and even expected, for the women interviewed to create narratives in which they cast themselves as helpless victims, beleaguered by the decisions of others. Women like Elizabeth Watts and Bettie Perdue Woodall did not choose this path. Instead, they chose to create narratives of survival rather than narratives of victimry.

Final Thoughts

At the beginning of this chapter, I explained the way in which the Moore tornado on May 20, 2013 and Cherokee and Creek women's narratives of the Civil War destruction have become intertwined in my memory and understanding. As the calendar would fittingly have it, I finished my work on this chapter just shortly after Memorial Day, a holiday established after the Civil War as a day of remembrance for the dead and reconciliation for the country. On the eve of Memorial Day 2013, thousands of Oklahomans gathered at a church in Moore to formally mourn those who lost their lives in the tornado. Listening to the service on the radio, I found that it at once echoed and presaged traditional elements of Memorial Day ceremonies in two notable ways: by remembering those who had died violently and by seeking some sort of "reconciliation"—in this case the resolution or understanding of the tragic events and our path forward, through and from the tragedy.

The people of Moore, almost wiped out, have been left with no choice but to rebuild their homes and lives and are becoming reconciled to doing so with the help of the Oklahoma community as well as people across the United States. I do not know whether the Moore tornado will be "memorialized," but it will certainly be remembered. I find myself asking how the Cherokee and Creek women managed to "reconcile" or resolve all that had happened to them, even though as Elizabeth Watts bluntly stated, "The Cherokee Nation was almost wiped out."[47] My answer lies in the words of Watts, "they never gave up," and in Woodall's story of the willingness of neighbors to pull together to rebuild. As other scholars have noted, the old chimneys were the original monuments of the U.S. Civil War in Indian Territory.[48] Monuments of the Civil War usually depict soldiers, thus commemorating and memorializing the war memories of men. The old chimney standing alone suggests a different kind of monument altogether. To me, the lone chimney serves to commemorate the war memories of Cherokee and Creek women, memorializing not devastation, but, significantly, the persistent pursuit of hearth and home, of community, and of cultural continuance.

NOTES

Epigraph: Bettie Perdue Woodall, interview, September 20, 1937, vol. 100, ID 7551, Indian-Pioneer Papers Collection, Western History Collection, University of Oklahoma Libraries.

1. Grant Foreman, "Foreword," *Indian-Pioneer History*, Oklahoma Historical Society, 1937. The "Five Nations," also known as the "Five Tribes," were historically referred to as the "Five Civilized Tribes" and include the Chickasaw, Choctaw, Cherokee, Creek, and Seminole Nations.
2. Marita Sturken, *Tangled Memories: The Vietnam War, the AIDS Epidemic, and the Politics of Remembering* (Los Angeles: University of California Press, 1997), 3.
3. Sturken, *Tangled Memories*, 3.
4. Robert Penn Warren, *The Legacy of the Civil War* (1961; repr. Cambridge MA: Harvard University Press, 1983), 4.
5. Caroline E. Janney, *Burying the Dead but Not the Past: Ladies' Memorial Associations and the Lost Cause* (Chapel Hill: University of North Carolina Press, 2008).
6. Kirk Savage, *Standing Soldiers, Kneeling Slaves: Race, War, and Monument in Nineteenth-Century America* (Princeton NJ: Princeton University Press, 1997).
7. David W. Blight, *Race and Reunion: The Civil War in American Memory* (Cambridge MA: The Belknap Press of Harvard University Press, 2001), 2–3.
8. Jeff Fortney, "Lest We Remember: Civil War Memory and Commemoration among the Five Tribes," *American Indian Quarterly* 36, no. 4 (2012): 537.
9. Fortney, "Lest We Remember," 537.
10. Foreman, "Foreword."
11. Foreman, "Foreword."
12. Jerrold Hirsch, *Portrait of America: A Cultural History of the Federal Writers' Project* (Chapel Hill: University of North Carolina Press, 2003), 160.

13. Elizabeth Watts, interview, April 27, 1937, vol. 95, ID 0000, Indian-Pioneer Papers Collection, Western History Collection, University of Oklahoma Libraries.
14. Elizabeth Watts, interview, April 27, 1937, vol. 95, ID 0000.
15. Nancy Jane Rider, interview, November 17, 1937, vol. 76, ID 12143, Indian-Pioneer Papers Collection, Western History Collection, University of Oklahoma Libraries.
16. Nancy Jane Rider, interview, November 17, 1937, vol. 76, ID 12143.
17. Nancy Jane Rider, interview, November 17, 1937, vol. 76, ID 12143.
18. Bettie Perdue Woodall, interview, September 20, 1937, vol. 100, ID 7551, Indian-Pioneer Papers Collection, Western History Collection, University of Oklahoma Libraries.
19. Bettie Perdue Woodall, interview, September 20, 1937, vol. 100, ID 7551.
20. Bettie Perdue Woodall, interview, September 20, 1937, vol. 100, ID 7551.
21. Bettie Perdue Woodall, interview, September 20, 1937, vol. 100, ID 7551.
22. W. David Baird and Danney Goble, *Oklahoma: A History* (Norman: University of Oklahoma Press, 2008), 105–12; David A. Nichols, *Lincoln and the Indians: Civil War Policy and Politics* (Columbia: University of Missouri Press, 1978), 25–41; Arrell M. Gibson, *The Chickasaws* (Norman: University of Oklahoma Press, 1971), 259–68; David. A. Chang, *The Color of the Land: Race, Nation, and the Politics of Landownership in Oklahoma, 1832–1929* (Chapel Hill: University of North Carolina Press, 2010), 35–44; Clara Sue Kidwell, *The Choctaws in Oklahoma: From Tribe to Nation, 1855–1970* (Norman: University of Oklahoma Press, 2007), 57–71; Murray R. Wickett, *Contested Territory: Whites, Native Americans, and African Americans in Oklahoma, 1865–1907* (Baton Rouge: Louisiana State University Press, 2000), 6; Faye Yarbrough, *Race and the Cherokee Nation: Sovereignty in the 19th Century* (Philadelphia: University of Pennsylvania Press, 2007), 74–92.
23. David A. Nichols, *Lincoln and the Indians: Civil War Policy and Politics* (Columbia: University of Missouri Press, 1978), 25–41.
24. Nichols, *Lincoln and the Indians*, 25–41.
25. Elizabeth Watts, interview, April 27, 1937, vol. 95, ID 0000, Indian-Pioneer Papers Collection, Western History Collection, University of Oklahoma Libraries.
26. Nancy Jane Rider, interview, November 17, 1937, vol. 76, ID 12143, Indian-Pioneer Papers Collection, Western History Collection, University of Oklahoma Libraries.
27. Nancy Jane Rider, interview, November 17, 1937, vol. 76, ID 12143.
28. Nancy Jane Rider, interview, November 17, 1937, vol. 76, ID 12143.
29. Elizabeth Watts, interview, April 27, 1937, vol. 95, ID 0000, Indian-Pioneer Papers Collection, Western History Collection, University of Oklahoma Libraries.
30. Elizabeth Watts, interview, April 27, 1937, vol. 95, ID 0000.
31. Arrell M. Gibson, *The Chickasaws* (Norman: University of Oklahoma Press, 1971), 270.

32. Agnes Kelley, interview, August 19, 1937, vol. 50, ID 7229, Indian-Pioneer Papers Collection, Western History Collection, University of Oklahoma Libraries.
33. Elizabeth Watts, interview, April 27, 1937, vol. 95, ID 0000, Indian-Pioneer Papers Collection, Western History Collection, University of Oklahoma Libraries.
34. Elizabeth Watts, interview, April 27, 1937, vol. 95, ID 0000.
35. Elizabeth Watts, interview, April 27, 1937, vol. 95, ID 0000.
36. Elizabeth Watts, interview, April 27, 1937, vol. 95, ID 0000.
37. Elizabeth Watts, interview, April 27, 1937, vol. 95, ID 0000.
38. Elizabeth Watts, interview, April 27, 1937, vol. 95, ID 0000.
39. Elizabeth Watts, interview, April 27, 1937, vol. 95, ID 0000.
40. Elizabeth Watts, interview, April 27, 1937, vol. 95, ID 0000.
41. Bettie Perdue Woodall, interview, September 20, 1937, vol. 100, ID 7551, Indian-Pioneer Papers Collection, Western History Collection, University of Oklahoma Libraries.
42. Bettie Perdue Woodall, interview, September 20, 1937, vol. 100, ID 7551.
43. Bettie Perdue Woodall, interview, September 20, 1937, vol. 100, ID 7551.
44. Bettie Perdue Woodall, interview, September 20, 1937, vol. 100, ID 7551.
45. Bettie Perdue Woodall, interview, September 20, 1937, vol. 100, ID 7551.
46. Bettie Perdue Woodall, interview, September 20, 1937, vol. 100, ID 7551.
47. Elizabeth Watts, interview, April 27, 1937, vol. 95, ID 0000, Indian-Pioneer Papers Collection, Western History Collection, University of Oklahoma Libraries.
48. Fortney, "Lest We Remember," 541–42.

8   To Reach a Wider Audience

Public Commemoration of the Civil War in Indian Territory

Whit Edwards

Oklahoma public schools generally dedicate precious little time to Civil War history. American and even Oklahoma history textbooks often gloss over all but a few battles and generally omit almost everything west of the Mississippi River.[1] Only a few regionally focused textbooks mention Indian Territory in sections devoted to the Civil War, and those books offer only limited information on the subject.[2] University-level U.S. history textbooks barely mention Indian Territory in Civil War chapters.[3] Even popular Hollywood films about the war generally focus on events in the eastern theater. So, short of specialized university courses on Oklahoma history or Civil War history, where and how does the public learn about the war in Indian Territory?

Bringing historical research to the public consciousness through historical reenactments and "living history" has been my challenge since 1984. As a public historian, I have endeavored to uncover the fascinating and intricate details of Civil War events in Indian Territory and present them in a public forum with the hope of raising the awareness of the struggles and triumphs of Americans during the nation's most transformative event. Although I have employed numerous techniques for the presentation of subject matter uncovered through scholarly research, reenactments in various formats have proven most popular with the public. In my experience, historical reenactments have emerged as the best way to inform the public of the broad significance of wartime events in Indian Territory and to inspire them to further investigation about the Civil War in their home state.

Public history was originally defined as the separation of professional historians from amateur practitioners. However, the discipline of public history evolved into a professional field of historians trained to work in public settings. Today public history is also often referred to as applied history, a reference to the practitioners' expertise that allows them to make history relevant to a general audience.[4] Public historians commemorate the Civil War in several forums, including symposiums, theater productions, films, statuary, plaques, living history, and reenactments. These final terms—living history and reenactments—refer to a particular format of public history that involves costumed interpreters. Though slight differences exist between the two terms, for the purpose of this discussion both will be referred to as reenactments. Living history does not necessarily seek to reenact a specific event, but rather targets a general historic era based on scholarly research. A historical reenactment is a scripted educational activity in which participants follow a prearranged plan or script to re-create some aspects of a historical event. A reenactment is not as regimented as a theatrical play, but it does retain some of the characteristics.

Reenacting great battles as a way of commemorating historic events is not a modern phenomenon. Romans reenacted great naval battles in the Coliseum. The English reenacted their great 1815 victory at Waterloo just a few years after the battle occurred. Even veterans of the American Civil War reenacted many of the battles they had fought. Wild West shows of the late nineteenth century reenacted famous Indian battles, including the infamous 1876 Battle of Little Bighorn. Twentieth-century state fairs often included reenactments of World War II battles. Modern reenactments of battles of the American War for Independence and the Civil War have evolved through centuries of commemorations and reenactments. These commemorations have become a hobby for thousands of Americans. Indeed, the phenomenon of American Civil War reenactments has spread even to European countries.[5]

When Americans consider public commemoration of the Civil War, most likely think of the reenactments of epic battles such as Gettysburg, Fredericksburg, Antietam, or Chickamauga. Such huge events employ thousands of reenactors, hundreds of horses, and scores of artillery. Those reenactments, while impressive in scope and sometimes even visually stunning, rarely accurately depict the battles they represent. Four basic reasons explain this important shortcoming.

First, troop strengths in reenactment units are underfilled in comparison to actual troop strengths of the battles. Battle reenactments, including the very large national events, usually only field no more than one-third of the historic numbers of participants. Occasionally a reenactment features more artillery pieces than were actually present, particularly in Indian Territory. A prime example where this has happened is the reenactment of the battle of Round Mountain in Yale, Oklahoma, where the participants usually field three or four pieces of artillery despite the fact that there was a complete absence of artillery at the battle in 1861. This is typically done because artillery is a crowd pleaser and the sponsors are competing for the public's entertainment or leisure funds.

Second, the movements of the troops are most often restricted because of available, viewable space at reenactment battlefields. Moreover, many battles are not reenacted on the actual battlefields because of archeological preservation concerns. Terrain is often different than it was during the actual battle, and out of necessity, only portions of the battle are represented. Collectively, these restrictions and challenges mean that the representations of troop movements typically do not move in a proper time and space relationship to the actual battle. Such distortions could understandably mislead the audience with regard to the details of size, location, and speed of the battle.

Third, the reenactors themselves overwhelmingly do not accurately portray the troops of the engagement in five ways: girth, age, uniforms and accouterments, mindset, and especially in Indian Territory, race.

The generations of hobbyists who pursue reenacting are largely middle- or upper-income people who can afford the "authentic" uniforms, equipment, and travel. The reenactors are largely white, middle-aged men who are mostly graying and portly, not the lean young men who actually did the fighting. Most hobbyists buy one or two uniforms and use them no matter which battles they reenact. This is particularly true with regard to battles in the Trans-Mississippi theater, where uniforms were scarce for white Confederate soldiers and almost nonexistent for Indian troops. On the Federal side, Indian soldiers were garnished with a mixture of tribal regalia, while both the black troops and Indian troops were given ill-fitting uniforms and outdated equipment. Additionally, uniforms were altered in style over the four years of the conflict. So while reenactors don uniforms "accurate" for the time period, they are most often not accurate for the particular engagement.

Finally, reenactments rarely depict casualties of the battle in proper time and space. Reenactors typically choose not to "die" before they have a chance to "burn some powder." Thus, reenactment casualties usually occur after twenty minutes of fierce firing at close range and in close proximity to an available shade tree. Of course, this applies to reenactments of large and small battles alike, including Indian Territory battles such as Round Mountain, Perryville, Cabin Creek, and Honey Springs.

None of this diminishes the value of battle reenactments as Civil War commemoration. A commemorative reenactment brings graphic attention to the fierce struggle endured by Americans during the nation's deadliest and most significant conflict. Critics of reenactments often point to the reasons discussed in the preceding paragraphs to insist that statuary or plaques provide the more appropriate commemoration. However, despite the flaws inherent in reenactments, this form of public history excels in communicating history to an audience in ways unachievable in other forms of commemoration, especially statues and plaques. Battle reenactments draw large numbers of spectators, which serves as an exciting way to draw attention to Civil War history in heretofore unheralded locations such as Indian Territory. Simply put, an action-packed reenactment will draw an audience that a statue and plaque could never reach and might spark an interest among members of the audience.

For amateur and professional historians, there are numerous books written on the Civil War in the Trans-Mississippi and in Indian Territory.[6] For the average person with a passing interest in the Civil War or who just thought it might be interesting to witness a reenactment, the event provides a valuable avenue toward enlightenment. Battle reenactments are extensively covered by the local media because they are quite colorful and full of pageantry, which plays well for the media's purpose, far more than the unveiling of a statue or plaque or even the release of a well-written, well-researched book on the subject. Battle reenactments are also more widely attended than any other commemorative event. Reenactments therefore are the best tool for increasing awareness to the largest audience. This holds true especially for reenactments in Oklahoma, where very little is known of Civil War activity in the region.

Reenactments have introduced a new term into the consciousness of history professionals: "edutainment." Simply put, edutainment is an entertaining way of educating. Edutainment predictably has received mixed reviews from professional historians. Some dismiss it as watered-down popular history, while others recognize its power to reach large audiences. The term has been derived from the museum and historic site's need to compete for the leisure dollar the public spends on entertainment. The reenactment is not an exact re-creation of the historic event; rather, it is scholarly information presented in an entertaining format. The reenactment is an entertaining way to reach an educated, uneducated, or slightly aware public and inform that public about a multitude of historical subjects, including but not exclusively battles. Thus the reenactment is a tool to inspire further learning, reading, or even academic research into the subject at hand.

Once the public arrives at a battle reenactment, the reenactors have the opportunity to breech subjects ranging from a soldier's personal effects, equipment, and daily activities to agriculture of the time, medical achievements, courting, issues on the home front, music and literary endeavors, or tribal politics—almost anything pertinent to the period. Sometimes these subjects are addressed in a formal manner utilizing lectures and demonstrations presented at specific times and locations. Some subjects are presented by the reenactors in less formal settings and with less structure around the camps. While it is true that some reenactors are less informed than others, the vast majority of participants are amateur historians anxious to share their knowledge.

Those reenactors and professional public historians alike face the usual challenges that come with attempting to attract the general public to history, but they also encounter challenges and opportunities unique to the study of the Civil War in Indian Territory. Probably more so than any other theater of the conflict, the war in Indian Territory provides an opportunity to examine the wartime experience of a diverse population. The region was home to several sovereign Indian nations, some of which were slaveholders, and numerous Plains tribes, who resided primarily in the western portions of the territory. If the subject of the Civil War was not complex enough, in the study of wartime Indian Territory, students and historians encounter the added complexities of tribal governments, their interactions with Federals and Confederates, and of course intertribal relations. These complexities challenge public historians but also offer opportunities for those who wish to use reenactments as a way to educate the public.

The biggest challenge for the planner of reenactments is the limited involvement of the American Indians and African Americans as active participants. Most American Indians and African Americans traditionally have not embraced this part of their history, perhaps because it has been institutionalized as a white man's war. Among the African American community this attitude is changing rapidly. The instigation for this change, at least in part, was a popular movie called *Glory*. This single movie did more to educate the public about African Americans' proactive role in their emancipation than school textbooks had done since the Civil War.[7] As a consequence, African Americans began reenacting in larger numbers to continue the educational movement. The first African American unit formed during the war was not the famous unit portrayed in the movie, but rather the First Kansas Colored Volunteers. They were also the first to see action and spent most of their service in Indian Territory. Today, there remains an active reenactment group of the First Kansas Colored Volunteers in Oklahoma continuing the education.[8]

Unfortunately there has not been such an event for the American Indians, nor is there likely to be such an event. The African American wartime experience, while powerful and important, is less complex than the multiple and sometimes conflicting American Indian experiences with the war. Each tribe in the territory, whether one of the five "Civilized" tribes or a Plains tribe, had an independent and unique experience with the war. The tribes of the Cherokees, Creeks, Seminoles, Delawares, and Osages fielded troops for both sides of the national conflict. The underlying reasons for the divisions within these tribes did not necessarily follow the same reasons the national conflict divided the United States. The Choctaws and Chickasaws sided wholly with the Confederacy, while the Quapaws and Senecas sided wholly with the Union. In addition to the "white man's war," traditional tribal disagreements raged among the Plains tribes and between those tribes and the tribes who resided in the eastern portion of the territory. These complexities are too numerous and consequentially too large of a subject to breach in our public schools; therefore, they typically are not addressed. Not only is the general public unaware, but for the most part so are tribal members. Unfortunately, tribal histories often treat the Civil War with the same disdain that characterizes their discussion of general relations with the United States.[9] There is little effort within the tribes to educate their members on their particular situation during the conflict. That and the institutional factor largely explain the limited participation among tribal members in reenactments.

Thus the planner of reenactments of Civil War events in Indian Territory must carefully craft the message to the media. Because the media will only briefly cover the event, the presenter must choose sound bites, quotations, or images that can best summarize the message that should be promoted. To further the cause the planner may consider hiring paid American Indian actors to portray some of the leading roles. While this may disturb many of the volunteer reenactors, it would be worth the effort. The media will focus on the key players; consequently, their images will be those that are used both in reporting the event and in advertisement. This is a simple marketing strategy to further educational goals and, more important, might spark an interest among tribal members. A reenactment of Gen. Stand Watie's surrender serves as a prime example of how this has worked in Oklahoma. To bring attention to the fact that the war ended in Indian Territory, when the last Confederate general, a Cherokee, surrendered months after Gen. Robert E. Lee had surrendered at Appomattox, an American Indian was hired to play the role of Stand Watie. The media captured the event and highly publicized it. While it is true that Oklahoma textbooks do feature this event in their discussions of the Civil War, Oklahoma is perhaps one of the few states to do so. The media attention of the event, however, was covered statewide both in the press and on television. The event was such a success that Oklahomans petitioned to have the U.S. Postal Service release a commemorative stamp of the event. A stamp was indeed released. American Indians, like any other group, are more likely to remember and embrace their history if they see themselves portraying it. With this acceptance, more American Indians will get involved in reenacting. With more American Indians reenacting, the authenticity factor and education value are increased.

The success of the surrender commemoration points up the significant opportunities to create reenactments of events other than battles from the Civil War in Indian Territory. Fort locations, tribal grounds, historic homes, and theater or school venues all offer viable outlets for reenactments of societal drama or conflicts. Subject matters are numerous as well, from all aspects of political interactions to internal family strife. Most of the candlelight tours conducted by the Oklahoma Historical Society at their fort and battlefield locations have attempted to do just that. These tours take the visitors through several vignettes as though the visitors were looking through a window of time observing the dramas being played out in front of them. The subject matter changes depending on the theme or storyline of the tour. Home theater in historic homes follows the same format as the candlelight tours at the forts or battlefields but uses the different rooms in the house and historic grounds as the dramatic setting. These multiscene vignettes allow presentations of the different perspectives of a given subject. In a fort setting you would be able to show the diverse perspectives, officers, enlisted men, wives, refugees, and civilian contractors, to mention a few. In a historic home you could present the head of the household, the family members, slaves, and perhaps visitors or unwelcome occupiers of the home all with different perspectives of a given subject. Another venue following in a similar format to present a multitude of perspectives is a cemetery tour, where the interred step out of the shadows to discuss aspects of their life or their views on a certain subject. All three of these formats are highly scripted, much like theater.

Ultimately, entertaining presentations of historical events and personalities often inspire the research that expands our knowledge of that material, and of course the more that is known about a particular subject, the easier that knowledge is to convey. Because of this, Hollywood movies and professional historic sites actually share an important connection. Hollywood is in the entertainment business, and in a way so are historic sites; both venues compete for the same leisure dollar and leisure time of the public. There are numerous famous movies that utilize the Civil War as a backdrop: *Gone With the Wind* (1939), *The Red Badge of Courage* (1951), *The Horse Soldiers* (1959), *Shenandoah* (1965), and countless others. These movies did little to advance authentic portrayals of soldiers' uniforms, equipment, or military decorum, but that criticism misses the point.[10] The filmmakers valued the story, not the details, and of course the stories in these movies revolved around historic events. These films, although not always depicting a portrayal of events accurate enough to suit the serious historian, likely inspired many to academic research and helped to keep alive the public interest in all things Civil War. Later, as a result of rejuvenated interest in Civil War films and the war itself, and in part helping to inspire that rejuvenation, Hollywood made movies such as *Glory* (1989), *Gettysburg* (1993), and *Lincoln* (2012), where filmmakers devoted more attention to historic detail.[11] Reenacting events in Indian Territory will evolve in much the same manner. Reenacting in general has already followed this pattern. In early Civil War Centennial commemorating reenactments, Federal troops wore "blue jeans and blue work shirts," while the Confederates wore "grey gas station uniforms" and coveralls.[12]

The most important thing in Civil War commemoration is the communication of the human dimension, the powerful stories of the people who sacrificed and endured such incredible hardships and struggles. So whether a white man is wearing a uniform representing an American Indian fighting for one side or the other, or an American Indian is in a uniform from the Confederate Army of Northern Virginia, it is the story that is most important. The details will reveal themselves as people are inspired toward investigation, and reenactments provide such inspiration like no other historical medium.

NOTES

1. Holt, Rinehart and Winston, *Call to Freedom* (Woodbury CT, 2003); Jay J. Wagoner, *Oklahoma* (Norman OK: Thunderbird, 1987); Ann Hendrichs, *Oklahoma: This Is Your Land* (North Mankato MN: Compass Point Books–Capstone, 2003); Michael A. Martin, *Oklahoma: The Sooner State* (New York: Gareth Stevens, 2003).
2. David W. Baird, *The Story of Oklahoma* (Norman: University of Oklahoma Press, 1994); Gibbs Smith, *Oklahoma, Our Home* (Salt Lake City UT: Gibbs Smith, 2007).
3. James Murrin, Paul E. Johnson, James M. McPherson, Alice Fahs, Gary Gerstle, *Liberty, Equality, and Power* (Belmont CA: Thomason Wadworth, 2007); Robert A. Divine et al., *The American Story* (New York: Pearson Longman, 2007); George Brown Tindall and David Emory Shi, *America: A Narrative History* (New York: W. W. Norton, 2013).

4. Ian Tyrrell, *Historians in Public: The Practice of American History, 1890–1970* (Chicago: University of Chicago Press, 2005), 209; G. Wesley Johnson, "The Origins of the Public Historian and the National Council on Public History," *Public Historian* 21, no. 3 (Summer 1999): 167–79; Jill Liddington, "What Is Public History? Publics and Their Pasts, Meanings and Practices," *Oral History* 30 (Spring 2002): 83–93.
5. Robert Lee Hadden, *Reliving the Civil War: A Reenactor's Handbook* (Mechanicsburg PA: Stackpole Books, 1999).
6. Whit Edwards, ed., *The Prairie Was on Fire: Eyewitness Accounts of the Civil War in Indian Territory* (Oklahoma City: Oklahoma Historical Society, 2001); Annie Heloise Abel, *The American Indian as Slaveholder and Secessionist: An Omitted Chapter in the Diplomatic History of the Southern Confederacy* (Cleveland OH: A. H. Clark, 1919); Wiley Britton, *Civil War on the Border*, 2 vols. (Ottawa KS: Heritage, 1994); Britton, *The Union Indian Brigade in the Civil War* (Ottawa KS: Heritage, 1994); George W. Grayson, *A Creek Warrior for the Confederacy: The Autobiography of Chief G. W. Grayson* (Norman: University of Oklahoma Press, 1988).
7. James M. McPherson, *Drawn with the Sword: Reflections on the American Civil War* (New York: Oxford University Press, 1996), 99–109.
8. John David Smith, "Let Us All Be Grateful That We Have Colored Troops That Will Fight," in John David Smith, ed., *Black Soldiers in Blue: African American Troops in the Civil War Era* (Chapel Hill: University of North Carolina Press, 2002), 20.
9. John Joseph Mathews, *The Osage: Children of the Middle Waters* (Norman: University of Oklahoma Press, 1961); Grace Steele Woodward, *The Cherokees* (Norman: University of Oklahoma Press, 1963); Edwin C. McReynolds, *The Seminoles* (Norman: University of Oklahoma Press, 1957); J. Leitch Wright, Jr., *Creeks and Seminoles* (Omaha: University of Nebraska Press, 1986); Russell Thornton, *The Cherokees* (Lincoln: University of Nebraska Press, 1990); Brice Obermeyer, *Delaware Tribe in a Cherokee Nation* (Lincoln: University of Nebraska Press, 1998); Robbie Ethridge, *Creek Country* (Chapel Hill: University of North Carolina Press, 2003).
10. McPherson, *Drawn with the Sword*, 99–109; Gary W. Gallagher, *Causes Won, Lost, and Forgotten: How Hollywood and Popular Art Shape What We Know about the Civil War* (Chapel Hill: University of North Carolina Press, 2008), 1–14.
11. Gallagher, *Causes Won, Lost, and Forgotten*. See esp. the introduction and chaps. 2 and 3.
12. John Reid, "The Centennial Reenactment of First Manassas, Blood in Bull Run: The Battlefield Today," *Hallowed Ground Magazine* (Spring 2011), http://www.civilwar.org/hallowed-ground-magazine/spring-2011/the-centennial-reenactment-manassas.html.

CONTRIBUTORS

Brad Agnew is a professor of history at Northeastern State University and the author of *Fort Gibson: Terminal on the Trail of Tears* (Norman: University of Oklahoma Press, 1989).

Christopher B. Bean is an associate professor of history at East Central University and the author of numerous articles in scholarly journals and a forthcoming book that examines the sub-assistant commissioners of the Freedmen's Bureau in Texas during Reconstruction.

Bradley R. Clampitt is an associate professor and chair of the Department of History and Native American Studies at East Central University and the author of *The Confederate Heartland: Military and Civilian Morale in the Western Confederacy* (Baton Rouge: Louisiana State University Press, 2011).

Amanda Cobb-Greetham is Coca Cola Professor, director of Native American Studies at the University of Oklahoma, and author of *Listening to Our Grandmothers' Stories: The Bloomfield Academy for Chickasaw Females, 1852–1948* (Lincoln: University of Nebraska Press, 2000).

Clarissa Confer is an associate professor of history and director of the LaDonna Harris Indigenous Peoples Institute at California University of Pennsylvania and the author of *The Cherokee Nation in the Civil War* (Norman: University of Oklahoma Press, 2007).

Whit Edwards was the site director of the Starr Family Home State Historic Site in Marshall, Texas, former director of education and special programs for the Oklahoma Historical Society, and the editor of *The Prairie Was on Fire: Eyewitness Accounts of the Civil War in the Indian Territory* (Oklahoma City: Oklahoma Historical Society Press, 2001).

Richard B. McCaslin is a professor and chair of the Department of History at the University of North Texas and the author of numerous books, including *Tainted Breeze: The Great Hanging at Gainesville, Texas, 1862* (Baton Rouge: Louisiana State University, 1994), *Lee in the Shadow of Washington* (Baton Rouge: Louisiana State University Press, 2004), and *A Distant Thunder: The Civil War in the Trans-Mississippi* (forthcoming, University of Nebraska Press).

Linda W. Reese is a retired history professor who taught at East Central University and the University of Oklahoma. She is the author of *Trail Sisters: Freedwomen in Indian Territory, 1850–1890* (Lubbock: Texas Tech University Press, 2013) and *Women of Oklahoma, 1890–1920* (Norman: University of Oklahoma Press, 1997).

F. Todd Smith is a professor of history at the University of North Texas and the author of several books, including *From Dominance to Disappearance: The Indians of Texas and the Near Southwest, 1786–1859* (Lincoln: University of Nebraska Press, 2005), *Colonial Louisiana and the Gulf Coast Frontier, 1500–1821* (forthcoming, University of Nebraska Press), and *The Wichita Indians: Traders of Texas and the Southern Plains, 1540–1845* (College Station: Texas A&M University Press, 2000).

INDEX

Acaquash (Waco chief), 101
Adair, George Washington, 54–55
Adair, William Penn, 31, 54–55, 70–71
African Americans. *See* blacks
Arkansas Post, 28
Arkansas River, 22, 72, 89, 97, 99, 104–5; as supply route to Fort Gibson, 31–32, 77; as Union-Confederate boundary, 27, 29, 31, 32–33, 41, 77

Ballard family, 46
Banks, Nathaniel P., 31
Baylor, John R., 90
Bird Creek, skirmish at, 21
blacks: effects of Civil War on, 55–58, 132–49, 177–78; legal status in Indian Territory, 55; and Reconstruction, 112, 115–19; as soldiers, 8, 28–29, 31, 33, 75, 134, 175, 178; towns founded by, 143; wartime suffering of, 38–39, 133–34, 138–39. *See also* freedpeople; slavery
Blain, Samuel, 91, 92
Blight, David W., 156, 157
Blunt, James G., 26, 28, 34; assumes Federal command in Kansas, 24; invasion of Indian Territory ordered by, 24–25; and Perryville,

battle of, 29; removed from command, 30
Boggy Depot, Indian Territory, 30, 34, 132
Bogy, Lewis V., 143
Booth, John Wilkes, 78
Boudinot, William Penn, 51
Brazos Reserve, Texas, 89–90
Brewster, Jacob D., 27
Brown, Joseph, 140
Buchanan, James, 66
Burgess, Mary, 52
Bushyhead, Buck, 134, 138
Butler, Ed, 57

Cabell, William L., 29
Cabin Creek, first battle of, 28, 175
Cabin Creek, second battle of, 33–34, 77
Caddo tribe. *See* Wichita Agency tribes
Camp Napoleon Conference, 10–11, 78
Canadian River, 70, 91
Cane Hill, Arkansas, 27
Carruth, E. H., 96, 97–98
Checote, Samuel, 143–44
Cherokee Freedmen, Association of, 140

Cherokee Nation, 1–2; Confederate treaty of 1861, 27, 74; internal divisions, 64–65, 67, 68, 70, 74, 83n11, 116, 125, 134–35; refugees from, 48; unionists among, 20, 21, 25, 30, 39; Union soldiers from, 42. *See also* Five Nations; freedpeople; Reconstruction

Chickasaw Nation, 1–2, 41; reaffirms commitment to CSA (1864), 30–31; as refugee haven, 51–55, 77, 163–64. *See also* Five Nations; freedpeople; Reconstruction

Choctaw Nation, 1–2, 41; reaffirms commitment to CSA (1864), 30–31; as refugee haven, 51–55, 77, 163–64. *See also* Five Nations; freedpeople; Reconstruction

Chollar, J. J., 103, 104–5

Chustenahlah, battle of, 21–22, 49, 70

civilians, 38–59; avoiding military service, 40–41; children, affected by war, 46–47, 49, 52, 53, 54, 70, 75, 105, 163–64; and Chustenahlah, battle of, 21–22, 38, 49, 70; communications disrupted, 47; material shortages among, 43, 45–46, 47, 51, 52–53, 57, 59, 77; wartime suffering of, 8, 12, 21–22, 30, 38–39, 45–50, 75, 134, 138–39; uncertainty during war, 38–41, 42, 50, 75–76. *See also* refugees; women

Clausewitz, Carl von, 19, 35

Clay, Henry, 134

Cleveland, Grover, 140

Cloud, William F., 29

Coachman, Ward, 144

Coffin, William G., 68, 73, 99, 101

Comanche tribe. *See* Plains tribes

Cooley, Dennis Nelson, 111–12, 135–37

Cooper, Douglas H., 25, 29, 32–33; apologizes to Chickasaws and Choctaws, 30–31; arrest of Pike suggested by, 26; arrests suspected Union spy, 40; assumes command of Indian Territory (CSA), 34; assumes command of Indian Troops, 72; and campaign against Opothleyahola, 21–22, 49; and Chickasaw and Choctaw Confederate alliance, 21; Choctaw-Chickasaw regiment organized by, 69; commands southern Indian Territory (CSA), 28; concedes territory north of Arkansas River, 27; leads attack on Fort Smith (1864), 32; orders raid north of Arkansas River (1863), 30

Cowskin Prairie, Indian Territory, 74, 136

Craig, John N., 140

Creek Nation, 1–2; internal divisions, 47, 64, 69–70, 71, 114, 116, 125; refugees among, 48–53; unionists among, 20–22, 39; Union soldiers from, 42. *See also* Five Nations; freedpeople; Reconstruction

Curtis, Samuel R., 23, 76

Davis, Jefferson, 22; and command changes, 26, 28; and Indian alliances, 67, 69, 94

Davis, William B., 140

Debo, Angie, 64, 120

Delaware tribe, 48

Doaksville, Indian Territory, 35, 51

Douglas, Stephen, 66

Drew, John T., commands Cherokee regiment, 20, 22, 23, 24, 69, 73

Emancipation Proclamation, 136, 145
Emory, William H., 91, 93–94

Falconer, Henry, 71
Fall River, 97, 98
Federal Writers' Project, 153, 158, 167
Fields, Franklin A., 144
First Kansas Infantry (Colored), 28–29, 134, 178
Five Nations, 2, 64; choosing sides in Civil War, 4–7, 8–9, 19–21, 39, 40–41, 71, 160–64, 178; and Christianity, 9, 65, 121–22, 135; Confederate alliance, terms of, 69, 72; Confederate soldiers from, 19–35, 42, 43, 69; conflicts among, 9, 39, 40–41; effects of Civil War on, 9, 12, 13–15, 67, 70–71, 73, 78, 79–80, 113, 135; freedpeople and, 12, 112, 115–19, 126, 132–49; governments in, 3, 141–42; as nations, 16n4; and Plains tribes, 6, 16n4, 41, 112, 135; progressives versus traditionalists, 121–23; removal to Indian Territory, 2, 4, 64, 145, 148; scalping allegations against, 23; and slavery, 5, 9, 13–14, 65, 67, 79, 133, 135–37, 141–42, 144–45, 149n3; surrenders of, 10–11, 34–35, 77–78; and Texans, 19–20; unionists among, 20, 21–22, 25, 30. *See also* Cherokee Nation; Chickasaw Nation; Choctaw Nation; Creek Nation; Reconstruction; refugees; Seminole Nation
Foreman, Grant, 158, 159, 167
Fort Arbuckle, Indian Territory, 89; evacuated by Union forces, 6–7, 19, 68, 93–94; location of, 6; as refuge for Wichita Agency tribes, 97, 99

Fort Ben McCulloch, Indian Territory, 24, 93–94
Fort Cobb, Indian Territory, attacked by Union Indians, 96–97; established, 91; evacuated by Union forces, 6–7, 19, 68, 93–94; location of, 6; occupied by Confederates, 96
Fort Davis, Indian Territory, 22, 27, 72
Fort Gibson, Indian Territory, 25, 31–32, 72, 163; and Creek Agency, 143, 144; described, 17n10, 22, 41; and refugees, 54, 76–77; as target for Confederate forces, 28, 34; under Union control, 27, 29, 30, 33, 50, 75
Fort Leavenworth, Kansas, 25, 94, 101
Fortney, Jeff, 156–57, 158
Fort Scott, Kansas, 26, 29, 34
Fort Smith, Arkansas, 32, 34, 147; attacked by Confederates (1864), 32; captured by Federals (1863), 29; as Confederate headquarters (1863), 28; and Freedmen's Bureau, 138; location of, 6; postwar council meeting, 11, 80, 111–13, 132–33, 135–37, 138, 139; as Union base, 50, 77
Fort Sumter, South Carolina, 6
Fort Towson, Indian Territory, 17n10
Fort Washita, Indian Territory, 52; evacuated by Union forces, 6–7, 19, 68, 93–94; as headquarters for Cooper, Douglas, 30; location of, 6; and refugees, 55, 71
Fourteenth Amendment, 136, 145
Freedmen's Bureau, 138
Freedmen's Oklahoma Association, 146
freedpeople, 12; and emancipation, 58, 136–37; and Reconstruction, 112, 115–19, 126, 135–49
Furnas, Robert W., 25, 27

Gano, Richard M., 31, 32, 33
Gardner, Elsie, 57
Gibson, Arrell M., 135
Glory (film), 177–78, 181
Gookins, Milo, 98, 99–102
Gourd, Oce, 77
Grant, Ulysses S., 139
Greeley, Horace, 25
Green Peach War, 144

Halleck, Henry W., 22, 139
Hanley, Aminda, 75
Harjo (Sands), Oktarharsars, 69, 116, 142, 143–44
Harjo, Lochar, 144
Harlan, James, 78, 111, 137, 139, 143
Harris, Cyrus, 20, 147
Harrison, Benjamin, 148
Hayes, Doc, 56–57
Helena, Arkansas, 28
Henderson, Henry, 134
Hendrix, Annie Eliza, 70, 71
Hicks, Hannah, 43, 44–45, 46
Hicks, John, 46–47
Hindman, Thomas C., 26, 27, 28
Hirsch, Jerrold, 160
Hitchcock, Daniel Dwight, 40, 41, 47
Hitchcock, Isaac, 40, 43
Hodge, Alvin, 52
Holmes, Theophilus H., 26, 28
home front. *See* civilians
Honey Springs, battle of, 28–29, 75, 134, 175
Hunter, David H., 22, 24

Iesh (Nadaco chief), 96, 97
Illinois River, 54
Indian-Pioneer Papers, 12, 153–55, 158–60
Indian Territory, 1; Civil War and, 1–15; Civil War military campaigns in, 19–37; conditions after Civil War, 9, 13–15, 78, 79–80, 160–64; conditions before Civil War, 2–3, 9, 64–67; evacuated by Union military forces (1861), 6–7, 19, 41, 68, 93–94; population of, 2; surrenders in, 10–11, 34–35; Union and Confederate interest in, 3–4, 7–8. *See also* Reconstruction; slavery
Ingraham, Edward H., 24
Island, Harry, 141, 142

Janney, Caroline, 155
Jenkins Ferry, battle of, 31
Johnson, Andrew, 143
Johnson, Charles B., 94
Johnson, Robert, 66, 141
Jones, Evan, 67, 73
J. R. Williams (steamboat), 31–32, 77
Jumper, John, 21, 33, 69

Kansas, Department of, 22
Kansas-Nebraska Act, 66, 67
Keetoowah Society, 67, 75–76
Kelley, Agnes, 164
Kickapoo tribe. *See* Plains tribes
Kievet, Joyce Ann, 121
Kiowa tribe. *See* Plains tribes
Knights of the Golden Circle, 67

Lane, James M., 24, 34, 74, 79
Lee, Robert E., 78, 179
Leeper, Matthew, 93, 94
Lincoln, Abraham, 5, 6, 22, 25, 35; amnesty offered to Indians by, 76; assassinated, 78; elected president of the United States, 67; and Emancipation Proclamation, 136, 145; and Indian allegiance, 68, 69–70, 72, 73, 74; meets with John Ross, 73–74; postwar plans for Five

Nations, 78; and Reconstruction, 78–79; and Union military strategy, 19; unpublished proclamation to Five Nations, 74; and Wichita Agency tribes, 100
Little Arkansas River, 98, 100, 101, 102, 104
Louisiana Purchase, 89

Mankiller, Wilma, 64, 83n11
Manus, Sallie, 79
Marmaduke, John S., 31
Marsh, William H., 23
Maxey, Samuel Bell, 32, 34; assumes command of Indian Territory (CSA), 30; transferred to Texas, 34
McCulloch, Ben, 20, 22; death of, 23
McIntosh, Chilly, 20–21, 29, 69
McIntosh, Daniel N., 20–21, 24, 29, 69, 143
McIntosh, William, 21
McReynolds, Edwin C., 70
Medicine Lodge Treaty, 124
memory (Civil War), 12–13, 153–69, 172–81; and Civil War scholarship, 155–58; and film, 177–78, 180–81; and Indian involvement in Civil War, 160–64; and public history, 172–81; and rebuilding after Civil War, 164–68; and reenactments, 173–81; and women, 153–55, 160–69
Mexican War, 89
Micco, Coweta, 142
Mikko, Heniha, 141
Mississippi River, 8, 172
Missouri, Department of, 22, 26
Moore, Oklahoma, 154, 168
Moses, Lonian, 58
Mulroy, Kevin, 141
Muskogee, Oklahoma, 160

Nail, Jonathan, 54
Native Americans. *See* Five Nations; Plains tribes; Wichita Agency Tribes
Nave, Charley, 134
Neighbors, Robert S., 90, 91
Neosho, state of, 66

Ocherash (Tawakoni chief), 101
Oklahoma, name, 2; territory, 132, 148; state, 148, 157, 167, 168, 172, 176, 178, 179
Oklahoma Historical Society, 153, 180
Okmulgee, Indian Territory, 122, 123, 143
Olmstead, George, 147
Opothleyahola, 71; escape to Kansas (1861), 20–22, 38, 48–49, 51, 61–62n29, 72, 133–34; followers of join Union regiments, 73; and neutrality, 69–70; and slavery, 142

Parker, Ely S., 119–20
Pea Ridge, battle of, 22–24, 72
Pegg, Thomas, 136
Penateka Comanches. *See* Wichita Agency tribes
Perryville, battle of, 29, 175
Phillips, William A., 27, 30, 31, 34, 73; alleviates civilian suffering, 46; biographical information, 25; delivers amnesty offer to Five Nations, 76; victimizes civilians, 75
Pike, Albert, and Five Nations-Confederate alliances, 20, 21, 68, 69, 71, 94; Fort Davis constructed by, 22, 72; and Hindman, Thomas, 26; and Pea Ridge, Battle of, 22–24; and Plains tribes, 69; resignation from Confederate service, 26, 72; takes command of Indian troops, 22; and Wichita Agency tribes, 69, 94–95

Pin Indians. *See* Keetoowah Society
Pitchlynn, Peter P., 10, 54
Plains tribes. 2–3, 124–25; and Five Nations, 6, 41, 112, 135; and Wichita Agency tribes, 2, 90, 91, 93–94, 95, 104–5, 124–25
Pock Mark, Jim, 99
Poison Spring, battle of, 31
Pomeroy, Samuel, 74, 79
Prairie Grove, Arkansas, 27
Price, Sterling, 22, 32, 34
public history, 12–13

Quantrill, William C., 29–30, 31, 38, 42, 75

Rattlinggourd, John, 77
Reconstruction, 110–26; and Cherokee Nation, 113, 116–17, 118, 122–23, 125, 139–40; and Chickasaw Nation, 80, 113, 115–16, 117, 118, 122–23, 125, 139, 144–48; and Choctaw Nation, 80, 113, 115–16, 117, 118, 122–23, 125, 139, 144–48; and consolidated Indian government, 122–23; and Creek Nation, 113–15, 116, 118, 122–23, 125, 139, 140–44; and Five Nations, 79, 80–81, 110–26, 136–49; and freedpeople, 112, 115–19, 126, 135–49; in Indian Territory, 11–12, 14, 110–26; and progressives versus traditionalists, 121–23; and railroads in Indian Territory, 119–20; and Seminole Nation, 113, 116, 122–23, 125, 139, 140–41; and Wichita Agency Tribes, 124–25
Red River, 24, 29, 52, 89, 93, 163; as boundary for Indian Territory, 66, 88, 90, 91, 97, 106
Red River War, 125

refugees, 47–55, 61–62n29, 148; Five Nations citizens as, 75, 76–77, 78, 133–34, 138–39, 163–64; Wichita Agency tribes as, 88, 95, 96–102
Republican Party, 5–6
Rider, Nancy Jane, 40–41, 161, 163
Robinson, Ella, 74
Rogers, Will, 70
Ross, John, 9, 20; captured by Union forces, 25, 72–73; home burned, 30, 44, 135; leaves Indian Territory, 73; meets with Lincoln, Abraham, 73–74; and neutrality for Indians, 68; opposes state of Neosho, 66; signs treaty with Confederacy, 69; rivalry with Stand Watie, 44, 54–55, 68, 74, 135
Ross, Lewis, 58
Round Mountain, battle of, 21, 174, 175

Salomon, Frederick S., 25, 26
Sanborn, John B., 139
Saunt, Claudio, 116, 119
Savage, Kirk, 155–56
Schofield, John M., 26, 27, 28
Second Kansas Cavalry, 29
Second Kansas Infantry (Colored), 134
Sells, Elijah, 102, 103, 137
Seminole Nation, 1–2; internal divisions, 64, 65, 69, 125; refugees from, 48–53; unionists among, 39; Union soldiers from, 42. *See also* Five Nations; freedpeople; Reconstruction
Seneca Nation, 119
Seward, William H., 5, 66
Shanklin, Henry, 102–3, 104, 105
Shelby, Joseph O., 26

Shiloh, Battle of, 24
slavery, 1, 5, 13–14; emancipation and, 58; Union armies and, 58; in wartime Indian Territory, 55–58. *See also* Five Nations
Smith, Dan, 52
Smith, Edmund Kirby, 28, 31
Smith, Edward P., 146
Smith, James M. C., 143
Steele, Frederick, 31
Steele, William, 29; relieved of command of Indian Territory (CSA), 30; takes command of Indian Territory (CSA), 28
Stinnett, Mary, 56
Strout, Eliza Daniel, 138–39
Sturken, Marita, 155

Tahlequah, Indian Territory, 20, 30, 41, 44, 70
Texas Revolution, 89, 96
Texas Road, 24, 25, 28, 30, 33
Thirteenth Amendment, 145
Thirteenth Illinois Infantry, 23
Thirty-Third Illinois Infantry, 24
Thomas, George, 91
Thompson, Victoria, 56
Threat, Jim, 57
Tinah (Kadohadacho chief), 96, 98, 99, 105
Tonkawa tribe, attacked by Union Indians, 96–97. *See also* Wichita Agency tribes
Toshaway (Penateka Comanche chief), 98
Trail of Tears, 165
Turner, James Milton, 140, 146
Twenty-Ninth Texas Cavalry, 28–29

United Daughters of the Confederacy, 157

United States of America, 1, 6; Indian policies of, 4, 5–7, 9, 11–14, 110–11, 124–25, 148. *See also* Reconstruction

Van Buren, Arkansas, 27
Van Dorn, Earl, 22–24, 90
Verden, Oklahoma, 10
Verdigris River, 49, 97
Vicksburg campaign, 28

Walker, Martha Gibson, 51–52
Walker, Tandy, 31, 32
Warren, Robert Penn, 155
Washington, George (Whitebead chief Showetat), 89, 91, 97, 103
Washita River, 10, 89, 91, 99, 103–6
Watie, Sarah, 57
Watie, Stand, 20, 22, 24, 28–30, 57; and Barren Fork Creek, battle of, 30; and Cabin Creek, first battle of, 28; and Cabin Creek, second battle of, 33–34, 77; and Chustenahlah, battle of, 49; assumes command of Confederate Indians, 34; attacks Fort Smith (1864), 32; captures *J. R. Williams*, 31–32, 77; commands mixed-blood Cherokee unit, 69; and Pea Ridge, battle of, 23; promoted to brigadier general, 32; rivalry with John Ross, 44, 54–55, 68, 74, 135; surrender of, 35, 78, 79, 179
Watts, Elizabeth, 160–69
Weer, William, 25, 26
Western History Collection, University of Oklahoma, 158
Wichita Agency, 2–3, 88–106; attacked by Union Indians, 96–97, 124; established, 91; tribes served by, 6, 88; villages near, 91–92. *See also* Wichita Agency tribes

Wichita Agency tribes, 2–3, 88–106; alliance with Confederacy, 10, 94–95, 124; and cattle trade, 98; background before Civil War, 88–93; choosing sides in Civil War, 9–10, 93–95, 178; effects of Civil War on, 9–10, 13–15, 88, 93–106, 124–25; familiarity with Indian Territory, 89; and Lincoln, Abraham, 100; refugees among, 88, 95, 96–102, 124; and Plains tribes, 2, 90, 91, 93, 95, 102, 104, 104–5, 124–25; and Reconstruction, 124–25; removal from Texas to Indian Territory, 4, 9, 90–91, 124; return to Wichita Agency (1867), 88, 103–6, 124; surrenders of, 10–11; and Texans, 4, 9, 89–93, 94, 95; as tribes, 16n4

Wichita tribe. *See* Wichita Agency tribes

Williams, James M., 134

Wilson, Mary Mackey, 54

Wilson's Creek, battle of, 69

women, 38–59; alone in wartime, 41, 42, 43–44, 46–47, 50, 52–53, 56–57, 75, 75–76; Indian Territory and, 8, 12; male responsibilities assumed by, 52–53, 56; and memory, 153, 160–69. *See also* refugees

Woodall, Bettie Perdue, 153, 161–62, 166–68, 169

Worcester, Samuel, 65

Works Progress Administration, 133, 134, 153, 158

Wortham, James, 104

Wright, Allen, 80, 147

Yale, Oklahoma, 174

Young, William C., 19, 94, 95

www.ingramcontent.com/pod-product-compliance
Lightning Source LLC
Chambersburg PA
CBHW030624230426
43661CB00053B/2133